Whose Homosexuality? Which Authority?

Homosexual Practice, Marriage, Ordination and the Church

Edited by

Brian Edgar
and
Gordon Preece

ATF Press
Adelaide

Contents

Editorial

Homosexuality has been, and still is, a double-bunger of an issue in the churches and society, hence this double issue of *Interface*. Homosexual practice, ordination and marriage are divisive issues as recent debates and threatened (and, to some extent, actual) church splits amply demonstrate. Witness the splintered state of the Australian Uniting Church into differing presbyteries, the Reforming Alliance, the Assembly of Confessing Churches and other groups. Also note the worldwide Anglican Churches' increasingly loose federation and informal theological alliances, precipitated by the moves by the Canadian Anglican Diocese of New Westminster to recognise gay marriages and the US New Hampshire Diocese to ordain a practising homosexual bishop, Gene Robinson. They have provoked major ecclesiological problems for both churches.

The project, of which this double issue of *Interface* is the culmination, started when one of the editors (Preece)—in his then capacity as Director of the Centre for Applied Christian Ethics (CACE)—was asked to organise a conference on homosexuality. This conference was aiming to facilitate a discussion that would generate more light than heat and lessen the possibility of a damaging split over the issue. It fell on his last Saturday in the job and seemed like an invitation to go out 'with a bang not a whimper'. Fortunately, a highly successful conference, for one hundred and sixty, was held on 26 June 2004 at Ridley College where 'iron sharpened iron' in a constructive and charitable atmosphere. Face-to-face contact, including lunch before the conference, encouraged a convivial atmosphere, a forum rather than a point-scoring debate, where the ball is played rather than the man or woman. At all times in this debate we must remember we are talking not just about another, but to a brother or sister. It is said that noted Anglican theologian Oliver O'Donovan disciplined himself while writing a chapter on homosexuality by reading sections to a man dying of AIDS. That would be a good discipline for all of us.

Originally intended as a book, this bumper journal follows up the highly successful book dealing with the homosexuality issue, *More Than a Single Issue* edited by Murray Rae and Graeme Redding (ATF Press, 2000). This featured mainly New Zealand authors examining the issue in the church with contributors from a range of perspectives. This issue of *Interface* picks up on recent further developments, particularly in the Australian Anglican and Uniting Churches. It aims to facilitate helpful discussion of the homosexual issue going beyond the first book and the Anglican Church Doctrine Commission's *Faithfulness in Fellowship* (Melbourne: John Garratt, 2001). It also has a more even representation of viewpoints than the latter which featured only two small contributions from Evangelicals. It does this, as the contributor list shows, by having representatives of the more liberal and conservative positions (for want of better terms) writing on each part of the Wesleyan quadrilateral—Scripture, tradition, reason and experience—as well as other theological topics—Trinity, ecclesiology, anthropology and marriage—in relation to homosexuality.

By adopting this method we believe we were able to tease out the 'more than a single issue' authority issues, or the sources of moral insight behind the issue, so that people are not simply talking past each other as often happens in such debates and forums. Hence the title *Whose Homosexuality? Which Authority?* which is an adaptation of Alasdair MacIntyre's *Whose Justice? Which Rationality?* We have chosen the contributors from both sides of the debate, all with a commitment, we believe, to genuine theologically-based argument. Each of the contributors has considerable expertise and experience within the particular area that they have been assigned. We tried to ensure sufficient representation of women among the contributors and regret that only three could participate.

The contributors, except one (an American Anabaptist, Mark Thiessen Nation), are overwhelmingly Australasian. Unfortunately other overseas articles we sought to use—by Eugene Rodgers, Douglas Farrow and David Matzco McCarthy's—were prohibitively priced. Thus the balance is tilting in a slightly more conservative direction, despite our best efforts.

Opinions obviously vary about the origins, relative priorities amongst the authorities as well as the distinctiveness and usefulness of the Anglican/ Wesleyan quadrilateral. Sociologist Martyn Percy argues that Anglicanism's use of the quadrilateral goes back to Richard Hooker (1554–1600) and implicitly predates him all the way back to tenth century Jewish philosopher Saadia Ben Joseph (882–942 AD).[1] That quadrilateral—in the views of John Wesley, the Anglican fathers Thomas Cranmer and Richard Hooker, and the historic Christian orthodoxy—is seen as a ladder of hierarchical authority.

---

1. Martyn Percy, *Power and the Church: Ecclesiology in an Age of Transition* (London: Cassell, 1998), 174 and n 49.

Graham A Cole, a contributor to this volume, shows that Thomas Cranmer, the architect of Prayer Book Anglicanism, in his homily on the Lord's Supper, used Scripture as the governing norm, with tradition and reason as *ad hoc* supports, to refute Roman Catholic views of the sacraments.[2]

On the other hand, the quadrilateral today is often seen as a table of four equal authorities. This is partly due to the fact that a ladder is a limited image unless we remember also that traffic moves up and down the ladder—we read Scripture through tradition, reason and experience as the term 'hermeneutical circle' implies. Robert Carroll somewhat cheekily describes the quadrilateral as 'the dodo's incorporative principle by which everyone wins'.[3] On this principle Scripture and tradition only count when they agree with experience and reason. This denies the otherness and distinctiveness of Scripture and tradition.

Former Australian Anglican Primate Peter Carnley, while warmly affirming of Richard Hooker's articulation and use of the trilateral of Scripture, tradition and reason (Wesley added experience) as representing the best of Anglicanism, does not regard it as 'a distinctively Anglican way of doing theology'. The difficulty with talk of a distinctive Anglican theological method, expressed in the catchcry 'scripture, tradition and reason', is that Roman Catholic and Greek Orthodox theologians, or Lutheran or Uniting church theologians, would probably also agree, not to mention Christians of many other denominational traditions. Therefore I do not see that there is anything distinctively or uniquely Anglican about the method of doing theology using this threefold court of appeal.[4]

This may well be true, but it adds to the value of the tri- and/or quadrilateral in an ecumenical context, and the broader relevance of our volume, rather than detracting from it.

Percy speaks of 'fundamental weaknesses of the quadrilateral in the context of postmodernity', particularly as in contemporary Anglicanism it provides a process but no product: it fails to proscribe belief or behaviour; it is all methodological throat clearing, no conclusion or clear voice, a trumpet with an uncertain sound. So, using the quadrilateral pluralistically we often

---

2. Graham A Cole, 'Paley and the Myth of "Classical Anglicanism"', *The Reformed Theological Review*, 54/3, (September-December, 1995): 98–102.

3. Robert Carrol, *Wolf in the Sheepfold: The Bible as a Problem for Christianity* (London: SPCK, 1991), 62.

4. Peter Carnley, *Reflections in Glass: Trends and Tensions in the Contemporary Anglican Church* (Pymble, NSW: HarperCollins, 2004), 82–3.

arrive at opposite conclusions.[5] This will be apparent from the essays in this volume which we now proceed to summarise (with the more liberal argument first). Nonetheless, this framework provides a useful way of framing the issues and making explicit the often implicit prioritising of authorities behind the arguments so that we can know 'The *More* Than a Single Issue' that we are really arguing about.

Scripture

Keith Dyer, in seeking 'A Consistent Biblical Approach to '(Homo)sexuality' does a lot of ground-clearing work concerning the cultural baggage that we bring to biblical texts as well as that of the biblical texts themselves. He sees those texts as anchored much more strongly than some conservative commentators in the culture of the times. For instance, he sees the Sodom narrative as more a condemnation of gang rape than of homosexual practice. And while Paul *was* strongly opposed to Gentile exploitative and promiscuous 'homosexuality', that does not imply condemnation of committed and mutually enriching homosexual relationships.

Yet even if 'homosexuality' in all its forms is still viewed as sinful, there are no New Testament grounds to single out 'homosexuals' as more sinful than others, or to refuse them church membership or training. We should be welcoming and affirming of homosexuals.

The clear focus of New Testament 'sexual' exhortations is on *porneia*—promiscuous, abusive, obsessive and exploitative sexuality (whether 'hetero-' or 'homo-' but mainly the former). There are no grounds for a 'witch-hunt' of Christians with a same-sex orientation. Yet there is a clear mandate in Jesus' ministry to the marginalised (including prostitutes and adulterers) for support of 'homosexual' persons in our churches and for legal justice for 'practising homosexuals'—especially to care for AIDS/HIV victims.

In 'Scripture and Homosex: Addressing the Key Texts', Graham A Cole first explores what it means to call the Bible 'Scripture' and then the implications of the various texts relating to homosex. The key Old and New Testament texts (Genesis, Judges, Leviticus, Romans, 1 Corinthians and 1 Timothy) are all negative about same-sex sexual behaviour but, it is noted, the texts are approached in different ways which can change the implications for today. Cole evaluates a series of these approaches which argue that the texts are morally primitive, are in need of reinterpretation or do not deal with

---

5.   Martyn Percy, *Power and the Church* (London: Cassel and Co, 1998), 176.

committed monogamous same sex relations and concludes that all the attempted reinterpretations of the biblical texts are unconvincing. When normative questions are asked of the scriptural testimony it must be concluded that same-sex sexual expression, when in the service of power and/or violence, or in the service of a pagan lifestyle, is against the Scriptures. Sexual expression outside God's design is not a Christian option and the divine design is heterosexual not homosexual. To live otherwise is foolish and not wise.

Tradition

In her chapter, originally from *Faithfulness in Fellowship,* Muriel Porter argues that Christian tradition has always seen homosexual practice as wrongful. However, there has been ambivalence concerning the degree of its sinfulness. For long periods of Western church history, homosexual acts were regarded as no worse than gluttony. But at other times, they have been regarded as the worst abominations, deserving death.

Porter sees the church's attitude to homosexuality as following secular trends, not biblical interpretation. The church was most condemnatory in periods when heterosexual sex was most tightly controlled (for example: during the war against clergy marriage in the eleventh and twelfth centuries, or during the conformist Victorian era). Traditional teaching on homosexual activity needs to be paralleled with teaching on heterosexual activity. The latter includes teaching now scorned by the church, such as suspicion of sexual pleasure even within marriage, or (in the Protestant, Anglican and Orthodox churches) artificial contraception.

The basis for the most persistent and influential Christian teaching against homosexuality has not been solely, or even pre-eminently, biblical but instead that it was viewed as 'against nature', or non-procreative. This drew as much on echoes of pre-Christian philosophies as on Scripture. Once the way was opened to non-procreative sex, in logic and principle it was also opened to homosexual sex.

Gordon R Preece's 'Democracy of the Dead' is written as a defence of tradition. Firstly, drawing upon but critiquing sociologist Anthony Giddens' *Runaway World*, he asks why tradition in its broadest, not specifically Christian sense, is a dirty word in (post)modern democratic and novelty-obsessed societies.

Secondly, Preece critiques journalist-historian Muriel Porter's Whig-progressivist (Herbert Butterfield) reading of the Christian tradition as stepping-stones to our present progress on homosexuality and sexuality in her *Sex, Marriage and the Church: Patterns of Change*[6] and in *Faithfulness in Fellowship*. Porter's revisionism is more journalistic argument for Giddens' 'democracy of the emotions'[7] than genuinely historical and traditional in the sense of GK Chesterton's 'democracy of the dead'. He does not go into detail refuting revisionist readings of church tradition on homosexuality, taking them as largely refuted by the consensus of historians and weight of evidence. Instead he addresses the presuppositions of such arguments, as exemplified by Porter's works. He argues that the key changes in church teaching on sexuality were as much due to changes in biblical interpretation as secular thought.

Reason and Science

Mark Thiessen Nation's essay inviting us to 'Come Let Us Reason Together' is partly an exercise in conflict resolution, as one might expect from a Mennonite. Rather than polarising, it charts different positions regarding homosexual practice along a spectrum. First, it marks out common ground. (1) The social and biological sciences present a set of puzzles we do not yet fully understand. (2) We affirm that the Bible is centrally authoritative for Christian faith and morality. (3) The handful of biblical texts directly on homoerotic relations, at face value, speaks negatively. (4) Those texts must be included in a more comprehensive biblical framework for sexuality, theology and ethics. (5) Church tradition can teach us today concerning sexuality in general and homosexual relations in particular. (6) Christians should love their neighbours as themselves. This would include practising homosexuals and people who believe homoerotic behaviour to be wrong. (7) If the church shifted positions on homosexual relationships, a parallel supportive monogamous arrangement for gays and lesbians is being suggested to that prevailing for heterosexuals. (8) Homoerotic behaviour is the issue not homosexual persons.

Second, Nation names a few issues leading some to use strong rhetoric: we are dealing with real people not abstractions; we are dealing with real fears; there is a legitimate concern that our culture is in moral decline. Third, he invites people who disagree to hear the potential flaws in their own arguments as well as to hear others' views. Finally, he offers some potential ways forward for the church. While keeping his own position in the background for

---

6. Muriel Porter, *Sex, Marriage and the Church: Patterns of Change* (Melbourne: Dove, 1996).
7. Anthony Giddens, *Runaway World: How Globalisation is Reshaping our Lives* (London: Profile, 1999), 64–5.

most of the essay, he concludes that it is reasonable for us to ask whether or not revisionist readings of homosexuality (and sexuality), currently common, are for convenience sake. It is reasonable to argue the burden of proof rests with those challenging the church's historical consensus that the plain sense of Scripture is right, that homosexual activity is wrong. But the latter position must be upheld with humility, and great pain.

David Clarke's chapter on 'Scientific Reason and Homosexuality' summarises the contribution of science to the issue of homosexuality. Those looking for evidence supporting a deterministic psychological or biological view of homosexuality, will be disappointed, as will those holding that homosexuality is a mere matter of choice. The evidence, especially regarding heritability, displays great variability concerning genetic and environmental influence. It is therefore probable that for some people genes are critical and that for others social and psychological factors are more prominant in determining sexual orientation. Either way, science can never answer the moral question of the good or evil of any action. That answer lies elsewhere. But science may provide knowledge and understanding to inform our responses to people with sexual orientation different to ours. Homosexuality is not just a choice, certainly not an easy choice. But nor is it determined. Sexual orientation develops in a person, shaped by a succession of choices made in an encircling biological and social environment. Understanding an individual's sexuality involves understanding their unique history and, simultaneously, the human need for intimacy and dignity, and an element of ambivalence in all relationships.

Experience

Peter Sherlock in 'On Being a "Gay Anglican"' presents an insider's view of the experience of a practising Christian gay. It brings home the reality that we are dealing with real people not academic abstractions in this question. His alternative vision for the way out of the mess he sees the church in over the question is to encourage gay and lesbian people to stand up and offer their visions for the church, and to encourage other Christians to help make that vision a reality.

The elements of his vision are several. First, let us stop reading Scripture as a rule book and instead seek the Holy Spirit's fresh inspiration to re-open the Scriptures in all their penetration of 'the craziness of human experience'. Let us celebrate the completeness of Christ's inside knowledge of our humanity and sexuality. 'Perhaps we need to re-examine what our guiding passages of Scripture are. Must we take the "seven texts" referring to homosexuality? Why should we begin with the model of man and wife offered by Genesis? What would happen if we used, say, Ezekiel 23:19–20 as our dominant hermeneutic for interpreting difficult texts—if you haven't read it, I strongly recommend trying a few different translations.'[8]

Second, we must stop seeking rules for entry into heaven but rejoice in the presence of God and the angels and celebrate the joy and despair brought by human companionship, so well revealed in the gospel accounts of Jesus and his followers. It is heart-breaking to watch the Anglican communion's increasing division, 'towards separating the elect from the damned and determining who is worthy of sacramental grace whether in the form of holy orders, or marriage'. This contrasts with the Christ who embraced everyone when he ascended the cross.

Finally, we should consider the vocation of all baptised people who are called by God's people to ordained ministry, including homosexual men and women, whether in relationships or not.

The question of what wholeness in Christ means is also central to Debra Hirsch's account of her longstanding ministry in Melbourne with those with a homosexual orientation. The conviction that an individual's goal should be to grow in relationship with God, and that wholeness in Christ is primarily about discipleship and not the pursuit of heterosexuality (something which, for many, isn't attainable or even desired) led to the development of Purple Heart ministry. In 'The Least of These . . .' Hirsch shows how Christ brings change to all, but while some people may come to experience heterosexual response, this is not a possibility for all individuals. Hirsch demonstrates the varieties of experience with four real stories of people who have all tried to understand and deal with their homosexuality with integrity. All changed, but in various ways, and some now experience heterosexual response.

Hirsch also discusses celibacy and the fairness of asking those with a homosexual orientation to deny themselves genital sexuality. The problem is that modern society over-rates genital activity and consequently under-rates social sexual relationships, that is, genuine intimacy without genital contact. Wholeness can be found without having sex. Celibacy can be one of the sacrificial acts of discipleship which are a part of the Christian life for all, whether homosexual or not.

---

8. See this journal, 124.

Trinity and Anthropology

Opposition to the idea that homosexuality was biologically determined (rather than a complex mix of biology, social upbringing and personal affirmation) brought together two dialogue partners with very different positions on the appropriateness of homosexual relations for Christians. In 'Sexuality, the Image of God and the Doctrine of the Trinity' Brian Edgar recounts a public debate in print and in person with another ordained minister who was a self-professed, active homosexual. The discussion included honest questions like, 'What is the weakest and most vulnerable aspect of my own position?' as well as the more usual form of debate presenting one's strongest arguments. The dialogue demonstrated the incompatibility of theological and biblical approaches and the fact that changes to the traditional ethical stance of the church could not be made to anyone's satisfaction by the simple addition of homosexual relationships alongside heterosexual ones. A gay ethic is not simply a traditional ethic with genders switched around; it is usually an ethic (or set of ethics) of a completely different order altogether. The most problematic aspect of the case for a revised Christian ethic is the scriptural material, given that revisionist interpretations (from Bailey, Scroggs, Spong, Boswell and others) have failed to be convincing. Consequently, those seeking to justify homosexual practice have tended to move on to other forms of argument. The most difficult aspect of the case for a traditional Christian ethic revolves around the question of *why* scripture says what it does about homosexuality. The answer comes from an examination of two important theological concepts: humanity being made in the image of God, and the Trinitarian nature of God.

In 'Whose Language? Which Grammar?' Bryden Black contrasts the 'diversity' and 'inclusivity' which are central expressions of the cultural pluralism resulting from the emancipatory agenda of autonomous human reason found in the Enlightenment and postmodernity, with a very different form of discourse about the world which is grounded in a Christian theology of creation by the Triune God. The consecration of an openly practising gay bishop in the USA is taken as an example of the functioning of these alternative forms of discourse with their different belief systems and moral evaluations. Black argues that a Christian theology of creation and a gospel that is both inclusive and exclusive has the explanatory power to render intelligible what others aspire to via 'diversity' and 'inclusion'. From within the scheme of discourse of the European story of the last three hundred years homosexuality, bisexuality, transsexuality—and of course heterosexuality—

are 'natural' and 'equal' and their denial is a form of 'injustice'. These are the assumed plausibility structures achieved via a sociology of knowledge applied to human sexual behaviour sanctioned by a politically plural state predicated upon a perceived autonomous humanity. The counter thesis, offered by Black, is that the eventual outcome of secular Western liberalism may very well be a counterfeit life—not least on account of a sterility which has already begun to manifest itself in patterns of sexual homogenisation, incapable of reflecting authentically the fruitful divine image among the human (Gen 1:26–31).

Ethics and Marriage

Virtue ethics, with its emphasis on character and moral practices, provides an alternative approach to sexuality compared with the more usual focus on searching for guidance in biblical rules and principles. In 'Sexuality and the Virtues or "Whose Marriage, which Sexuality?"', Denise Cooper-Clarke begins by observing that most contemporary liberal argument for the acceptance of long-term committed homosexual unions utilises virtue theory in order to emphasise the quality of homosexual relationships and the virtues of love, honesty and mutuality. But theological liberalism—which is an aspect of the dominant ideology in Western society (liberal individualism)—is really unable to sustain any virtues except the values of choice and independence of mind. Individual autonomy, sincerity and authenticity, may be said to constitute the cardinal virtues of liberalism. Ultimately, as MacIntyre argues in *After Virtue,* post-Enlightenment moral argument is incoherent and unsustainable. In short, Cooper-Clarke argues that the adoption of a virtue theory framework does not necessitate a revision of Christian sexual ethics, so long as one is clear which tradition, which narrative, which practices and which virtues are being talked about. In the Christian tradition the virtues relating to sexuality can only be specified within the practices of marriage and celibacy, which are in turn sub-practices of the church's practice of witness.

Eschatology

In a concluding chapter Gordon R Preece examines firstly the homosexuality issue in the context of the disillusioned 'morning after' modernity flavour of the highly rated US TV show *Sex and the City*'s portrayal of 'Postmodern Sex Etiquette or Bed Manners'. He secondly contrasts this with the Augustinian motif of the City of God, presenting a narrative theology of homosexuality in a creation, fall and redemption framework that makes sense of the mystery of sexuality. He looks at our created 'sexual ecology', our fallen condition of sexual idolatry and ideology, and the redemptive possibilities of sexual therapy set within a Christian form of social construction aimed at the City of God.

Preece uses the eschatological City of God motif to relativise the social locations of both inner-city 'bobo' (bourgeoisie) sexual expressivists and 'burbo' (suburban) family values advocates in the light of our fundamental identity in Christ and destiny towards the City of God.

Hopefully this edition of *Interface* will shed more light on, and bring more personal warmth to (while taking away some of the heat), the complex questions surrounding sexuality, and homosexuality in particular. It is the fervent prayer of both editors that this will be the case and we thank the contributors for the spirit in which they have helped towards making it possible.

Gordon R Preece and Brian Edgar

Contributors

Bryden Black, PhD, is an Anglican priest who has ministered in Zimbabwe, England, Australia and is currently in New Zealand. In Australia he was head of the Department of Evangelism in the Diocese of Melbourne and an associate priest at the Port Melbourne parish.

David M Clarke, PhD, is Head of Consultation and Liaison Psychiatry and Primary care Psychiatry at Monash University Medical Centre, Associate Professor in the Discipline of Psychological Medicine at Monash University and Victorian Chairman of the Christian Medical and Dental Fellowship of Australia (CMDFA). He is currently researching suffering and demoralisation and their relation to meaning, purpose and spirituality, as particularly experienced by people with cancer and other serious illness.

Denise Cooper-Clarke is a medical doctor and bioethicist currently completing a PhD through the University of Melbourne on medical practitioners' attitudes towards euthanasia. She is a member of the Ridley College Centre for Applied Christian Ethics (CACE) Board and of Christians for Biblical Equality and attends St Columb's Anglican Church Hawthorn.

Graham A Cole, ThD, is Professor of Biblical and Systematic Theology at Trinity Evangelical Divinity School in Deerfield, Illinois and formerly lecturer at Moore Theological College and principal of Ridley College, University of Melbourne. He is the author of many articles.

Keith Dyer teaches New Testament at Whitely College Melbourne and is Chair of the Academic Board of Melbourne College of Divinity.

Brian Edgar, PhD, is Public Theology spokesperson for the Australian Evangelical Alliance, a member of the Theological Commission of the World Evangelical Alliance and formerly lecturer in Theology and Ethics at the Bible College of Victoria.

Debra Hirsch was Director of Purple Heart (formally Exodus, South Melbourne), a pioneering ministry to gays and lesbians. She has recently worked with the Salvation Army with poor and marginalised people and now works with Forge, a missional training agency.

Muriel Porter, PhD, is a member of the General Synod Doctrine Commission and General Synod Standing Committee and until recently was Senior Lecturer in Journalism at RMIT University. She is now an honorary research fellow in the History Department, University of Melbourne, where she is focusing on a number of research and writing projects. Her most recent book, *The New Puritans: the Rise of Fundamentalism in the Anglican Church*, was published by MUP in 2006.

Gordon R Preece is Director of the Macquarie Christian Studies Institute (www.mcsi.edu.au). He was formerly Director of the Ridley College Centre for Applied Christian Ethics at the University of Melbourne and Lecturer in Ethics and Practical Theology at Ridley. He is also Vice-Chair of the Zadok Institute and Commissioning Editor for *Perspectives*. He is an ordained Anglican minister and author, co-author, editor of ten books and many articles on work and ethical issues.

Peter Sherlock is an Australia Research Council Postdoctoral Fellow in the Department of History at the University of Melbourne. He worships at St Peter's Eastern Hill, Melbourne, and is the founding president of Changing Attitudes Australia.

Mark Thiessen Nation is an Associate Professor of Theology at Eastern Mennonite Seminary, Harrisonburg, Virginia, USA. He is the editor or co-editor of five books and the author of *John Howard Yoder: Mennonite Patience, Evangelical Witness, Catholic Convictions*.

1

A Consistent Biblical Approach to '(Homo)sexuality'[1]

Keith Dyer

Placing 'Bible' and 'homosexuality' together in the one sentence always provokes questions. Some questioners are genuinely puzzled, some are angry: 'Why do we continue to ask what the Bible says about "homosexuality" when the few verses that do seem to refer to it are very clear in their meaning (particularly Lev 18:22; 20:13 and Rom 1:26–8)?' 'Surely the incessant re-opening of this question is evidence itself of the moral bankruptcy of the Western church as it tries to twist the "plain sense" of Scripture to legitimate its own selfish and lustful behaviour?' 'How can we possibly justify the time spent on discussing the "deviant sexuality of a tiny minority" in the face of such major human disasters as hunger, poverty, war, genocide and environmental degradation?' 'How can we fail to see that opening the door to "homosexuality" in the church will undermine the Christian family and begin a slippery slide that will lead inevitably to pedophilia, bestiality and all kinds of immorality?' These are the sorts of questions that generate so much heat that they often threaten to derail any discussion before it begins.

1. Do we really have to go here yet again?

Yes we do. Not because of pressure on the church from gay lobby groups or because of some new argument that will change people's minds on the issue. The attitudes of people are changed not by arguments or exegesis, but by personal encounters with a friend or a family member who is found to be 'homosexual' and Christian. After that comes the need for exegesis and

---

1. I use '(homo)sexuality' in the title to indicate that any discussion of 'homosexuality' needs to be undertaken within the wider context of human sexuality. I use the words 'homosexuality' and 'heterosexuality' in inverted commas throughout this paper to indicate that they are relatively recent constructions and have no direct Biblical equivalents.

reinterpretation, as we seek to understand this new reality in the light of our traditions—just as the early Christians struggled to come to terms with the presence of the Spirit in uncircumcised Gentiles, against all their biblical expectations. It is simply not possible, however, to explore the biblical traditions about 'homosexuality' without first addressing some of the questions above that lurk like unexploded land-mines in the strife-torn field of discussion. We will never clear the ground completely, but it will help at the outset if we can agree that we stand a better chance of finding a way forward if we negotiate it together, rather than by remaining in entrenched positions, lobbing texts like hand-grenades and laying more land-mines to destroy each other. So to begin with, here are a few brief reflections on the questions above, taken in reverse order.

1.1 The slippery slope to sexual immorality?

One way to describe the central issue is to ask whether 'homosexuals' can ever express their sexuality with another person in a moral way, or whether all 'homosexual' activity is immoral by nature as far as the Bible is concerned. This issue will be examined here assuming the wider framework of loving and mutual *human* sexuality. Of course, 'homosexuality' like 'heterosexuality' *can* be expressed in immoral ways, but to suggest that there is some kind of inevitable progression from 'homosexuality' to pedophilia and bestiality, or other forms of abusive, exploitative and promiscuous sexuality, is to pre-judge the issue (Rom 2:1!); or worse, it is to stoop to the level of scaremongering and homophobia. Christians do this all too often, unfortunately, whether from ignorance or fear is not always apparent.[2] How can one enquire honestly whether it is possible to live morally as a 'homosexual' person in a committed relationship, if the very idea of 'homosexuality' is bracketed alongside pedophilia and bestiality? Can we not see the difference between consenting and committed adults, and the exploitation of children and animals? Sexual

---

2.   Even Robert Gagnon's otherwise careful analysis of the arguments degenerates to this level in places, particularly towards the end of his book. He refuses to admit the possibility of long-lasting, committed and faithful 'homosexual' relationships—the very relationships that our churches and laws will not recognise or support. He then quotes alarming statistics about health issues, pedophilia and promiscuity which are based on the outlawed 'homosexual' community, and cites their plan for 'the total annihilation of societal gender norms'. Robert AJ Gagnon, *The Bible and Homosexual Practice: Texts and Hermeneutics* (Nashville: Abingdon, 2001), 482. This is as valid as quoting the extreme views of some in the pornography industry and the statistics from their victims to point out the dangers of 'heterosexuality'.

relations with a child or an animal can *never* be truly mutual or non-exploitative, those between consenting adults can be, though are not necessarily so. Are we seriously suggesting that all 'homosexuals' are uncontrollably promiscuous and exploitative by nature? Certainly there is ample evidence today that sexual idolatry and immorality know no limits to their appetite and expression, and that they can justify all manner of unspeakable evils in their pursuit of power and gratification. But this is a 'heterosexual' problem every bit as much as a 'homosexual' one, and there is no necessary progression of obsessions on the way to the inevitable disintegration that lust produces in the lives of its devotees.

For some, the very mention of the word 'homosexual' is a threat to the Creator's 'heterosexual' order; setting up a polarity rather like 'bad' is to 'good' and 'chaos' is to 'order'. This position could be argued persuasively if, rather like *The Da Vinci Code* suggests, there were a God and Goddess in heaven and all of creation bore their 'heterosexual' imprint. Yet the Genesis account (Gen 1:27) and its affirmation by Jesus (Mk 10:6; Mt 19:4) and indirectly by Paul (Gal 3:28) make it plain that we are created in God's image as humans (*adam*) 'male *and* female', which is deliberately expressed inclusively rather than as the dichotomous 'male *or* female'.[3] Our human sexuality is a wholistic continuum, not a bifurcated polarity, and this both reflects the image of God and is in turn reflected in creation by a wondrous diversity. This in no way threatens the importance and sacredness of 'heterosexual' marriage and procreation, which are obviously central to God's continuing re-creation of humanity and of most living organisms. But not all! In the animal kingdom, the sexuality of creatures like the seahorse and the snail provide wonderful exceptions to 'prove' (as in 'test') the rule. With reference to human sexuality, the Jesus tradition affirms that 'there are eunuchs who have been so from their mother's womb, and eunuchs who have been made so by humans, and eunuchs who have made themselves so on account of the kingdom of heaven. Let the one who is able to comprehend this, comprehend it' (Mt 19:12).[4] Of course, 'heterosexuality'—whether we

---

3. Galatians 3:28 is sometimes mistranslated this way, but the Greek is explicit: 'male *and* female', as in the Hebrew of Genesis 1:27. The polarity 'male or female' *does* occur in the Hebrew Bible, but is reserved for discussions of particular people, typically a 'male or female slave' in the Torah. It does not occur in the New Testament.

4. We are mistaken if we assume that the point of the saying is that eunuchs (like the preceding divorcees, so the argument goes) can't 'have sex'. Clearly they can't if

speak of physical features, gender roles or orientation—describes the majority of God's created order, but it has never been universal or mandatory. As Jesus says: some are born different, and this calls for our understanding.

Whereas it is possible and desirable, therefore, to affirm 'heterosexuality' as the created 'norm', it should be done so without denying the natural existence of other realities along the spectrum between maleness and femaleness. By their nature, 'norms' can never be absolutes since they exist only in relation to other minorities. Accepting this reality does not threaten the 'norm', but strengthens and defines it more clearly. It would pose a far greater threat to Christian 'heterosexual' marriage to insist that it should be imposed on all humans regardless of their physical sexuality and orientation. The trauma of those Christians whose partners eventually discover they are 'homosexual' or perhaps 'asexual' is testimony to the problems caused by the unhelpful and unbiblical imposition of a uniform 'heterosexuality' on all humans.[5] As Christians, we should allow the celibate and the eunuch to qualify our 'heterosexuality'; the validity of the single life (Jesus and Paul?!) to limit our expectations and glorification of marriage; and the presence of the abused and the prostitute to challenge our sexual idolatry. We haven't even really begun to ask what role the affirmation of the 'homosexual', the 'intersexual' and the 'transsexual' might play in awakening the church to its full glory as the body of Christ.

1.2 More important issues?

Yes, there *are* more important issues facing Christians today that affect the lives of many more people and which must therefore take priority, but that is no excuse to avoid the question altogether and thereby ignore those 'homosexuals' living on the margins of our churches and our society. This is not just an issue concerning private morality and sexual preference. It is a

---

sex is defined from a male perspective, but that definition is one of those aspects of patriarchal dominance still awaiting the transforming power of the Gospel (1 Cor 7:4b! See further below). J David Hester's 'Eunuchs and the Postgender Jesus: Matthew 19.12 and Transgressive Sexualities', *Journal for the Study of New Testament*, 28 (2005): 13–40, corrects the traditional misinterpretation that the eunuch is a symbol of inevitable celibacy.

5. I recall evangelists in my youth proclaiming: 'You are not in God's perfect will until you have found God's perfect partner' (a 'heterosexual' relationship being assumed, of course). Combine this with Western romantic mythology and the 'cult of The Wedding' and a very real threat to 'marriage and the Christian family' emerges—namely a divorce rate amongst Christians that is not that different to the rest of the population.

justice issue—an issue of righteousness in the private *and* public spheres—and a matter of life and death for some in our community so traumatised by the perils of discovering their sexual identity and orientation that they live in constant fear and even take their own life. Sadly, this seems to be particularly true of young men in Christian circles, though this is not a claim that can be substantiated with 'hard statistics'—only by the retrospective reflections of pastors, counsellors and grieving families.

I sometimes wish that I could avoid this whole topic in the hope that it might one day go away. But it won't, and I can't. I am not pressing for a militant campaign to force church authorities to change their mind on this matter. Rather, I simply wish to argue in support of those local congregations that are both welcoming *and* affirming of faithful Christian 'homosexuals' who are already in our midst—or perhaps who have been forced out of Christian fellowship by the church's stand on these issues—and to support the wider claims of justice for all 'homosexuals' before the law.

1.3 A problem of Western decadence?

'Homosexuality' and related issues are not just a problem within 'decadent Western societies', though they might be spoken about more openly in those communities that have the vocabulary and freedom to permit discussion of what is still unspeakable within some languages and cultures. There are, and always have been, forms of 'homosexual' expression within *all* human cultures (and within the wider animal kingdom), just as there also have been those who never mate or marry and those born with ambiguous sexual organs. The question is whether the biblical witness to what is appropriate sexual behaviour applies to all humans equally—or whether 'some are born more equal than others.' This should not be seen as a 'heterosexual versus homosexual' debate, but rather as a discussion undertaken with an awareness of the full spectrum of human sexuality: including physical characteristics, orientation and the social construction of gender roles. These are issues that lurk in the background of all human societies, and whereas some may rightly be preoccupied with more urgent problems such as hunger and war, the abuse of sexuality by entrenched patriarchies must not be ignored in the process of meeting other needs. It is salutary to note that those who protest most strongly against even discussing these issues may have the most to hide: this is a truth that applies not only at the individual level, but especially in those cultures where there are entrenched patriarchal interests in preserving the *status quo.*

1.4 The plain sense of Scripture?

Those who appeal to the 'plain sense' of Scripture about this and other issues—as if there does not even need to be any further discussion of what the Bible says—are in danger of reducing God's Living Word to a book of dead letters: immutable laws written in ink, or on stone (2 Cor 3:3). We are not called to be defenders of unchangeable rules, for we are 'competent to be servants of a new covenant, not in a written code but in the Spirit; for the written code kills, but the Spirit gives life' (2 Cor 3:6). From the beginning, we followers of Jesus have been painfully slow to accept that God's transforming Spirit has had new things to teach us about circumcision, food laws, ethnicity, the animal kingdom, slavery, the poor, males *and* females, and the environment. To some, the written code about these matters was, and is, crystal clear and absolutely unchangeable. Yet great changes have slowly taken place as Christian communities have taken seriously the power to 'bind and loose' (Mt 16:19; Jn 20:22–3) on these issues—to live out what the Spirit of the living God has written on their hearts (2 Cor 3:3)—often in defiance of ecclesial and secular authorities. Despite their human shortcomings, Paul of Tarsus, Francis of Assisi, William Wilberforce, Martin Luther King, Desmond Tutu, Mother Theresa, Elizabeth Schüssler Fiorenza and their like, have lived the way of Jesus and shown us much about 'God's-will-on-earth-as-it-is-in-heaven'. We should at least be open to the possibility that there is yet more to learn and put into practice in other areas too—even including our human sexuality. Heaven knows the church has not handled sex well throughout the centuries.

It may well be that our careful exegesis still leads us to what seem to be unambiguous meanings in the biblical text. There is still the task, however, to interpret how those meanings are to be applied in the present context, and by what authority. This is not to say that context determines meaning, nor is it to surrender to relativism, but to recognise the truth that Scripture itself is produced in, and interpreted by, a matrix of culture, tradition and the community of the faithful. This inevitably involves, under the guidance of the Spirit that undergirds the whole process, an examination of the assumptions that we bring to the text and that the text brings to us.

2. Some assumptions that we bring to Scripture

2.1 The way we understand the Bible

I have already alluded above to the ongoing struggle to discern the Living Word within the written Word in the context of the 'binding and loosing' community of faith. The starting place for this process is *not* the Law or community traditions, good and necessary though they may be, but those very people put at risk by the traditions. The ethics of the way of Jesus are always clarified and described at the margins of humanity—'inasmuch as you have done it for the least of these . . .' (Mt 25:40,45)—and stand in continuity with so much of the prophetic and wisdom literature (such as the recurring concern for 'the orphans and widows'). No follower of Jesus can afford to ignore the plight of any marginalised or ostracised group, whatever their religious or moral categorisation in relation to the 'norms' of culture or tradition.

Our interpretation of the biblical text is therefore a divinely biased reading. However much we might struggle to do it, we need to read from 'below the text'—to problematise our position of power, and from 'within the text'—to challenge our assumption that we already know what the text means. The inspiration and authority of the Bible belongs with God and is mediated through the faith community; it is not carved immutably in stone (2 Cor 3:3) or preserved in ossified traditions. It is manifest most powerfully in the Spirit of Jesus when the 'understory' intrudes into the dominant narratives of the 'normal' power structures—the 'overstory'. This happens precisely at those places (in the area of sexual relationships), where unjustly treated and abused women stand up for their rights (Gen 21:8–21; 38:1–30), or their mutilated bodies scream out through the retelling of their story (Jud 19; Hos 13:16; Amos 1:13); where the stereotype of the despised eunuch is challenged (Is 56:3; Jer 38:7f; Mt 19:12; Acts 8:27f), and the possibility of same-sex relationships is hinted at (1 Sam 18:1–4; 19:1; 20:30–1!; 2 Sam 1:26; Mt 8:5–13);[6] and where women of ambiguous reputation touch, and are touched, by Jesus (Mk 5:21–43; 14:3–9; and parallels). These texts should not be avoided in any discussion of human sexuality. They must not be swept conveniently under the mat of a simplistic reading of the law or a vigorous assertion of

---

6. The exact nature of the relationship between Jonathan and David cannot be established from these texts, of course—but nor can the suspicion of a sexual relationship be dismissed out of hand: note the shame alluded to by Saul (1 Sam 20:30–1). As for the relationship between the centurion and his boy-servant, 'the worst case' might well have been suspected from a Jewish perspective in the absence of Luke's commendation of the soldier (Lk 7:3–5). The possibility of such an obvious assumption about the Roman military does not seem to trouble Jesus and/or Matthew. See Theodore W Jennings and Tat-Siong Benny Liew, 'Mistaken Identities but Model Faith: Rereading the Centurion, the Chap, and the Christ in Matthew 8:5–13', *Journal of Biblical Literature*, 123 (2004): 467–94, for detailed arguments in support of this type of interpretation. They push them too far, but still . . .

dogma. They do not, in themselves, overturn the law—but they must qualify, inform and guide our interpretation and application of the law.

For these reasons we cannot simply affirm, nor blandly dispense with, the Levitical purity codes, either selectively or as a whole. They must be wrestled with and reinterpreted in the light of God's ongoing and transforming revelation. For example, the strict prohibitions surrounding menstruation (Lev 15:19–33) are radically reinterpreted by the 'understory' of Jesus' scandalous encounter with a woman who can't stop bleeding ('. . . for twelve years', Mk 5:25) and one who is just beginning ('. . . for she was twelve years old', Mk 5:42). These two stories of two daughters (Mk 5:21–43) are interwoven and inseparably linked by the touching of Jesus, and by the symbolic use of the two twelves, to make it absolutely clear that 'thus all women are declared clean'. A little later in a similar but more explicit way, 'all foods are declared clean' (Mk 7:19b and the food laws in Lev 11) in yet another subversive Jesus story. Thus the 'understories' of Jesus (and of the prophets and others), radically challenge and transform the dominant patriarchal narratives and traditions. It would be foolhardy indeed simply to quote Leviticus 18:22 and 20:13 (whichever way they are interpreted) as the final word on 'homosexuality' in the Bible![7] It would be just as unwise to ignore them altogether as antiquated and irrelevant. When we tackle them further below, we should approach them with a desire both to understand their intent within their own literary and social context, and their relationship to the ongoing transforming revelation of God, particularly as found in Jesus Christ.

---

7. Invariably the response to this sort of argument is that if the Jesus tradition overturns all the Levitical purity codes, then what happens to the prohibitions regarding incest, for example. Again, 'overturn' or 'negate' are not the right words—they belong to later Christian supercessionism, not to the way of Jesus. Jesus reinterprets the law in transformative ways and in ways that challenge patriarchal power. We must be consistent therefore, and reinterpret the laws against incest in this same way. That is, whereas Leviticus 18 (astonishingly) neglects to prohibit sexual relations between a father and his daughter (is this to preserve absolute patriarchal rights?!), it may be inferred that the Jesus tradition (as also later Rabbinic traditions) would challenge this potential for patriarchal abuse and reinterpret these codes in transformative and life-giving ways that affirm the mutuality and non-exploitative nature of responsible sexual relationships. Sometimes the way of Jesus requires stricter laws than the Levitical codes (see Mt 5:20)!

2.2 The way we understand sexuality

Our discussions of sexuality in society and church often reflect the powerful influence of modernist binary opposites—male *or* female; heterosexual *or* homosexual—as if to obscure deliberately the realities that exist between these polarised options. This is most clearly demonstrated at the physical level, but applies equally well to gender role construction and sexual orientation. Modern medicine has tried to resolve every sexually ambiguous birth in the direction of male *or* female (it *is* the first question people ask, after all), but the apparent success of the surgery and/or hormonal treatments has often been short-lived. Somewhere around one to two percent of all babies born have some ambiguity regarding their 'maleness' or 'femaleness', and this ambiguity persists for many of them (and for others not in that narrow physically defined minority) throughout their lives.[8] Even though some of them may not have the genital equipment to fit the 'normal heterosexual paradigm', is it not possible for them to marry and have sexual relations? Are they not also made in God's image and capable of faithful and committed love, and of expressing it physically? Or is marriage and sexual intimacy reserved only for 'heterosexual' couples with the requisite bust size and penis length? Heaven forbid!

Some progress towards challenging dominant stereotypes in the social construction of gender roles seems to have been made in recent years. The macho-man is no longer the only masculine role model on offer, and women are not restricted to purely domestic paradigms of femininity. We now recognise that a man who enjoys cooking and domestic chores may well partner a woman who prefers outdoor activities, even though some temporary adjustments may be necessary if they have children. There are still some Christians who quote the household codes (Col 3:18–19; Eph 5:21–33; 1 Pet 3:1–7; 1 Tim 2:8–15; Tit 2:3–5) as proof texts in support of the continued subordination and domestication of women, but they can only do so by ignoring the original context and intent of those codes, and the many examples of female leaders in the 'understories' of the earliest Christian communities.[9]

---

8. The statistics are notoriously difficult to establish, but see the careful articles by biologist Anne Fausto-Sterling, 'The Five Sexes: Why Male and Female Are Not Enough', *The Sciences* (March/April 1993): 20–5; and 'The Five Sexes, Revisited', *The Sciences* (July/August 2000): 18–23 (both available on-line).

9. The explanation '. . . so that, even if some of them do not obey the word, they may be won over without a word by their wives' conduct' (1 Pet 3:1b) indicates clearly

There is often great emotion and fear generated when it comes to challenging the polarity between 'heterosexual' and 'homosexual' orientation. Some would still prefer to describe 'homosexuality' as a perversion of 'heterosexuality' rather than as the other (less populated) end of a social continuum, and to fear the 'threat' of 'bisexuality' lurking somewhere in the middle. The looming spectre of an aggressive 'homosexuality' that perverts our youth and breaks up marriages often follows not far behind in such understandings. Clearly there *are* immoral and predatory manifestations of 'homosexual' behaviour, just as there are in even larger numbers amongst 'heterosexuals'. But we must be careful here not to let truth as well as love become the victims of our fears, for 'God has not given us a spirit of fear; but of power and love, and of a sound mind' (2 Tim 1:7).

This is not the place to revisit the evidence and arguments over the causes and prevalence of 'homosexual' orientation. We do need to be aware, however, of some of the issues and be suspicious of those who simplify them into neat polarities with black and white answers, lest we find ourselves in the company of those who questioned Jesus, seeking Yes/No answers in order to trap him. Surely it is time to confront the implications of this truth that has become apparent amongst us: there are, and always have been, faithful 'homosexual' Christians in our churches, who do not have the gift of celibacy, and who long to live in a stable, committed relationship with the church's blessing. Yet regardless of our decisions about this within the *ekklesia,* Christians concerned for public morality surely should support the efforts of all 'homosexuals' to gain State recognition for their committed relationships, so that they have full rights before the law, including adoption where appropriate. Whether we approve of 'homosexual' relationships or not, or whether we want to use the term 'marriage' in this context or not, some kind of State recognition is an obvious step to affirm for the greater public good. Long-term stable relationships are better for everyone concerned, and can only enhance the institution of 'heterosexual' marriage by providing a different option for those who are not gifted by God in that way.

---

that these codes (modified from the Greek philosophers) were adopted as an apologetic/evangelistic strategy to win over the non-believing husbands of Christian women who were otherwise in potential danger for rejecting the patriarchal gods. As for women leaders, they abound in the Pauline greetings—sometimes despite the patriarchal bias of our translators! See, for example, Phoebe, letter-bearer, patron of Paul and minister of the church at Cenchreae (Rom 16:1–2); Prisca/Priscilla; Junia, prominent among the apostles (Rom 16:7); Lydia, foundation member and patron at Philippi (Acts 16:11–40), and many others 'mentioned in passing'.

Our assumptions about these issues will shape the way we interpret those biblical texts that intersect with these concerns. It is better that we seek to clarify them first in order to open ourselves to the often very different assumptions that the world of the text brings to us.

3. Assumptions that Scripture brings to us

3.1 Sex as patriarchal power and propagation

References to sex in the Bible reflect both the patriarchal assumptions of the Ancient Near East and the subversive challenges of God's way to that patriarchy. Thus, sex is described, defined and regulated from a male point of view: it is penetrative, ejaculatory and its purpose is to perpetuate the male line. A man plants his seed in a woman, who provides the 'fertile' or 'barren' soil for the seed to grow. There is no awareness of any egg provided by the woman. It is the male seed that provides everything necessary, and thus it is the woman's fault if she proves to be 'infertile'.[10]

Yet at the same time, as argued above, the transforming nature of God's progressive revelation is evident in the persistent 'understories' of faithful 'infertile' women, of prostitutes and of other women of dubious or ambiguous origins. Their vision of justice and their shameless and unshakable faith in God, keep alive the tensive nature of the Living Word within the written word. It is this Living Word that is incarnate in Jesus Christ and embodied again in the Pauline communities and texts. Astonishingly, neither Jesus nor Paul makes any reference to the procreative purposes of sexual intercourse or 'marriage'. In their understanding, sexual relations are not just a means to that end, it would seem. Equally astonishing is the mutuality of sexual relationships implied in the teaching of Jesus (Mk 10:11–12!) and described by Paul. That a woman's body is not her own but her man's (1 Cor 7:4a) is stating the obvious in the ancient world, but to go on to claim the reverse— that a man's body belongs to his woman (1 Cor 7:4b) is revolutionary indeed in a world where sex was an expression of power.

It was assumed in the wider ancient world that men constituted the powerful end of the sex spectrum, and that women were the 'weaker sex'—

---

10. Or indeed, if she allows any foreign seed to grow in her! It is always 'the woman caught in adultery' (which threatens the purity of the male line), rather than the man who is caught in adultery (since he may be expected to sow some 'wild seed').

really also 'inferior males' but with their genitals turned inwards.[11] So for a 'man to lie with a man' and penetrate him was to show supremacy over him, humiliate him and treat him like a woman, rather like the way that 'homosexual' rape functions in our prisons. By definition then, same-sex intercourse could not happen between continuing social equals: one man would have to lose face. Thus 'homosexuality' in the ancient world was invariably described in terms of unequal relationships: typically older men penetrating younger, often pre-pubescent, youths. The nature of such relationships was inherently exploitative, and despite their prevalence in the Greco-Roman world, there was considerable criticism of them from some philosophers and especially from Jewish writers. It appears that ongoing 'homosexual' relationships between equals (in age or status) were not made public or discussed openly, no doubt because of the shameful implication that the penetrated partner would be understood to be 'weak' and not truly 'male'. For these reasons, the public face of 'homosexuality'—and of Gentile immorality in general as far as the Jews were concerned—was pederasty: the relatively common and promiscuous exploitation of young teenagers and boys (often slaves) by the wealthy and powerful. This is the background against which Paul writes.

3.2 Public and private porneia

It is no surprise then, that *porneia* (better translated generally as 'immorality' than more narrowly as 'fornication') is used to head the lists of vices in many Pauline letters (1 Cor 5:10,11; 6:9; Gal 5:19; Eph 5:3,5; Col 3:5; 1Tim 1:10; see also Jesus in Mk 7:21). It acts as the opposite heading to *agape* ('gift love', the source of all true loves) which introduces the lists of virtues (Gal 5:22) and is used much more pervasively throughout the Pauline letters. Lest we think that Paul is obsessed with sexual sin, we should note that his positive use of *agape* occurs at least five times more frequently than *porneia,* and that the sins of greed and pride are also commonly targeted. We should also note that Paul's focus in naming *porneia* as one of the prime evils of his age is not on 'private relationships between consenting adults' or on the violation of some deep purity taboos. Unlike the Levitical codes and some of the 'Christian' equivalents in every age since, Paul does not legislate or pronounce judgment on exactly how or when married couples should express their sexuality, nor does he limit sex to procreative purposes only. He leaves the expression of sexuality within a committed relationship to the imagination

---

11. See, for example, Thomas Laqueur, *Making Sex* (Cambridge: Harvard University Press, 1990), 4.

and mutual benefit of the participants, and encourages them not to abstain for too long (1 Cor 7: 2–5). But when it comes to the abuse of sexuality, Paul is fearless in confronting the ways in which it affects the wider social networks of church and society (see 1 Cor 5–7). The victims are affirmed as cleansed members of the community (1 Cor 6:11).

For Paul, *porneia* is sexual idolatry, which becomes manifest in abusive, promiscuous, exploitative and obsessive sexual behaviour: worshipping the creature rather than the Creator (Rom 1:24–32). The consequences of this idolatrous behaviour included all the excesses widely known to occur at orgies and dinner parties amongst the rich and famous in the first century: the exploitation of slave girls and boys for the gratification of guests and the lewd entertainments of dancing girls, boys and animals. Indeed, members of some of the Pauline communities had been caught up in this abusive behaviour (1 Cor 6:11, 'and this is what some of you were'). Whether some of the slaves in the Corinthian community were still abused against their will is not clear, but Paul is adamant that sexual abuse and exploitation should not continue to happen amongst the community of the faithful (1 Cor 6:12–20). We still tend to overemphasise the role of the individual (private purity codes) in applying these ethics—but Paul makes it abundantly clear that it is not just our bodies that 'are members of Christ' (1 Cor 6:15); it is the body of all of us ('the body of youse/y'all', plural!) that is 'the temple of the Holy Spirit' (1 Cor 6:19). *Porneia,* whether 'hetero-' or 'homo-', is not just a sin against one's own body, but against the body of Christ—the *ekklesia.*

There is no doubt that sex has again become an idol for many in our age, but I think that often the evangelical defence of 'heterosexuality' is just as guilty of this idolatry as the aggressive sectors of the 'homosexual' community. Sexuality (of any kind) should not be spoken of as *the defining* aspect of our personality. We are made in God's image as humans who have been given the potential for sexual relations—a potentiality that is never realised or remains very ambiguous for many. There is no question that heterosexual marriage and procreation are affirmed throughout the biblical traditions, but never to the exclusion of those people that patriarchal structures tend to marginalise: the 'single' person, the 'barren' woman, the widow, the orphan and the eunuch. With this brief sketch of some of the cultural assumptions of the text and its context in mind, we can now approach the biblical traditions with greater sensitivity and openness.

4. At last: the texts about 'homosexuality'

The arguments for and against 'homosexuality' are at their strongest when they appeal to the consistent revelation of the whole canon rather than to specific texts. Those arguing for the exclusivity of the 'heterosexual' norm throughout creation, will point to the paradigmatic nature of the Genesis stories of the creation of male and female and their endorsement by Jesus and Paul. Those arguing for the acceptance of 'moral homosexuals' within the church will point to the love command of Christ as the centre of the canon and make their case accordingly. Both sides can construct an argument with some coherence across various biblical traditions, and marginalise those particular texts that don't fit the case so well. The dominant 'heterosexual interpretation' will tend to downplay the significance of those texts and 'understories' that destabilise the 'norm'. A reading that seeks to claim room in God's house for the sexually marginalised—whilst still 'fleeing *porneia*'—has some hurdles of its own.

For there *are* a few biblical texts that seem to refer explicitly and negatively to sexual activity between people of the same gender.[12] It seems

---

12. The literature on the Bible and 'homosexuality' grows rapidly by the day. I have found the following books particularly helpful: *Homosexuality in the Church: Both Sides of the Debate,* edited by Jeffrey S Siker (Louisville: Westminster John Knox Press, 1994). The chapter by Richard Hays, re-published in *The Moral Vision of the New Testament* (Edinburgh: T and T Clark/HarperCollins, 1996), is one of the most compassionate and fair defences of the traditional 'no-to-homosexuality' position, in my opinion. Surely as Christians we can move at least this far in our understanding! *Biblical Ethics and Homosexuality: Listening to Scripture,* edited by Robert L Brawley (Louisville: Westminster John Knox Press, 1996); *Homosexuality, Science, and the 'Plain Sense' of Scripture,* edited by David L Balch (Grand Rapids: Wm B Eerdmans, 2000); *The Way Forward? Christian Voices on Homosexuality and the Church,* edited by Timothy Bradshaw (Grand Rapids: Wm B Eerdmans, 1997/2003); *Homosexuality and Christian Community,* edited by Choon-Leong Seow (Louisville: WJK Press, 1996); and Willard M Swartley, *Homosexuality: Biblical Interpretation and Moral Discernment* (Waterloo: Herald Press, 2003) are all outstanding examples of open and vigorous Christian debate on these issues. Stanley J Grenz's *Welcoming but not Affirming: An Evangelical Response to Homosexuality* (Louisville: WJK Press, 1998) is a very accessible and fair defence of the traditional position, and Gray Temple's *Gay Unions, In the Light of Scripture, Tradition and Reason* (New York: Church Publishing, 2004) does the same for the pro-'homosexual' arguments. Thomas E Schmidt, *Straight and Narrow? Compassion and Clarity in the Homosexual Debate* (Leicester: IVP, 1995), was regarded by some evangelicals as the best

that the Jewish legal codes were unique in the ancient world in specifically banning 'men-lying-with-men-as-with-a-woman' and in prescribing the death penalty for offenders (see Lev 18:22 and 20:13).[13] On the other hand, female 'homosexuality' ('lesbianism') is not mentioned in the Jewish Scriptures at all, probably because from a patriarchal perspective, women can't have 'real sex' together at all because no 'seed is planted'.[14] Of course we cannot simply derive a position on 'homosexuality' directly from these Jewish texts, since they are part of the purity codes which Jesus continually reinterpreted, explicitly and implicitly (as argued above). It would also seem somewhat arbitrary for us to endorse uncritically the laws prohibiting male same-sex genital activity and not those connected with wearing mixed-yarn garments (Lev 19:19), eating 'black-pudding' (Lev 17:12), clean and unclean foods (Lev 11), women and childbirth (Lev 12), shaving hair and marriage by capture, and so on. Many of the Levitical laws we *would* want to affirm unequivocally (such as those banning child sacrifice and bestiality)—but the point is that we have to re-evaluate each tradition separately, based on the

---

defence of the traditional church position against homosexuality until replaced by Gagnon's *The Bible and Homosexual Practice*. To my mind, Gagnon's exhaustive investigations lack the compassion and fairness of Hays' and Grenz's work, and are biased by an insistence on preserving absolute 'gender boundaries' (male *or* female!) and on a 'homophobic' reading of the First Testament narratives (so that he finds implied 'homosexuality' in the Ham/Noah story amongst many others, but not in the David/Jonathan accounts, for example. See 1 Sam 20:30–3; 2 Sam 1:26).

13. The Sodom and Gomorrah stories do not help to clarify the issues. At most, they rightly indicate disapproval of threatened homosexual gang rape (but a surprising lack of disapproval of Lot offering his virgin daughters instead to protect the visitors), though the main issue in the story seems to be the violation of the hospitality codes for strangers. In the Bible and other Jewish literature, Sodom stands condemned for its pride, wealth, failure to welcome visitors, and immorality (in general, rather than homosexuality in particular, see Ezekiel 16:49, and the strange reference in Jude 7 to 'other flesh', meaning the angels?). It is a much later development that coins the word 'sodomite' meaning 'homosexual'. In fact neither 'sodomy' or 'homosexuality' are Biblical (or even first-century) terms or concepts as such.

14. As Jacob Milgrom concludes: 'Female sexual relations are nowhere prohibited in Scripture, nor anywhere else (to my knowledge) in the Ancient Near East. Surely, lesbianism was known!' *Leviticus 17–22: A New Translation and Commentary,* The Anchor Bible, volume 3A (New York: Doubleday, 2000), 1568. This raises some questions about the traditional interpretation of Romans 1:26 as a reference to 'lesbianism'(see further below).

further revelation of God through Jesus Christ. Part of this process is to seek to understand the social and literary context of the texts in question, so that we can evaluate the relationship between the intent of the codes and the later transformative traditions.

The prohibition in Leviticus 18:22 is situated in a list of codes regulating sexual relations. Many scholars have attempted to describe the underlying principle(s) that explains this rather odd collection of prohibitions and that connects it to the wider holiness codes in the surrounding chapters. Are they arcane purity codes that can be dismissed out of hand as irrelevant today? Is there some kind of obsession with improper 'mixing' of body fluids (semen/blood/anal fluids), as with the bans on 'mixing' yarns and 'mixing' cooking utensils?[15] Is it a concern for the wastage of human seed that underlies the texts banning 'non-productive' sexuality? There may be an element of truth in each of these explanations, but the most coherent arguments for a unifying theme are those of Jewish commentator Jacob Milgrom: 'the common denominator of the entire list of sexual prohibitions, including homosexuality, is procreation within a stable family'.[16] This is shown to be so by the dual concern in chapter 18 for protecting family relationships from exploitative patriarchal sexual abuse (Lev 18:6–18), and for avoiding sexual and behavioural practices that were thought to be inherently non-productive or 'anti-procreational' (intercourse with a menstruant; sacrificing offspring to Molech; intercourse between males, or with animals, Lev 18:19–23).[17] Milgrom adds the suggestion that the 'legal reason for interdicting anal intercourse is the waste, the nonproductive spilling, of seed—the equivalence of Onanism (Gen 38:9–10)'. But as he points out himself, the sin of Onan was not the spilling of his seed but the refusal to continue his brother's line and thus the rejection of the responsibility to

---

15. This sounds plausible, but why then isn't 'heterosexual' anal intercourse explicitly banned?

16. Milgrom, *Leviticus 17–22*, 1568.

17. Milgrom argues the case in detail, *Leviticus 17–22*, 1568. Note that a small percentage of women are at their most fertile during the seven days they are 'off limits', thus rendering them 'barren' through no fault of their own. Gagnon, *The Bible and Homosexual Practice*, 118, is not sure what to do about the naming of sex with a woman during these seven days as an abomination (Lev 18:24–30; Ez 18:6; 22:10), and thus equivalent to 'homosexual' sexual relations in some way. He nevertheless concludes that it is one of the requirements that 'no longer have force today' (121, 137–8), without really explaining why it doesn't, but the ban on 'homosexual' relations in 18:22 does.

procreate.[18] A more precise understanding of the Levitical problem with male 'homosexuality' would be that it is a deliberate avoidance of the responsibility to procreate—a planting of seed (as distinct from a spilling) where it cannot grow.

If Milgrom's underlying principle behind Leviticus 18 ('procreation within a stable family') sounds almost evangelical in its formulation, his suggested solution to the problem of interpreting Leviticus 18:22 comes from another direction altogether:

> Thus from the Bible we can infer the following: presumably, half of the world's homosexual population, lesbians, are not mentioned. Over ninety-nine percent of the gays, namely non-Jews, are not addressed. This leaves the small number of Jewish gays subject to this prohibition. If they are biologically or psychologically incapable of procreation, adoption provides a solution. I hope the Eternal, in love and compassion, will reckon their spilled seed as producing fruit.[19]

How then does the Gospel affirm or transform this text? If it is the mixing and purity concerns which dominate the interpretation, then the examples of Jesus and the bleeding women in Mark 5 and the food laws in Mark 7 provide a strong challenge to any insistence on the letter of these codes. If Milgrom is correct that the underlying concern is for procreation within a stable family, then we must note that this procreational imperative is nowhere affirmed by Jesus or Paul, and least of all by current population trends. The context of a 'stable family' may be seen as a particular concern of Christian ethics in continuity with the teaching of Jesus about children (Mk 10:13–16) and honouring parents (Mt 15:4; 19:19), yet the nature of the 'family unit' in the earliest Christian communities was never the 'nuclear family' (a 'heterosexual' couple with 1.8 children?) so fiercely defended by the Christian Right. The 'family' affirmed in the Jesus traditions and the Pauline communities, is the extended family, the 'fictive kinship group', the 'hospitable household', where no man is called father/patriarch (Mt 23:9; see

---

18. Otherwise masturbation would also be condemned as wasting seed, but it isn't. The Rabbis did condemn masturbation later on, 'but it is their enactment, not that of Scripture.' Milgrom, *Leviticus 17–22*, 1567–8.
19. Milgrom, *Leviticus 17–22*, 1787.

also Mk 10:29–30). This is the radical vision of the family that transforms the patriarchal Greco-Roman world. For today's church to support the adoption of 'unwanted' children by responsible 'homosexual' couples (and other 'fictive kinship groups') would be consistent with such transforming initiatives in a world of broken families. Perhaps Milgrom's Jewish exegesis of Leviticus 18:22 is not so different to a truly evangelical exegesis after all?

The Gospels say nothing explicitly about 'homosexuality' as such. Indeed there are only three texts in the New Testament which might be related directly to the topic (1 Cor 6:9; 1 Tim 1:10 and Romans 1:18–32).[20] The meaning of the word first found in Corinthians and then the Timothy text—*arsenokoites* ('man-bedder'/'lying with a male'; the modern terms *arse* and *coitus* are a *later* development)—is much disputed. The word seems to pick up the Greek translation of the Leviticus texts about 'men lying with men', but it can be argued that it carries the added connotation of male prostitution and the economic exploitation of sex rather than 'homosexuality' as such. The other term used in the Corinthian text, *malakos,* means 'soft' or 'effeminate' (in a first-century sexist way), which seems to confirm this connection with prostitution since it is used as the slang word for the 'passive homosexual partner' (who were younger men/boys in Greco-Roman culture). Yet it is also used of men who eat too much, read too many books or engage in heterosexual sex too often![21] Thus it can be argued that what Paul is opposing here is *exploitative* 'homosexual' relationships (namely, male prostitution and older men abusing young boys/slaves)—just as he also opposes exploitative heterosexual relationships—rather than opposing the possibility of a loving, long-term relationship between two same-sex adults. Indeed, there is no clear

---

20. The texts in Matthew that Schmidt, *Straight and Narrow?* refers to are rather less clear (Mt 18: 6–9). At best they might be used against pedophilia ('anyone who causes one of these little ones to stumble . . . ' Mt 18:6), but this would apply to 'heterosexuals' at least as much as to 'homosexuals'.

21. See Dale B Martin, '*Arsenokoites* and *Malakos*: Meanings and Consequences' in *Biblical Ethics and Homosexuality,* edited by Brawley, 117–36. It is thus very difficult to know how to translate the term in today's world—perhaps 'indulgent', 'lazy' or 'lacking self-control' would be best. John H Elliott, 'No Kingdom of God for Softies? Or, What Was Paul Really Saying? 1 Corinthians 6:9–10 in Context,' *Biblical Theological Bulletin,* 34 (2004): 17–40, despairs of a clear translation of these words: 'it is possible but not certain that *malakoi* and *arsenokoitai* denoted effeminate and domineering male partners respectively in abusive or commercialised sexual relationships. This meaning, however, is a supposition based on what is known about the culture of Paul's world and on semantic possibilities (but not certainties) of the words themselves' (36).

evidence of any specific reference to same-age same-sex sexual relationships in Paul or in any other ancient literature.[22] Rather it is pederasty that is the focus of Paul's criticism, and the assumption in most literature of the day (and in Romans 1) seems to be that this exploitation of young males by older men occurs when those men have grown weary of promiscuous heterosexual relations.

Even so, the argument that Paul only refers to exploitative or promiscuous same-sex relationships seems to be more difficult to sustain in connection with the Romans 1:18–32 (26–8) text, which contains a descriptive reference to men-lying-with-men, including *perhaps* the only biblical reference to 'lesbianism'. This is not totally clear, however, since the emphasis is that the women are no longer under the authority of their husbands ('*their* women exchanged natural relations for unnatural', Rom 1:26), and the exact nature of the unnatural relations is not certain, though the presumption should be that it involved sexual penetration, or else the contrast with 'natural relations' loses most of its force. Again, from the assumed patriarchal perspective of the text, any 'lesbian' activity between women would be seen as just 'foreplay' before the 'real sex' of penetration and ejaculation. Therefore bestiality is more likely being alluded to here (see Lev 20:16)—especially given what we know of the lewd entertainments at some Greco-Roman dinner parties—though no doubt Paul would also have disapproved of other kinds of public female sexual lewdness.[23] It is clear, however, that the wider context shows that Paul is not prescribing ethical standards in Romans 1–3 so much as describing what he sees as the fallen condition of humanity (Gentile *and* Jew, see Romans 3:9). So in Romans 1:26–8 he merely reflects the typical Jewish perceptions of 'immoral pagan Gentiles' before hitting his Jewish colleagues with the truth that they are no better off (Rom 2:17f)—even if they don't practise 'homosexuality', amongst other things. *All* have fallen short—*all* are saved by grace—whereupon ethical standards must be worked out anew in the light of that grace.

Clearly Paul *was* emphatically opposed to the exploitative and promiscuous 'homosexuality' widely known to have been practised in Gentile circles at that time. Just what he would have said about two 'homosexuals' in

---

22. See Herman C Waetjen, 'Same-Sex Sexual Relations in Antiquity and Sexuality and Sexual Identity in Contemporary American Society', in *Biblical Ethics and Homosexuality*, edited by Brawley, 103–16.

23. The language used by Paul in this section is very similar to that used by Philo, Josephus and other Jewish critics of Gentile immorality.

a committed and mutually enriching relationship is not at all clear. Such relationships were kept quiet then, as they still have to be for many today—and especially in the church.

Yet even if we were still to view 'homosexuality' in all its forms as sinful, there are certainly no grounds in these New Testament texts for Christians to single out 'homosexuals' as such or to regard them as more sinful than others, or to refuse them church membership or training. Do we refuse membership (or even ordination) to those who have a tendency towards greed or gossip and who occasionally yield to the temptation? What is the church's record on disciplining all ministers who have a tendency to commit adultery? As Hays, who opposes the ordination of 'homosexuals', puts it: 'If they ('homosexuals') are not welcome (in the church), I will have to walk out the door along with them, leaving in the sanctuary only those entitled to cast the first stone'.[24]

5. Just what is the Spirit saying to the churches?

The wider context is always helpful to return to in this debate. The clear focus of New Testament exhortations about sexual ethics (which themselves must be balanced by the far more frequent exhortations about wealth, pride, gossip, divisive behaviour, and so on) is on *porneia*—promiscuous, abusive, obsessive and exploitative sexuality (whether 'hetero-' or 'homo-' but predominantly the former). There are certainly no grounds for a fear-driven 'witch-hunt' of those in our churches who have a same-sex orientation/ temptation. Indeed, more positively stated, there is a clear mandate in the ministry of Jesus to the marginalised (including prostitutes and the adulterous) for us to support 'homosexual' persons in our church communities and to fight for justice for 'practising homosexuals' under our legal system—and especially to care for those who may be suffering from AIDS/HIV. Our ethics—if we wish to follow Jesus—should be formulated from our position of solidarity with those living and suffering at the margins of society.

Certainly Christians may justifiably oppose the aggressive 'homosexuality' seen in some aspects of the 'Gay' street marches and the promiscuous 'homosexuality' that is found in some of the night clubs and bars—but our protests will only be legitimate insofar as we spend even more time protesting against the aggressive and promiscuous 'heterosexuality' that dominates far more of our media and society. Furthermore, we should be able

---

24. Hays, 'Awaiting the Redemption of Our Bodies', in *Homosexuality in the* Church, edited by Siker, 14.

to expect that Christians will show the world how discussion on these issues can be carried out in a loving and truthful way, so that fear, 'homophobia' and 'heterosexism' do not dominate the debate as so often happens, but rather the 'the spirit of love, peace and a sound mind'. Would it be such a threat to the good order of creation and of the church for us to acknowledge the truth that some of our past heroes in the faith were 'practising homosexuals' (assuming for a moment that we all agree on what that phrase might mean)?

I have a dream—pretentious though it may be for me to say it in this way—I have a dream that one day all people may come to value and express (if they choose) their sexuality in accord with the biblical principles of mutuality, commitment and love, and thereby accept and embrace themselves and each other as God's beloved regardless of their sexual orientation or genital equipment. I have a dream that even though different parts of the church will no doubt continue to disagree on these matters (as also on abortion, divorce and remarriage, women and ministry, slavery, head-coverings, pork and a host of other issues), they will respect each other's right and responsibility to 'bind and loose' (Mt 16:19; Jn 20:22–3) on these difficult issues, and trust God to reveal the consequences over time. This dream is a thoroughly biblical dream in upholding the persistent (but never absolute) Divine affirmation of monogamous heterosexual relationships in both Testaments, and in opposing *porneia*—exploitative, promiscuous, obsessive and abusive forms of sexuality—which the biblical accounts also never shy away from confronting. This dream is also a transformative one, in that it envisions an even more inclusive gathering of God's elect—reaching beyond the comfortable norms of blinkered tradition to embrace those who have been made to feel they can never belong.

2

Scripture and Homosex: Addressing the Key Texts[1]

Graham A Cole

1. Introduction

Our topic is an important one. In the Anglican Communion—to cite one example—there is great controversy over the consecration of Bishop Gene Robinson as the Episcopal Bishop of New Hampshire, which the *Windsor Report* released in October 2004 has not settled.[2] Bishop Robinson is not only divorced but is in a same-sex union. For some his consecration is a gospel blessing: a matter of social justice. The gospel on this view is about God setting things right in the world. Part of that setting right involves giving the poor and those marginalised because of sexual 'orientation', race or religion a place at the table and a share in the commonwealth. For others, especially in Africa, the church's interaction with its Muslim neighbours has become all the more difficult because of the consecration. Homosex to Muslims is a great sin and the consecration of Robinson is symptomatic of Western decadence.

---

1. Often these days a distinction is drawn between a same-sex orientation and same-sex sexual behaviour. As far as I can see, the Scripture writers do not know this distinction. So for our purposes I will focus on same-sex behaviour or homosex. 'Homosex' is being used increasingly to refer to same-sex, sexual activity as opposed to homosexuality as a sexual orientation, which may or may not express itself in same-sex, sexual practices. The writer learned from Dr Robert Priest, an anthropologist at Trinity Evangelical Divinity School, that in certain South American countries the male who penetrates another male is not considered a homosexual. However, any male willingly so penetrated is regarded as a homosexual. But both have been involved in homosex. Hence the usefulness of the term as it does not beg the questions of orientation versus practice

2. The Windsor Report of *The Lambeth Commission on Communion* was a study undertaken at the request of the Archbishop of Canterbury on the legal and theological implications flowing from the decisions of the Episcopal Church (USA) to appoint Gene Robinson as one of its bishops.

Moreover, to many African Anglicans the consecration is a betrayal of the Faith. In particular, the consecration is perceived as a disavowal of biblical authority.

What are Christians to make of such controversy? How does Scripture speak to these complex questions? As Dietrich Bonhoeffer lamented long ago in his classic work *Life Together,* there is too much argument from experience and life in the churches and not enough of 'the Scripture argument'.[3] By 'the Scripture argument' he meant where Scripture is the norm, providing the ultimate court of appeal in matters of faith and life.

But such a sentiment raises a prior question: What does it mean to call our Bible 'Scripture'? Then the next question becomes: What does Scripture actually have to say about homosex? Let's look at each of these questions in turn before briefly considering some differing interpretative approaches to the scriptural texts and then drawing some conclusions.

2. Scripture: God's book and the church's book

When I speak of the Scriptures I am not referring to merely some literature of ancient Israel and the early church. Some theologians do, however. For them the Scriptures represent human groping after God, of varying degrees of inspiration and quality. In contrast, theologian David Kelsey states the traditional view rather well, when he writes: 'To call this collection "Holy Scripture" is to judge that it is not merely an anthology of texts, but that it ought to fill an indispensable and decisive function at the very centre of the church's life with the holy God'.[4] My own approach is more the traditional or, better, the classical one as found in the reformers of the sixteenth century and as presented in the formularies of my own Anglican tradition: namely, the Book of Common Prayer and the Thirty-Nine Articles. I say 'classical' because many a Roman Catholic and Eastern Orthodox believer would hold a like view.

But what exactly is that view mentioned above? Formally speaking, Scripture, on this view, is construed as God's word in human words. A double agency story is required to do justice to the internal testimony of Scripture: a divine one of inspiration and a human one of its writing. Just as in our Christology (doctrine of Christ) we may be bewitched by a lurch to the right

---

3. Dietrich Bonhoeffer, *Life Together* (New York: Harper, 1954).
4. David Kelsey, 'Scripture, Doctrine of', in *A New Dictionary of Christian Theology*, edited by Alan Richardson and John Bowden, revised edition (London: SCM, 1983), 528.

or the left, so too with Scripture. A lurch to the right turns Scripture into a monophysitism (one naturedness) of only divine authorship. In the ancient church some argued that Christ was truly God but only apparently human (for example Docetism). A lurch to the left reduces Scripture to a merely human word about God and us. This is a monophysitism of only human authorship. In the ancient church some argued that Christ was not God but a human prophet only (for example the Ebionites). Islam holds a similar view today. But just as orthodox Christology predicates a truly divine nature and a truly human nature of the one Person of Christ so too, classically, Scripture is seen as a divine book and a human one.

The resulting doctrine of Scripture is a highly sophisticated one. True, what the Bible says, God says. But that old saw can mask a huge amount of theological work that underlies such a claim. Indeed, a plethora of technical terms has been generated in an attempt to get to grips with the reality of Scripture as God's word written: special revelation, inspiration, supremacy, sufficiency, canonicity, inerrancy, infallibility, clarity to name a few. My point is that on analysis the classical view of Scripture, as the inspired authoritative Word of God, is a complex theological notion that catches up a whole cluster of subordinate notions such as the ones mentioned above. In many ways it is like the notion of Trinity which, as BB Warfield argued so long ago, although not found in Scripture *per se*, takes us more deeply into the sense of Scripture than merely quoting texts can do. It is a master concept that gathers up the otherwise *disjecta membra* (discrete parts) of the scriptural testimony into a coherent whole.[5] Likewise, I maintain, the classical notion of Holy Scripture takes us more deeply into the human and divine reality of Scripture than any other proposal to date.

Put another way, when I speak of Scripture, especially Holy Scripture, I speak out of the context not of the world, nor of the academy but of the church. Thus I speak as a theologian rather than an historian of religious ideas—albeit a Christian one—or as philosopher of religion or as an academic in the field of religious studies. As a Christian theologian I am looking for what is normative in Scripture: namely, what in Scripture should bind my conscience in today's world? However, it is one thing to have such a high view of Scripture. It is another to interpret Scripture aright.

With regard to matters of interpretation or hermeneutics our Reformers still have much to teach us. They adopted the Analogy of Faith: Scripture is to

---

5. BB Warfield, *Biblical and Theological Studies* (Philadelphia: Presbyterian and Reformed, 1952).

interpret Scripture, Scripture is not to be interpreted against Scripture and plain Scripture is to interpret obscure Scripture. Our Anglican formularies reflect these principles. I would add a fourth principle: Scripture is to be interpreted genre by genre. A parable is to be seen as such in contrast to a proverb or a psalm and so forth. Moreover, when texts are appealed, to they need to be placed in their contexts, in their arguments, in their books, in the canon in the light of the flow of redemptive history. For example, many an Old Testament regulation no longer applies literally. Tabernacle worship regulations are a case in point. However, the theological principles underlying such texts may still be of particular relevance: God is to be approached God's way not ours.

So much for generalities and scene setting—what about the specific texts that refer to same-sex behaviour?

3. The key scriptural texts

In the canon of Scripture there are seven crucial texts for our consideration: four are in the Old Testament and three in the New.[6]

---

6. There is a fourth text in the New Testament if Jude 7 is counted. However, it is not clear that Jude has homosexuality in mind or sex with angelic beings—'other flesh' (Greek)—as constituting the offence and so I have not included it. For a scholarly engagement with the texts see Richard B Hays, *Moral Vision of the New Testament: Community, Cross, New Creation: a Contemporary Introduction to New Testament Ethics* (San Francisco: HarperSanFrancisco, 1996). Also see the important article by David F Wright, 'Homosexuals or Prostitutes: The Meaning of ARSENOKOITAI (1 Corinthians 6:9, 1 Timothy 1:10)' *Vigilae Christianae*, 38, (1984): 125–53. For a radical, same-sex reading of the texts and others see Daniel A Helminiak, *What the Bible Really Says About Homosexuality*, millenium edition (New Mexico: Alamo Square Press, 1999). Helminiak treats sympathetically the arguments that Ruth and Naomi were lesbian lovers, and that Saul tried to kill David because of a same-sex love triangle involving his son, Jonathan, and that Jesus healed a centurion's boy slave, who was also his same-sex lover, and did so without condemnation. The exegesis is unconvincing in the extreme. Also see Dan O Via and Robert AJ Gagnon, *Homosexuality and the Bible: Two Views* (Minneapolis: Fortress, 2003). As New Testament scholars, Via and Gagnon take different approaches to the question of the propriety of homosex. Via supports committed same-sex unions. Gagnon opposes the notion. Both agree, importantly, that the biblical texts that refer to homosex 'condemn it unconditionally (93)'.

3.1 Key Old Testament texts

The Genesis 19 text deals with the story of the judgment of Sodom and Gomorrah, and the rescue of Abraham's nephew Lot. As the story unfolds, the angelic visitors to Lot's house come under threat from the men of the city who demand that they come out and be known sexually by them. This sordid story is about inhospitality, about sexual humiliation, power and violence. Same-sex rape is on view (Gen 19:5). Severe judgment follows. In Judges 19 there are some similar themes. The Levite and his concubine are shown hospitality in Gibeah. But the men of the city demand that the Levite come out and be known sexually by them (Judg 19:22). Again on display are inhospitality, threatened sexual humiliation, power, violence and same-sex rape. The Levite responds to the threat by providing his concubine to them. She subsequently dies. Over and over again in the latter part of the book of Judges the point is made that in those days there was no king in the land (Judg 18:1; 19:1 and 20:25). Hence such outrages occurred.

The two key Leviticus texts are in a section of Leviticus known to scholars as the Holiness Code. Israel is not to be religiously and morally like the nation it left behind (Egypt; Lev 18:1–5), nor to be like the nation to whose land it was going (Canaan; Lev 20:22–4). Same-sex male sexual behaviour merited death (Lev 18:22 and 20:13). Such behaviour like that of Egypt and Canaan were abominations. Other behaviour that belonged to the pagan cluster included child sacrifice, sex within certain family relations and sex during a woman's menstruation.

In sum, there are only negative texts in the Old Testament about same-sex behaviour. What is not treated in any Old Testament texts is a same-sex monogamous sexual relationship, a matter to which we shall return at a later stage.

3.2 Key New Testament texts

Romans 1 is part of an argument that extends to Romans 3, which asserts that the whole world—whether Jewish or Gentile—stands guilty before God for turning away from its Creator. In the first chapter, Gentiles in particular are on view and same-sex behaviour is presented by Paul as an expression of God's judgment upon them (Rom 1:26–7). He gives people up to what they set their hearts on. Disordered sexual expression is an example of this. According to Paul it is *para phusin*: that is to say, 'against nature.' Chapter 4 introduces the counter example of Abraham and Sarah as NT Wright suggests.[7] Abraham

---

7. NT Wright, 'Interview with Anglican Bishop NT Wright of Durham, England' http:/www.nationalcatholicreporter.org/word/wright.htm

and Sarah show the godly way, which acknowledges God, is thankful, is obedient to the divine will, is a union of male and female, and is fertile. The Genesis 1 mandate of fruitfulness is back on track through faith.

In 1 Corinthians 6:9–11, Paul writes of the Corinthians' past pagan life, which included active and passive roles in same-sex behaviour (*arsenokoites* and *malakoi*, respectively]. Those who live like that won't inherit the kingdom of God. All this is past tense because the gospel has changed their lives.[8] This text is consistent with the Romans 1 presentation, as is the final one, which is 1Timothy 1:10. Lawless behaviour is contrary to the gospel and that includes active same-sex behaviour (*arsenokoites*).

In sum, there are only negative texts about same-sex sexual behaviour in the New Testament. But interestingly, the language of abomination is not used, in unlike the Leviticus text.[9] And again, what is not thematised in any New Testament texts is a same-sex monogamous sexual relationship.

4. Some approaches to the key texts

The question now before us is to how such texts are to be approached today.

4.1 The texts-are-morally-primitive approach

On this view, the biblical writers were people of their time and ill-informed on same-sex matters. Bishop Richard Holloway puts it this way:

> allowing the living scripture of our own experience to challenge the dead letter of the written law . . . acknowledging that it witnesses to an earlier, no longer appropriate, attitude to human relationships.[10]

The bishop sees the Scripture as the church's book but begs the question about Scripture as God's book. Such an approach is not consistent with a high view of Scripture.

---

8. Both the NRSV and NIV take *arsenkoitai* to mean 'male prostitutes'.

9. Perhaps the reason for the absence of abomination language is that according to Romans 1 same-sex sexual expression is an outworking of judgment rather than grounds for judgment.

10. Richard Holloway, *Godless Morality: Keeping Religion Out Of Ethics* (Edinburgh: Canongate Books, 1999), 80ff.

4.2 The texts-need-reinterpretation approach

D Sherwin Bailey, for example, in 1955 argued that Genesis 19 is about inhospitality rather than same-sex behaviour.[11] As for Romans 1, John Boswell in 1980 maintained that the text was about heterosexuals acting as homosexuals and therefore in a perverted way as far as their natures were concerned.[12] A few years later, Robin Scroggs argued that Paul was writing about sexual abuse: namely, pederasty.[13] William L Countryman in 1988 suggested that Romans 1 is talking about the contravention of the social conventions about purity.[14] Examples could be multiplied. Such views may be consistent with a high view of Scripture but how exegetically well founded is at issue.

4.3 The texts-prove-too-much approach

On this view if Christians condemn homosexual behaviour because of scriptural testimony then, by analogy, those same Christians must sanction slavery. Bishop John Shelby Spong offers this line of argument.[15] Other examples cited are women's ordination, and divorce and remarriage. The argument runs that if one maintains that same-sex sexual relations are immoral then so too is women's ordination, and divorce and remarriage. But the question to be faced is whether these are apple-and-apple comparisons or apples-and-oranges comparisons?[16]

---

11. D Sherwin Bailey, *Homosexuality and the Western Tradition* (London: Longmans, Green and Co, 1955).

12. John Boswell, *Christianity, Social Tolerance and Homosexuality: Gay People in Western Europe from the Beginning of the Christian Era to the Fourteenth Century* (Chicago: University of Chicago Press, 1980).

13. R Scroggs, *Homosexuality in the New Testament: Contextual Background for Contemporary Debate* (Philadelphia: Fortress Press, 1983).

14. William L Countryman, *Dirt, Greed and Sex: Sexual Ethics in the New Testament and Their Implications for Today* (Philadelphia: Fortress Press, 1988).

15. See Sally Cloke, 'Spong takes on Scripture's "terrible texts"', in *The Melbourne Anglican*, November 2003.

16. In particular, there are different kinds of slavery described in Scripture, especially in the Old Testament. A Hebrew who has become a slave through debt is not analogous to the Gentile captured in war. Again, in the New Testament the argument of Philemon appears to undermine slavery and in 1 Timothy 1 slave trading is one of the expressions of lawlessness that is contrary to the gospel. As for women's ordination, women's ministry is clearly a New Testament reality (Phil 4:2–3). The issue is the present day scope of their ministry. With regard to divorce and remarriage, the *prima facie* tensions between Matthew 19, Mark 10 and 1

4.4 The silence-of-Jesus approach

This position draws attention to the fact that none of the canonical gospels provides a text from Jesus on the subject of homosex.[17] There are texts concerning marriage and divorce (for example, Matt 19:1–12), texts concerning adultery (for example, John 8:1–11) but no texts concerning homosex. Jesus does refer to Sodom but the accent either falls on the hypothetical scenario that if Jesus had done his mighty works there then the people of that city would have repented (Matt 11:23) or on the judgment that did fall on the Sodom (Luke 17:28–9). With regard to the latter reference, on view is the very ordinary rhythm of Sodom's everyday life of eating, drinking and marrying. The argument runs that if homosex were that important an issue or if Jesus held strong opinions opposed to the practice then there surely would be a text. Instead there is silence.[18]

However, the argument proves too much. Jesus was silent on pedophilia and bestiality. So did he approve or tolerate such practices? Moreover, Jesus did speak about marriage and when he did his views were conservative. For him it was back to Moses and the primordial text of Genesis. One flesh union involves a man and a woman and could not be dissolved except under certain conditions (Matt 19:1–12). Indeed divorce is concession to the hardness of the

---

Corinthians 7 demand subtle theological treatment. In contrast, as we have seen, there are no positive texts about same-sex sexual behaviour in Scripture. See William J Webb, 'A Redemptive-Movement Hermeneutic: The Slavery Analogy' and 'Gender Equality And Homosexuality', in *Discovering Biblical Equality: Complementarity Without Hierarchy*, edited by Ronald W Pierce and Rebecca Merrill Groothuis (Downers Grove: InterVarsity Press, 2004), chapters 22 and 23 respectively.

17. See Victor Paul Furnish's the argument from the silence of Jesus on the subject of homosex in his 'The Bible and Homosexuality: Reading the Texts in Context', in *Homosexuality in the Church: Both sides of the Debate*, edited by JS Siker (Louisville, Kentucky: Westminster Knox Press, 1994), 18–35.

18. The silence may be more apparent than real. When Jesus addresses the matter of divorce, the exceptional circumstance, which provides grounds for divorce in both Matthew 5:32 and 19:9, is described in terms of 'sexual immorality' (ESV). In the Greek text, *porneia* is a very broad term that arguably covers all the sorts of sexual sin referred to in the Old Testament, according to Kevin Scott, *At Variance: The Church's Argument Against Homosexual Conduct* (Edinburgh: Dunedin Academic Press, 2004), 28–9. Also see the use of *porneia* as a descriptor in the Greek text of Mark 7:20–3 where Jesus speaks of the evils that come out of the human heart.

Graham A Cole

human heart. The argument from silence is a dangerous one to suggest. The absence of evidence is not necessarily evidence of absence.

4.5 The committed-monogamous-same-sex-relations-not-on-view approach
This position maintains that Scripture is uniformly negative about the kinds of homosex it describes. However, there is one kind of homosex that Scripture does not describe and therefore the question is an open one as to whether Scripture can be interpreted to proscribe this practice. A committed, monogamous, same-sex union does not fall under the biblical strictures. In fact such a union may embody all the positive values found in a heterosexual, one flesh union: love, faithfulness and kindness, for example. The writer has Christian friends who advocate and instantiate this view. But is it tenable? The problematic with this view lies in the consistent biblical teaching, canonically considered, that sees the proper context for one flesh union is that of heterosexuality.

Certainly, in the biblical writings, human sexuality, though it may be distorted by sin, remains a creation good. The Song of Songs is a marvellous depiction of the joys and embodiment as expressed in sexual arousal, desire and consummation (Song 7:1–8:4).[19] There is none of the ancient Greek view of the body as the tomb of the soul, nor of the later Manichaen flight from the physical. Likewise in the New Testament, Paul attacks the proto-Gnostic teaching that forbade marriage. For Paul, God's creation remains good and can be properly appropriated for human enjoyment in the context of the word and prayer (1 Tim 4:1–5). Paul's own teaching on the created order is then a dialectic, between the good creation continued (as in 1 Tim 4:1–5) and a creation which itself longs for redemption from futility (as in Rom 8:18–25).

There is, therefore, no room in a robustly biblical Christianity for the denigration of sexual union or, more generally put, life in the body. However, the relationally and morally proper context for sexual union is the marriage of male and female. The rationale for such a marriage, as presented in the Genesis story, is companionship and procreation (Gen 1–2). Elsewhere in the Old Testament the marital relationship is further described in covenant terms

---

19. See the excellent article by BG Webb, 'The Song of Songs: a love poem as Holy Scripture', in *Reformed Theological Review*, XLIX (1990): 91–9. Significantly Webb points out that in the LXX version *agapaō* is regularly used of the love between lovers (for example, 1:3,4,7). This is the word used in the New Testament for God's love for the world (John 3:16). Agape and eros are not necessarily antithetical.

(Mal 2:14). Indeed, again and again in the Old Testament the marital relationship becomes the metaphor for describing God's own covenantal relationship with his people (for example, Hosea and Ezekiel).

The New Testament evidence is of a piece with the older covenant. Jesus understands marriage in one flesh terms (Matt 19) as does Paul (I Cor 6). Hence for Jesus, divorce is a very serious moral concern and for Paul, sexual union with a prostitute can never be a casual matter.

In a biblical doctrine of the good, relationship brings responsibility. Covenants assume commitments and bring moral obligations. The proper context for the celebration of sexuality in one flesh union is marriage, which involves—in biblical summary—a leaving and cleaving, a commitment to companionship and procreation, and a public covenant of some kind. Hence the biblical obligations are clear, though unpopular, in today's permissive world: namely, fidelity within marriage, chastity outside of marriage. The will-to-relate in sexual union is, therefore, delimited by divine design. Put another way, there is moral grain to the universe and to plane against the grain risks splintering the wood. Likewise in human relations, to go against the created order is fraught with difficulty. It is unwise.[20]

5. My own approach and view

Given my high view of scriptural authority and my desire as a Christian to live under that authority, I look for the normative teaching of these texts. This requires wrestling with the meaning of the texts in their ancient context and then wrestling with their moral significance for life in today's world. On this view, what is described in a text needs to be distinguished from what is prescribed or proscribed in the text with sensitivity to their canonical locations in the flow of redemptive history. This approach also asks whether the texts provide limiting cases or precedents? If limiting cases then what about committed gay unions? Are they then exempt from scriptural criticism? Do such unions contravene deeper theological and moral principles? My view is that they do. To adequately address the question of committed gay unions

---

20. The question may be asked, 'What then could change the mind of the Christian with a high view of Scripture that makes all the above approaches untenable? What would the text need to say?' To be sure, if there was a homosex equivalent to the Song of Songs that celebrated the love between David or Jonathan, or, again, if Paul appealed to Philemon to accept the runaway slave Onesimus on the basis of not only his apostleship and their brotherhood in Christ but also as lovers, then faithfulness to Scripture would mean a rethink. But there are no such texts.

more needs to be said about the positive context for sexual union in the biblical accounts, especially about the covenant ideal of heterosexual union as marriage. This ideal is first found in Genesis 2:24, then reaffirmed by Jesus in Matthew's Gospel (Matt 19:4–6) and subsequently by Paul in his Ephesian letter (Eph 5:31) and illustrated in Song of Songs. Briefly put, this positive strand of the biblical presentation is particularly relevant to the question of the ideal for sexual expression. The divine design is heterosexual.

In my own view, when the normative questions are asked of the scriptural testimony the following may be said. Same-sex sexual expression, in the service of power and/or violence, is against the Scripture (Gen 19 and Judges 19). This equally applies to heterosexuals. Further, same-sex sexual expression in the service of a pagan lifestyle is against the Scriptures (an abomination according to Lev 18 and 20). This equally applies to heterosexuals and their sexual activity. Sexual expression outside God's design is not a Christian option (Rom 1, 1 Cor 6 and 1 Tim 1). The divine design is heterosexual not homosexual. To live otherwise is foolish and not wise.

6. Conclusions

There are no biblical texts that affirm same-sex sexual expression whether on view is the Old Testament or the New. In fact, the contrary is the case both in the Old Testament and the New. The attempted reinterpretations of the biblical texts to soften this feature of Scripture are unconvincing though often sincere. A more adequate approach to these complex questions would place the specific discussion of same-sex questions in the wider one of a scriptural view of sexuality, gender and its expression.

Put another way, the discussion of homosex needs to be placed in the bigger framework of a theology of human sexuality which addresses the questions of what the Christian ought to believe about human sexuality, how the Christian ought to live in the light of those beliefs, and what the church has to say to a world which does not subscribe to those beliefs. Such a wider discussion lies beyond the scope of this paper and I have addressed it in print in other places.[21]

---

21. For example, I have attempted that wider discussion in several places including: 'Sexuality in Biblical Perspective with Special Reference to Homosexuality', in *Current Concerns*, edited by Andrew Dirks (Armidale: EFAC, 1993), 3–13. A shorter version has appeared as ' Sexuality and its expression' in *Lukes's Journal*, 5/3 (August 2000): 4–8. Also see my 'Engaging Gay Advocates', *Trinity Magazine* (Spring 2005), 6–19.

3

Homosexuality in Christian Tradition[1]

Muriel Porter

Christian tradition has always treated homosexual practices—though not always homosexual love—as sinful. However, the degree of sinfulness it has accorded homosexuality has varied, creating a tradition that can best be regarded as ambivalent. For considerable periods in Western Christian history, homosexual activity has been regarded as no more sinful than gluttony; at other times, it has been regarded as the grossest of abominations, punishable by death.

It is worth noting that the condemnation of homosexuality has waxed and waned according to the secular environment. This condemnation has been strongest in periods when heterosexual activity was most stringently controlled, such as during the campaign against clerical marriage in the eleventh and twelfth centuries, or during the Victorian era, when heterosexual practice was subject to a rigid conformity. The traditional teaching on homosexuality needs always to be understood alongside traditional main-stream Christian teachings on heterosexual activities, which include teachings now generally abandoned by the church, such as the condemnation of pleasure in intercourse even within marriage, or—in the Protestant, Anglican and Orthodox churches—artificial contraception.

The basis for the most persistent and influential Christian teaching against homosexuality has not been biblical exegesis on its own, or even pre-eminently, but rather claims that it was 'against nature', which drew as much on continuing pre-Christian Western philosophies as on Scripture.

Sexuality and Scripture

Traditionally, the Jewish Scriptures have been interpreted as explicitly forbidding homosexual practices *per se*. Precisely what understanding of homosexual activity they condemn is the subject of modern debate among

---

1. This chapter appears by kind permission of the original publisher, with minor amendments.

Scripture scholars: is it the modern concept of a monogamous loving relationship between consenting adults of homosexual orientation, or is it ritualistic, coercive, or abusive same-sex practice that is condemned? This debate is engaged elsewhere in this report. It should simply be recorded here that male homosexual activity is forbidden in Leviticus 18:22 and 20:13. Judges 19:16–30 and Genesis 19:1–8 have traditionally been seen as providing evidence of God's judgment on homosexuality, though these texts have been the subject of significant reinterpretation in recent times.

The key New Testament text is Romans 1: 26–7, with other references in 2 Peter 2:6–7, Jude 7, 1 Corinthians 6:9–10 and 1 Timothy 1:10. Again, the same question of interpretation is brought to these texts by modern scholars.

Nevertheless, there can be no doubt that the early church believed it was building on the testimony of the Bible when it developed its opposition to homosexuality. This was not however the only reason for its opposition, or even the major one. It was strong in its opposition to homosexual activity of all kinds, at least in part because of the culture in which it came to birth. The early Church Fathers were in reaction to the Greco-Roman world, which was the context within which they developed their system of Christian ethics. High Greek culture, in the golden age of the fifth century before Christ, had regarded homosexual practices as entirely acceptable. Homosexual relationships were regarded as normal and valuable, an important part of male intellectual and emotional friendship. At a time when female company was purely for purposes of procreation and domestic and dynastic arrangements, strong male bondings were sought and celebrated. Physical homosexual relationships between older men and younger boys, particularly teachers and students, or masters and apprentices, were believed to 'enhance the learning process', though such relationships were only acceptable where the older man was the active partner.[2] Commercial exploitation and abusive relationships were condemned.

Greek philosophers in general preached an ethic of moderation, in sexual activity as in other aspects of life. They gave high importance to a doctrine of asceticism. But although Plato in his final work, *Laws*, insisted that sex must be restricted to married people and always potentially procreative to 'avoid the frenzied madness of love', thereby condemning homosexual activity, this was regarded as a highly idiosyncratic view. In general the philosophers did not distinguish between heterosexual or homosexual acts, so long as moderation was sought. The writings in this vein of Philo, a Jewish neo-Platonist of late

2.   David F Greenberg, *The Construction of Homosexuality* (University of Chicago Press, Chicago and London) 1988, 204–5.

first-century Alexandria, were especially influential on early Christian thinking.[3]

The period which covered the composition of the major books of the New Testament and beyond was, according to numerous contemporary writers, a time when several of the Roman emperors were renowned for their sexual licence and cruelty. Both adultery and homosexual licentiousness seemed to be common in certain aristocratic circles. Modern scholars question the 'Roman orgy' cliche, claiming that literary evidence of high-level sexual corruption is possibly more a metaphor for the political corruption and disintegration of the time, than a factual historical record. Whatever the real situation, though, the ideology of sexual corruption was clearly a powerful one. It is noteworthy that this ideology coincided with the early Christian persecutions, and so understandably had a powerful influence on the thinking of the early Christian theologians. Likewise, the scattered Jewish communities around the Mediterranean where Christianity began its missionary outreach, were uncompromising in their rejection of the supposed sexual lifestyle of the Greeks and Romans around them.

In the Jewish tradition, in any case, homosexual practices were regarded as a very serious matter. The prohibitions against them in the book of Leviticus were treated seriously. Homosexual activity was at least as grave as intercourse with a menstruating woman. As historian David Greenberg points out, though to modern minds the latter 'offence' seems utterly archaic and trivial, it needs to be accepted as a 'marker' of the seriousness with which ancient Palestine viewed homosexual activity. The menstrual taboo was an important one in primitive societies.[4]

Surrounded—and indeed nurtured—by such powerful influences, it is not surprising that the first Christian theologians developed a moral code that was harsh on all aspects of human sexuality, even sexual intercourse within marriage. Bodily pleasure was to be resisted in the name of a rigid asceticism

---

3. Greenberg, *The Construction of Homosexuality*. Various writers have pointed out their influence on St Paul, particularly in the key passage in Romans 1:19f. James Barr, *Biblical Faith and Natural Theology: the Gifford Lectures for 1991* (Oxford: Clarendon Press, 1993) 51–7 points out that Paul's terminology and thought-framework here is 'unmistakably Hellenic' in the pattern of both Plato, and of the Jewish writer Josephus, who taught that sexual intercourse was only lawful between men and women, and then only for the begetting of children. See also Brendan Byrne, *Romans* (Minnesota: Collegeville, 1996) 92–3.
4. Greenberg, *The Construction of Homosexuality*, 195–6.

that exalted a dualistic concept of human nature. Homosexual practice, because it had not even the excuse of procreation—the only acceptable reason for heterosexual activity, let alone the biblical sanction for marriage—was unambiguously sinful.

In particular, the competition from dualist Gnostic and Manichaean sects, which taught the sinfulness of sex and pleasure, and indeed the evil of procreation, provided a powerful additional impetus for the development of a strict Christian code of sexual conduct. Formulated by St Augustine of Hippo, once himself a Manichaean, this code has dominated traditional Christian teaching on sexuality.[5]

In part, this code was built on many pre-Christian ideas about 'nature' and natural law, ideas that were based on Platonic and Aristotelian concepts, and Stoic versions of 'natural morality'. St Paul adopted them formally into Christian teaching in the first chapter of Romans. A three-pronged analogy with nature was developed: first, sexual processes were compared to the sowing of a field; second, sexual behaviour in animals was compared to that of humans; third, there was an attempt to determine the natural functional structure of the sex organ.[6] Vern Bullough, an historian with a special interest in the history of Christian attitudes to sexuality, has written:

> In effect, the appeal to nature was a teaching device used to reinforce theoretical assumptions. It was not really based upon observations of what took place in nature since anything contrary to the preconceived notions was ignored. Procreation was the chief criterion for judging whether sexual activity was natural or unnatural, and anything that did not lead to procreation was regarded as unnatural.[7]

These principles became the fundamental 'rule of thumb' for judging everything connected with human sexual activity. So artificial contraception was condemned as 'against nature', marital relations that were not explicitly

---

5. See Vern L Bullough, 'Introduction: The Christian Inheritance', *Sexual Practices and the Medieval Church*, edited by Vern L Bullough and James Brundage (Buffalo, New York: Prometheus Books, 1982), 1–12 for a useful discussion of the Gnostic/Manichaean influence on Christianity.

6. Vern L Bullough, 'The Sin Against Nature and Homosexuality', in *Sexual Practices and the Medieval Church*, 56.

7. Bullough, 'The Sin Against Nature and Homosexuality', in *Sexual Practices and the Medieval Church*, 57.

procreative were 'against nature', and homosexual practices were 'against nature'.

Sexuality from Augustine to the Third Lateran Council

Homosexuality was condemned as unnatural and depraved by both St John Chrysostom and St Augustine of Hippo, both writing in the early fifth century. John Chrysostom was particularly harsh, and believed male homosexuals deserved to be driven from the church and stoned. At least part of Chrysostom's horror of homosexuality seemed to be linked to disgust with a male taking the passive role of a woman, and therefore ceasing to be male. In Greco-Roman society, the only males expected to accept the passive role in homosexual intercourse were youths, slaves or other lesser males, as it was regarded beneath the dignity of full citizens to 'play the woman'.[8] In Christian society, this violation of customary gender expectations may have been one factor in the history of attitudes to homosexuality. Traditional church teaching on heterosexual relations always insisted on what is facetiously known as the 'missionary position'. Any other position, particularly those where the female might have been 'on top', was categorically forbidden.[9] Is this a subliminal reason why the Christian church has been so concerned about male homosexuality and rarely about lesbianism, though lesbianism was well known in the Hellenic world?

In general, though, the hostility of Christianity's first theologians was 'directed to all sexual experiences not intended to lead to procreation within marriage— homosexual or heterosexual'. While some theologians, notably Tertullian, were more hostile to homosexuality, for Gregory of Nyssa, adultery was as serious as homosexual intercourse.[10]

The first significant legislation against homosexuality was enacted by the Emperor Justinian in the sixth century.[11] The development of anti-homosexual legislation in the later Roman Empire was probably as much based on a growing antipathy to sexual pleasure among non-Christian Romans as among

---

8. See Warren Johansson and William A Percy, 'Homosexuality', in *Handbook of Medieval Sexuality*, edited by Vern L Bullough and James A Brundage (New York: Garland Publishing, 1996), 158–9.
9. See Pierre J Payer, 'Confession and the Study of Sex in the Middle Ages', *Handbook of Medieval Sexuality,* 3–17, for a full discussion of marital sexual sins identified in the Medieval penitentials.
10. Greenberg, *The Construction of Homosexuality*, 227.
11. Greenberg, *The Construction of Homosexuality*, 230.

Christians. What is important to note in Justinian's legislation, however, is his condemnation of homosexuality on the basis that this crime threatened not just the individual, but the whole community: 'because of such crimes, there are famines, earthquakes and pestilences'. This rationale initiated a long tradition of making forbidden forms of sexuality the scapegoat for society's ills, suggesting that God sent plagues, earthquakes and, in recent times, AIDS as a punishment. This accords with the teaching of Leviticus, that defilements such as these would cause the people to be 'vomited out of the land'.[12] By the same legislation of Justinian, swearing and blaspheming were forbidden, and adultery was made a capital offence.[13]

So far we have used the word 'homosexuality' in the modern sense, that is, as pertaining to specifically male-to-male sexual acts. However, the word 'homosexual' is relatively modern. It was first used in 1869.[14] The concept of homosexuality as an innate sexual identity, affecting a certain proportion of the male population, is also a modern concept, a development from the nineteenth century medicalisation of the subject.[15]

The terms most commonly used in history were 'sodomy' and 'sodomite', derived from the biblical story of the destruction of the city of Sodom. (The sin for which Sodom was destroyed has in the past been interpreted as homosexuality.) However, numerous historians have pointed out that the term 'sodomy' was not historically used to imply homosexual activity exclusively. In medieval usage, sodomy was sin against nature, the worst category under the general heading of the deadly sin of lust. Sin against nature had itself three subdivisions: 'by reason of species' (with animals); 'by reason of sex' (with a person of the same gender); and 'by reason of manner' (with a person of the opposite sex, even a legal spouse, but in a manner that excluded procreation).[16] This last subdivision included heterosexual anal or oral sex— in other words, sex using the 'wrong orifice'. Some theologians classified 'coitus interruptus' and masturbation as sodomy, because both prevented procreation.[17] Homosexuality *per se* was not the 'primary category for

---

12. Greenberg, *The Construction of Homosexuality*, 232–5; Johansson and Perry, 'Homosexuality', 161.

13. Greenberg, *The Construction of Homosexuality*, 238–9.

14. Johansson and Perry, 'Homosexuality', 156.

15. Greenberg, *The Construction of Homosexuality*, 14; Robert Shephard, 'Sexual rumours in English politics: the cases of Elizabeth I and James I', in *Desire and Discipline: Sex and Sexuality in the Premodern West*, edited by Jacqueline Murray and Konrad Eisenbichler, (University of Toronto Press, Toronto, 1996) 114.

16. *Ibid.*

17. Greenberg, *The Construction of Homosexuality*, 275–6.

distinguishing acceptable sex from unacceptable', writes Greenberg; the principal distinction was the potential for conception.[18] In Christian tradition, then, the sin of sodomy has been condemned, but in recent times the definition of that 'sin' has changed markedly. Much that once came under that vague umbrella term—including masturbation and varied marital sexual relations—is no longer condemned.

Johansson has pointed out that another layer of meaning grew around the term 'sodomy' in the Middle Ages. It came to be associated with the mythical archetype of the satyr, which embodied the concept of rampant, uninhibited sexual appetite. It had demonic overtones. It also came to be connected with blasphemy. (Sexual intercourse between Christians and Jews, or Christians and Saracens, was classified as sodomy.[19])

The connection with heresy was also long-standing. The terms 'bugger' and 'buggery' for sodomites/sodomy are a direct link with heresy, as they are derived from names used for those who adhered to the Albigensian heresy, introduced into France in the thirteenth century by Bulgarians.[20] It is interesting to note that 'bugger' was a term also used for usurers, a class of people more consistently and rigorously condemned on the basis of Scripture by the church until the seventeenth century than homosexuals.[21]

The heresy link in fact increased the repression of homosexual activity, because of growing antipathy to Muslims (who were believed to practice homosexual sex freely) in the wake of the Crusades. From the thirteenth century on, stiff new secular penalties were introduced against homosexuality in Europe. The 'sodomite', like the heretic, was someone who had to be destroyed.[22] Inevitably, as sodomy came to be defined more narrowly as homosexual activity, it carried with it the emotive connotations of its earlier definitions.

Further, though there were occasional suggestions that some men were more inclined towards sex with other men than with women, the general assumption throughout Christian history has been that all men were capable of being tempted to homosexual sex. It was no different to temptation to commit

18. Greenberg, *The Construction of Homosexuality*, 265.
19. Johansson and Percy, 'Homosexuality', 157–8
20. Johansson and Percy, 'Homosexuality', 158; Greenberg, *The Construction of Homosexuality*, 20.
21. Johansson and Percy, 'Homosexuality', 158.
22. Greenberg, *The Construction of Homosexuality*, 276.

adultery or fornication or 'unnatural' sex with a woman. Homosexual sex was a form of sexual vice, not an identity.[23]

Other factors in the church had contributed to the development of a stricter attitude to homosexual practice. In particular, increasing pressure on clerical marriage had a marked and in some ways, unexpected impact. The campaign to outlaw clerical marriage began during the eleventh century, with a series of decrees which ordered the laity not to attend masses conducted by priests known to be in intimate relationships with their wives. (The theoretical situation at the time was that clergy were permitted to remain married after ordination, so long as they did not continue sexual relations with their wives.) Peter Damian, the eleventh-century Benedictine and Doctor of the Church renowned for his uncompromising teachings on personal austerity and mortification, was harsh in his condemnation of married clergy. He it was who elaborated the 'cultic purity' argument for clerical celibacy in its most extreme form:

> If, therefore, our Redeemer so loved the bloom of perfect chastity that he was not only born of a virgin womb, but also fondly handled by a virgin foster-father, and this while he was still an infant crying in the cradle, by whom, I ask, does he wish his Body to be handled, now that he is reigning in all his immensity in heaven? [24]

This same theologian, not surprisingly, was supremely harsh in his condemnation of homosexuality. He insisted that monks and clergy must be removed from their orders for any form of homosexual expression, but this met with considerable resistance. After much unsuccessful lobbying of the papacy, Pope Leo IX finally decreed that the penalty was only for those who persisted in practising sodomy.[25]

The church was far less amenable when it came to tolerance for heterosexual relations between clergy and their lawful wives. There is some suggestion that the anti-clerical marriage campaign, which culminated in the Second Lateran Council decree of 1139 forbidding clerical marriage, represented in some ways a struggle between homosexual and heterosexual clergy. Certainly, the church's actions in condemning and outlawing clergy marriage

---

23. Greenberg, *The Construction of Homosexuality*, 328f.
24. Quoted in Bernard Verkamp, 'Cultic Purity and the Law of Celibacy', *Review for Religious*, 30, (1971): 199–217. This reference, 217.
25. Bullough, 'The Sin Against Nature and Homosexuality', 61.

were far more severe than its actions against homosexuality, and came forty years before a council would condemn homosexuality.[26] When the Third Lateran Council of 1179 became the first ecumenical council of the church to rule on homosexual acts (clerics were to be deposed from office, and laymen excommunicated), it treated homosexuality as comparable in gravity to clerical marriage.[27] The same council also imposed sanctions on usurers, heretics, Jews, Muslims and mercenaries, and presaged a period obsessed by a quest for 'intellectual and institutional uniformity' in Europe.[28] During this period, there was a steep rise in popular hostility towards minority groups, including Jews and heretics.

Sexuality from the late Middle Ages to the Reformation

The late Middle Ages saw the development of a fear and loathing of homosexuality that at times became quite hysterical and irrational. Greenberg has suggested that the growing pre-occupation with homosexuality at this time was an 'indirect and unanticipated consequence of the efforts of church reformers to establish sacerdotal celibacy'. The elimination of heterosexual outlets for the clergy could only have fostered homoerotic feelings, as often happens among men deprived of female company on ships, in prison and in monasteries. (The eleventh and twelfth centuries witnessed the growth of a literary sub-culture celebrating homoerotic love, much of it emanating from the cloister. The writings of St Aelred of Rievaulx are an important example.) The need for emotional and physical intimacy can over-ride sexual orientation in such circumstances, Greenberg writes.[29]

It was against this background that the rediscovery of classical writings, including that of the Stoics, gave an impetus to a reinvigoration of the concept of 'nature' as the standard by which sexual activity should be judged.[30] In the last decades of the thirteenth century, St Thomas Aquinas gave detailed consideration to homosexuality in his *Summa Theologica*. He argued that homosexuality was not only contrary to reason, but also contrary to the natural order. There were four divisions in the 'sin against nature' for Aquinas: masturbation; bestiality; same-sex activity; and deviation from the natural

---

26. For a description of this struggle, see Muriel Porter, *Sex, Marriage and the Church: Patterns of Change* (Melbourne: Dove, 1996), 29–34.

27. Greenberg, *The Construction of Homosexuality*, 288.

28. Greenberg, *The Construction of Homosexuality*, 269ff.

29. Greenberg, *The Construction of Homosexuality*, 280–3.

30. Greenberg, *The Construction of Homosexuality*, 275.

manner of coitus (which was restricted to face-to-face contact, with the woman on her back). Of these, bestiality was the most grievous, followed by homosexual sex, then intercourse in an 'unnatural' position, with masturbation the least serious. In each case, the possibility of procreation was once more the key to deciding whether acts were natural or not.[31] These sins against nature were more serious, he argued, than adultery, seduction, or rape, even though these involved injury to others and were also contrary to charity. Aquinas held that as the order of nature was derived from God, its 'contravention was always an injury done to God, whether or not any offence was at the same time committed against one's neighbours'.[32] This offence to God was the more serious form of injury. It may be significant that Aquinas wrote the *Summa* from 1265, as civil law codes in Europe were increasingly legislating against homosexual practices. The death penalty was often prescribed, even for a single proved act.[33]

It is noteworthy that Aquinas' main line of argument was derived from the natural law theory, rather than from the Bible directly.[34] Though controversial in his own time and not established as the key Catholic moral authority until the sixteenth-century Counter Reformation, Aquinas's writings nevertheless have permanently established the 'natural' as the touchstone of Roman Catholic sexual ethics and by derivation, Protestant ethics as well. 'Since the teaching of Aquinas has remained in many respects the dominant influence in the theology of the Western Catholic Church', his writing has 'proved to be the definitive ground for all subsequent rejection of homosexual behaviour by the Catholic Church'. Vatican declarations on homosexuality up to the present continue to reflect Thomist thinking.[35]

The sixteenth-century Protestant reformers, though they came slowly to a higher view of women and marriage than their predecessors, made no

---

31. Bullough, 'The Sin Against Nature and Homosexuality', 65.

32. Bullough, 'The Sin Against Nature and Homosexuality', 65.

33. John Boswell, *Christianity, Social Tolerance and Homosexuality: Gay People in Western Europe from the beginning of the Christian Era to the Fourteenth century,* (Chicago: University of Chicago Press, 1980), 293.

34. However, the key Scriptural text cited against homosexuality is Romans 1:26–7, where Paul contrasts natural and unnatural intercourse. Brendan Byrne, *Romans,* (Minnesota: Collegeville, 1996), 92–3, claims this reference to natural law demonstrates Paul's dependence on Philo and Stoic concepts of natural law. Paul, Byrne writes, reflects the conventional Stoic sense of 'nature' as the established order of things. 'Central to that established order was the dominance of the male over female as far as gender relationships was concerned (69)'.

35. Peter Coleman, *Christian Attitudes to Homosexuality,* (London: SPCK, 1980), 132.

concession to homosexual behaviour. It continued to be, for them, one of the many manifestations of the sinfulness of fallen human nature. Between 1555 and 1678 in Geneva, there were sixty-two prosecutions for sodomy (resulting in thirty executions).[36]

Sexuality in British law

In England, sodomy cases, though rare, were heard in the ecclesiastical courts until the sixteenth century. They were always treated leniently. The first English secular law to deal with sodomy was an Act of 1533, instituted by Henry VIII in the aftermath of the formal break with Rome. In that Act, 'the abominable vice of buggery' was made a capital offence. The vice was defined as carnal knowledge 'by mankind with mankind or with brute beast or by womankind with brute beast'. It was harsh, but so was all Tudor criminal legislation. For instance, under Tudor law, vagabonds who refused to work on three occasions could be hanged.[37]

Re-enacted by Elizabeth I in 1563, this Act was only rarely enforced over the centuries that it remained on the law books. It was at first invoked only in connection with religious or political prosecutions. Walter Lord Hungerford was beheaded in 1540 for sodomising his servants over a period of years, but he was also convicted of harbouring a traitor.[38] Though the Act was more rhetoric than reality, its symbolic power was significant. The death penalty was finally removed in England in 1861. The result of the 1861 Act was that 'homosexuals who kept their physical activities private among themselves were left tolerably free from legal prosecution'.[39]

But that freedom was to be short-lived. In 1885, an infamous last-minute additional clause to the Criminal Law Amendment Act opened the gates to the prosecution of homosexual activities between consenting adult males. The Act itself was designed, among other things, to protect women and girls against sexual assault. The Labouchere amendment was supposedly designed to protect men and boys as well, given the large number of male prostitutes, and the high level of pederasty, in London at the time. But it was ill-considered and poorly worded, particularly in allowing the interpretation that private homosexual acts, as well as public assaults, were misdemeanours. The clause

---

36. Greenberg, *The Construction of Homosexuality*, 275.
37. Greenberg, *The Construction of Homosexuality*, 303.
38. Greenberg, *The Construction of Homosexuality*, 323.
39. Coleman, *Christian Attitudes to Homosexuality*, 140.

instantly became a 'blackmailer's charter'. It was under the provisions of this clause that Oscar Wilde and other high-profile victims were prosecuted. Given the high level of heterosexual immorality in London at the time, to which Parliament and society in general turned a convenient blind eye, the prosecution of homosexual men was gross hypocrisy.

What of lesbianism? It had been almost totally ignored in the Christian tradition, perhaps because male theologians and canonists were largely ignorant of, and uninterested in, female sexuality. Nor could it offend male concerns about passive and active roles. In 1921, there was an attempt in the British Parliament to legislate against 'acts of indecency by females'. The promoter, a Scottish Conservative lawyer, claimed 'lesbianism was sapping the highest and best in civilisation now as it had previously to a large extent caused the destruction of the early Grecian civilization and was still more the cause of the downfall of the Roman Empire'.[40] Another speaker claimed lunatic asylums were packed with nymphomaniacs, many women were having nervous breakdowns after being tampered with by members of their own sex, and the decline of the British race was imminent because lesbians were refusing to have children. Despite these extraordinary claims, the clause was passed by a large majority of votes. But some sanity entered the debate when the Bill reached the House of Lords. The clause was abandoned and the House of Commons did not seek to reintroduce it.[41]

The issue of the prosecution of consenting adult male homosexuals finally came up for scrutiny in Britain in the 1950s. The trigger was the exorbitant increase in the number of 'offences' known to police. Between 1931 and 1955 the annual number had grown from 622 to 6,644, with between a third and a half actually making it to the courts. The main reason for this jump was a change in police policy at the highest level, which encouraged police officers to step up the number of arrests in a crusade against 'male vice'. Another reason was the defection of Guy Burgess and Donald Maclean to the Soviet Union in 1951. Both men were believed to be homosexuals, and given the cold war paranoia about security, homosexuals were readily assumed to be prone to blackmail, thus endangering Western freedom. The final goad to reform was a series of trials of prominent men accused of homosexual activity, to all of whom harsh sentences were meted out.[42]

A vigorous public debate ensued. On the one hand, defenders of public morality saw the level of prosecution as a sure sign of post-war malaise and

40. Coleman, *Christian Attitudes to Homosexuality*, 159.
41. Coleman, *Christian Attitudes to Homosexuality*, 159–60.
42. Coleman, *Christian Attitudes to Homosexuality*, 161ff.

corruption in society, but on the other, more thoughtful people, including some church people, began to agitate for homosexual law reform. In the debate in the British Parliament calling for a royal commission, an important clause from a report by the Church of England Moral Welfare Council was read. That clause stated:

> In no other department of life does the State hold itself competent to interfere with the private actions of consenting adults. A man and a woman may commit the grave sin of fornication with legal impunity, but a corresponding act between man and man is liable to life imprisonment, and not infrequently is punished by very long prison sentences.[43]

In a nutshell, this was the main argument of most of those, including some prominent church leaders, who fought for the decriminalisation of homosexuality at that time. While the Church of England still regarded homosexual behaviour as sinful, for instance, officially it no longer believed it should be treated as criminal.

Bishop FR Barry, the Bishop of Southwell, a noted churchman who spoke for the Bench of Bishops, called on the House of Lords to 'disinfect' itself of the idea that the state of being a homosexual was necessarily 'in itself, something morally reprehensible'. It happened to a man 'like colour-blindness or paralysis'. It demanded sympathy, he said. However, he still adhered to the natural law argument formulated by Thomas Aquinas 700 years earlier: 'These forms of unnatural association are, of course, morally evil and sinful in the highest degree, because they are a violation of natural law', he insisted.[44]

Commentators have noted that church spokesmen in the British Parliament at this time were instrumental in disturbing the moral complacency among parliamentarians and opening the way for reform. Records of the crucial speeches at this time indicate that the Church of England had departed from the notion that homosexuality was of a different order of sexual sin from that practised by heterosexuals.[45]

The upshot of the parliamentary debate was the formation of the Wolfenden Committee, which deliberated for three years before producing its

---

43. Coleman, *Christian Attitudes to Homosexuality*, 164.
44. Coleman, *Christian Attitudes to Homosexuality*, 166–7.
45. Coleman, *Christian Attitudes to Homosexuality*, 166–7.

report in 1957. Its chief recommendation was the abolition of the law relating to private homosexual acts between consenting adults. It was not proper for the law to concern itself with what a man does in private, it said, unless 'it can be shown to be so contrary to the public good that the law ought to intervene in its function as the guardian of that public good'.[46]

It took ten years of intense public debate and repeated parliamentary attempts before the Wolfenden recommendation was finally enshrined in law in 1967. (Australian states would follow suit in the following decades, with Tasmania finally falling into line only in 1997.[47]) During those years, the reform was strongly supported by the Archbishops of Canterbury and York, as well as the General Assembly of the Church of England, the Roman Catholic Advisory Committee, the Methodist Conference, and the Quakers.

Recent debates

In more recent times in Britain, a 1995 General Synod working party report recommended that gay and lesbian families should 'find a ready welcome within the whole family of God'.[48] This was in line with the more cautious welcome extended by the earlier (1991) influential report by the Church of England's House of Bishops, *Issues in Human Sexuality*. While not able to commend same-sex partnerships, the bishops called on congregations to welcome gay people as members. The language is supremely cautious, but nevertheless surprisingly generous.[49]

The bishops' report, however, revealed that they were still responding to an understanding of human sexuality based on 'natural law' and specifically, procreative purpose. Heterosexual activity served 'the purposes of procreation', they wrote:

> Furthermore, since it is the interaction of the male and
> female genital organs which makes procreation possible,
> that too must be part of God's purpose . . . In short, the

---

46. Coleman, *Christian Attitudes to Homosexuality*, 168.

47. Homosexual acts between consenting male adults in private were decriminalised in South Australia in 1972 and 1975; the ACT in 1976; Victoria in 1981; NSW and the Northern Territory in 1984; Queensland and Western Australia in 1990; and Tasmania in 1997.

48. *Something to Celebrate: Valuing Families in Church and Society*, (London: Church House Publishing, 1995), 118.

49. *Issues in Human Sexuality: A Statement by the House of Bishop*, (London:Church House Publishing, 1991), 41.

biological evidence is at least compatible with a theological view that heterosexual physical union is divinely intended to be the norm.[50]

Heterosexual unions, in every way, reflected 'their essential place in God's providential order'. They were, therefore, truly 'natural' in a way that homosexual unions never could be.[51]

However, as early as 1958, a Lambeth Conference had decided that procreative purpose was not the sole key to what was acceptable for sexual behaviour. The 1958 Conference passed the following resolution on contraception:

> The Conference believes that the responsibility for deciding upon the number and frequency of children has been laid by God upon the consciences of parents everywhere: that this planning, in such ways as are mutually acceptable to husband and wife in Christian conscience, is a right and important factor in Christian family life and should be the result of positive choice before God. Such responsible parenthood, built on obedience to all the duties of marriage, requires a wise stewardship of the resources and abilities of the family as well as a thoughtful consideration of the varying population needs and problems of society and the claims of future generations.[52]

That the Lambeth reaffirmation of contraception came a decade before the Church of Rome would prohibit artificial contraception in *Humanae Vitae* is surely telling. However, the Anglican Church Fathers were still uncomfortable with real sexual freedom in marriage. In Resolutions 112 and 113, they condemned 'sins of self-indulgence and sensuality' in marriage, and commended 'self-discipline and restraint'. The ancient primacy of asceticism was still alive, if no longer as strong as it once had been.

The committee that had prepared these resolutions had produced a thoughtful report which examined carefully the arguments about the purposes

---

50. *Issues in Human Sexuality*, 36.
51. *Issues in Human Sexuality*, 36.
52. *The Lambeth Conference 1958*, Resolution 115 (London: SPCK, 1958).

of marriage. While it acknowledged the purpose of procreation, it gave equal weight to sexual union for relational reasons:

> Husbands and wives owe to each other and to the depth and stability of their families the duty to express, in sexual intercourse, the love which they bear and mean to bear to each other. Sexual intercourse is not by any means the only language of earthly love, but it is, in its full and right use, the most intimate and the most revealing; it has the depth of communication signified by the Biblical word so often used for it, 'knowledge'; it is a giving and receiving in the unity of two free spirits which is in itself good (within the marriage bond) and mediates good to those who share it. Therefore it is utterly wrong to urge that, unless children are specifically desired, sexual intercourse is of the nature of sin. It is also wrong to say that such intercourse ought not to be engaged in except with the willing intention to procreate children.[53]

This paragraph represents perhaps the most radical reversal in all the long centuries of Christian teaching on sexuality. It overturns not only the concept of procreation as primary cause, but also notions of marital sex as remedy for sin. At long last, it allows that sex is not only a valid expression of marital love, but actually the pre-eminent one. The implications of this historically novel attitude for sexual relationships in general, and homosexual relationships in particular, so far remain unexplored in official Anglican teaching.

In Australia, in the debate over decriminalisation of homosexuality activity, the Anglican Church revealed deep divisions. The Diocese of Melbourne followed the line taken by the Church of England. In 1971—a decade before the state law was changed—Melbourne Diocese's Social Questions Committee recommended the decriminalisation of homosexual acts between consenting adults in private; Melbourne Synod endorsed the recommendation in 1972. It was one of the first Australian churches to take such a stance. However, the Diocese of Sydney's committee, reporting two years later, called for a continuation of criminal sanctions against

---

53. *The Lambeth Conference 1958*, 147.

homosexuality.[54] Sydney Synod passed resolutions opposing government moves to decriminalise homosexual activity, or legislate to protect homosexual people from discrimination. In 1985—a year after the NSW law was changed—a sub-committee of the Diocese's Standing Committee, in a report on homosexuality and ministry, claimed that homosexual people who engaged in homosexual acts could not occupy any office or perform any ministry in a parish.[55]

The present situation

The mainstream Christian churches had, by the second half of the twentieth century, decided that they could no longer support the criminalisation of homosexual practices. The *sinfulness* of these practices remained a major theological issue as the century ended. Nevertheless the Western church has significantly changed its stance this century. Most mainstream churches are now agreed that homosexuality as an orientation is not evil *per se*, a considerable change from their earlier understanding. Most churches likewise have agreed that homosexual practice between consenting adult males in private should not be pursued as a criminal matter; this too is a significant change from their earlier collaboration with secular authorities.[56] All the churches, however, still officially regard homosexual practice as sinful to a greater or lesser degree.

What has brought about even this limited change? From the evidence examined, it is reasonable to argue that the change has been a response to a changing understanding of homosexuality in the wider community. From the mid-nineteenth century on, homosexuality has come to be seen first as an involuntary condition (often as a form of illness) and then as an identity. Homosexual behaviour, then, could no longer be seen as a form of criminal sexual vice, much as it might, in official church circles, still be regarded as

---

54. *Report on Homosexuality*, Diocese of Melbourne Social Questions Committee 1971; *Report on Homosexuality*, Diocese of Sydney Ethics and Social Questions Committee, Sydney, 1973.

55. See *Year Book of the Diocese of Sydney*, 1978: 249, and 1986: 245–6, 309–13. For these references, I am indebted to David Hilliard, 'Gender Roles, Homosexuality, and the Anglican Church in Sydney', in *Gender and Christian Religion*, Studies in Church History, volume 34 (Suffolk: Ecclesiastical History Society, 1998), 509–23.

56. The Anglican Diocese of Sydney was still calling for the continuation of criminal sanctions against homosexuality in 1977: *Year Book of the Diocese of Sydney* 1978: 249.

sinful. (Similarly, as we have seen, the harsh communal attitudes towards homosexuality in the late Middle Ages provided the cultural context in which the church developed a stricter theological condemnation of it.)

It is important to note that this changed understanding has prompted renewed examination of the scriptural references to homosexuality, and not vice versa. It is rarely a fresh understanding of Scripture that initiates changes to doctrine; rather, it offers a justification for changes already in process. The origin of these changes usually lies outside the institutional church. Similarly, the changing social understanding of homosexuality has prompted fresh interpretations of natural law theology, and particularly the arguments from natural law which have been traditionally used to ascribe sinfulness to homosexual practice.[57]

Many long-held theological teachings on human sexuality have changed down the centuries, at least in theory. The church no longer publicly declares women to be a lesser creation than men, though that was official teaching until the twentieth century. Celibacy is no longer officially promoted in the Catholic Church on the grounds that it is a holier lifestyle than marriage, though that was the main reason proffered in Christian tradition until very recently. The Anglican Church permits artificial contraception, at least within marriage, though the long tradition of the church had held that it was murder. Sexual pleasure within the marital relationship is affirmed in modern Christian teaching, though it was condemned universally by theologians until recent centuries. In most parts of the Anglican Communion, there is now recognition that marriages can and do die, and that new marriages can bring healing and grace. Theologians have recognised that their predecessors often misinterpreted or ignored Scripture, or at least misunderstood its meaning because of their mistaken understanding of human biology. This substantial revision of traditional teaching on human sexuality has largely been possible because the experience and insights of married clergy and more recently, female theologians, have been taken seriously.

The present debate on homosexuality is a logical development from these radical changes that have occurred in the church's teachings on women, marriage, sexuality, contraception and divorce. When the church viewed the human body with distaste, and all sexual expression, even within marriage, with suspicion, it was not surprising that the church condemned homosexual activity outright. When the church taught that heterosexual activity was only permissible for the express purpose of procreation within marriage, and

---

57. See Don Edwards, 'Natural Law and Homosexuality', *General Synod Doctrine Panel Report on Homosexuality* (work in progress, unpublished paper), June 1999.

condemned all other forms of heterosexual expression, let alone sexual pleasure, then logically homosexual expression had to be similarly forbidden. Only in recent times, as the church has come falteringly to understand that sexual expression is just as important for human relationship as it is for procreation, and has come to understand something of the complexity inherent in long-term sexual relationships, has it been possible for a fresh reassessment of homosexuality to develop.

4

'The Democracy of the Dead': Homosexuality and Tradition

Gordon R Preece

> Tradition means giving votes to the most obscure of classes, our ancestors. It is the democracy of the dead. Tradition refuses to submit to the small and arrogant oligarchy of those who merely happen to be walking about. All democrats object to men being disqualified by the accident of birth; tradition objects to their being disqualified by the accident of death.
>
> GK Chesterton, *The Ethics of Elfland*[1]

It seems like Muriel Porter and I drew the short straw. Tradition is not exactly a crowd-puller today, even if homosexuality is. I didn't advertise the conference from which these papers arose as the 'Christian Tradition and Homosexuality' or we might have had a much smaller crowd and readership. I know which side my bread's buttered on. Nonetheless I'm happy to address the issue of tradition, though I'd prefer to talk about Scripture, which I believe trumps tradition in the Anglican/Wesleyan quadrilateral that these papers are structured around. By Christian tradition the narrower, sixteenth-century Protestant sense refers to Christian creeds and the ecumenical councils of the first five centuries. This is second only to Scripture in authority. In the broader sense tradition means the generally accepted teaching of the church on matters of faith and morals. Homosexual practice fits the second sense as it is not directly an object of, or involve a statement of, salvific belief, such as the creeds. Nonetheless, it is a significant issue of Christian life, with implications for salvation (1 Cor 6:10). So what tradition in the second sense has to say about homosexual practice should be taken seriously, if not infallibly. This

---

1. In *A Motley Wisdom,* chosen and introduced by Nigel Forde (London: Hodder and Stoughton, 1995), 271.

broad tradition against homosexual practice needs corporate discernment, in the light of Scripture, reason, and experience, not contemporary consumerist disparagement.

Let me outline where I plan to go in this paper. First, drawing upon but critiquing sociologist Anthony Giddens, I will ask why tradition in its broadest, not specifically Christian, sense is a dirty word in democratic and novelty-obsessed societies today. Yet much, but not all, of that dirt should be worn as a badge of honour. Second, I will critique journalist-historian Muriel Porter's Whig-progressivist[2] reading of the Christian tradition on homosexuality and sexuality in her *Sex, Marriage and the Church: Patterns of Change*[3] and in the Doctrine Panel of the Anglican Church of Australia's *Faithfulness in Fellowship: Reflections on Homosexuality and the Church.*[4] Porter's revisionism is more journalistic argument for Giddens' 'democracy of the emotions'[5] than genuinely historical and traditional in the sense of GK Chesterton's 'democracy of the dead'. I will not go into detail refuting revisionist readings of church tradition on homosexuality, taking them as largely refuted by the consensus of historians and weight of evidence, instead addressing the presuppositions of such arguments as exemplified by Porter's works.

---

2. Herbert Butterfield, *The Whig Interpretation of History* (Harmondsworth, England: Penguin, 1973 [1931]) describes it as 'the tendency in many historians to write on the side of Protestants and Whigs, to praise revolutions provided they have been successful, to emphasize certain principles of progress in the past and to produce a story which is the ratification if not the glorification of the present'(9). The Whig historian 'is studying the past for the sake of the present', not its own sake (20). They take 'short cuts' using an anachronistic principle of selection and abstraction according to what fits a pattern of progress (28–30). In Butterfield's *Christianity and History* (London: Fontana, 1957), 'History Uncovers Man's Universal Sin', (57ff) and divine judgment shows 'those who rest their ultimate beliefs in progress are climbing a ladder which may be as vertical as they claim it to be, but which in reality is resting on nothing at all' (90).

3. Muriel Porter, *Sex, Marriage and the Church: Patterns of Change* (Melbourne: Dove, 1996).

4. *Faithfulness in Fellowship: Reflections on Homosexuality and the Church*, Doctrine Panel of the Anglican Church of Australia (Melbourne: John Garratt Publishing, 2001).

5. Anthony Giddens, *Runaway World: How Globalisation is Reshaping our Lives* (London: Profile, 1999), 64–5.

1. Why tradition is a dirty word

The first reason for the unpopularity of tradition in modern/postmodern societies is, according to leading English sociologist Anthony Giddens, due to a process of democratic detraditionalising 'at the core of the emerging global cosmopolitan society'. As he states:

> This is a society living . . . after the end of tradition. The end of tradition doesn't mean that tradition disappears, as the Enlightenment thinkers wanted. On the contrary, in different versions it continues to flourish everywhere. But less and less . . . is it tradition lived in the traditional way. The traditional way means defending traditional activities through their own ritual and symbolism—defending tradition through its internal claims to truth . . .

> It is entirely rational to recognise that traditions are needed in society . . . Traditions are needed, and will always persist, because they give continuity and form to life . . . Everyone in the academic world works within traditions . . . Without intellectual traditions, ideas would have no focus or direction . . . However, it is part of academic life continually to explore the limits of such traditions, and foster active interchange between them. Tradition can perfectly well be defended in a non-traditional way, and that should be its future . . . Traditions will continue to be sustained in so far as they can effectively be justified—not in terms of their own internal rituals, but as compared to other traditions or ways of doing things . . .

> This is true even of religious traditions. Religion is normally associated with the idea of faith, a sort of emotional leap into belief. Yet in a cosmopolitan world, more people than ever are in contact with others who think differently from them. They are required to justify their beliefs, in an implicit way, both to themselves, and others. There cannot but be a large dollop of rationality in the persistence of religious rituals and observances in a detraditionalising society. And this is exactly as it should be . . .

> [By contrast] Fundamentalism is beleaguered tradition. It
> is tradition defended in the traditional way—by reference
> to ritual truth—in a globalising world that asks for reasons
> . . . Yet fundamentalism isn't just the antithesis of
> globalising modernity, but poses questions to it. The most
> basic one is this: can we live in a world where nothing is
> sacred? I have to say, in conclusion, that I don't think we
> can. Cosmopolitans, of whom I count myself one, have to
> make plain that tolerance and dialogue can themselves be
> guided by values of a universal kind . . . Cosmopolitan
> morality itself needs to be driven by passion. None of us
> would have anything to live for if we didn't have
> something worth dying for. [6]

Giddens is more friendly to tradition than most sociologists, and yet cognisant of the problematic position of tradition in our global cosmopolis. He helpfully situates tradition somewhere between rational cosmopolitanism and fideistic fundamentalism. But here a tension in his account surfaces due to his polarity of secular, cosmopolitan reason and sacred passion. Tradition is to be answerable to cosmopolitan reason, to avoid irrationalism. But he allows fundamentalist or self-justifying tradition to question modernity's cosmopolitan reason in the name of sacred passion. Giddens is in a secular way exploring the tensions of the Wesleyan quadrilateral between tradition, reason and experience ('passion'?). He is aware that neither a mere ladder-like hierarchy, nor table-like equality of four equal legs, is satisfactory. Some things are sacred, fundamental, even *pre*-rational, though not necessarily *irrational*. The religious would say revelational.

Yet Giddens elsewhere emphasises 'a democracy of the emotions in everyday life', parallel to 'public democracy'. Here the political becomes personal. Giddens applies this democratic political metaphor to our topic of homosexuality: 'A democracy of the emotions would draw no distinctions of principle between heterosexual and same-sex relationships. Gays rather than heterosexuals have been pioneers in discovering the new world of relationships and exploring its possibilities.' In asking whether Western patterns will become universal he states boldly: 'it isn't a matter of *whether* existing forms of traditional family will become modified, but when and how.

---

6. Giddens, *Runaway World*, 43–5, 49.

. . . An emerging democracy of the emotions is on the front line in the struggle between cosmopolitanism and fundamentalism'.[7]

While partly agreeing with Giddens on emotional, especially male-female democracy, I find firstly, a lurking leftover from the secularisation theorists who assumed a linear progression of Western secular democratic models through history and geography in our global world. Yet the evidence from the highly religious global South (except Australasia), the US, and greater Europe and ironically, increasingly Islamic Europe, is that Western European secularisation is exceptional.[8] The previously standard secularisation thesis is another Whig progressivist historiography translated into sociology.

Secondly, while accepting the civil democratic liberties of homosexuals, I suspect Giddens' political metaphor misleads. It is a classical liberal or Whiggish category mistake to make secular democratic politics the prism through which all other relationships are viewed, whether religious hierarchical relationships with God, or personal, sexual and ecclesial relationships. Political categories should not precede theological or moral categories lest they lose a way of morally measuring themselves, becoming the measure of all things.[9] Compare American imposition of democracy on an intransigent Middle East—without a Renaissance, Reformation or Enlightenment—with the imposition of emotional democracy on all theological, ecclesial and sexual relationships, even when they go against the larger and longer 'democracy' of catholic tradition.

An ecclesial extension of Giddens' modern secular democratic argument represents a secular, imperial political takeover of the church polis and a denial of the rights of corporate entities to self-government. Against this despotic disenfranchising of tradition we need to re-enfranchise Chesterton's 'democracy of the dead' or tradition.

The former Dean of St Paul's London, Dean Inge, also displayed Chesterton's larger, longer sense of democracy when he said 'Democracy is

---

7. Giddens, *Runaway World*, 64–5.
8. Peter Berger, *The Desecularization of the World: Resurgent Religion and World Politics* (Grand Rapids: Eerdmans, 1999). Grace Davie, *Europe: The Exceptional Case* (London: Daron, Longman and Todd, 2002).
9. Butterfield's *Christianity and History* (143) critiques this democratic determinism acutely: 'those who in 1919 thought that since the world had become more liberal and democratic for a century it could now only become more liberal and democratic still—were actually handicapped in their historical knowledge, because they had run it into too rigid a pattern. They did not remember what a live thing history is, and how wilfully it may break away from the railway-lines which the prophets and pedants may have set for it'.

only an [extraordinarily successful with a century's hindsight!] experiment in government, and it has the obvious disadvantage of merely counting votes instead of weighing them'.[10] In matters of truth and ethics, votes need to be weighed against larger loyalties, as conscience votes recognise. And on the see-saw of truth, tradition is a way of weighing those votes to see if they pass the test of time and experience. When newsworthiness or opinion polls are baptised as prophecy, tradition is the church's orderly way of weighing prophecy (1 Cor 14:29) on the scales of Scripture and Spirit. It is how we humbly recognise that God's word did not originate or end with us, and that our alleged prophecy must bow to apostolic authority or be ignored (1 Cor 14:36–8).

Giddens' just concern for the rational testing and weighing of various traditions in cosmopolitan society was already addressed by Alasdair MacIntyre. MacIntyre argues for tradition as an ongoing argument about the interpretation of classic texts and a set of procedures for solving intellectual and ethical problems. Whichever interpretation solves the most pivotal problems becomes the reigning tradition.[11] Wilfred M McClay agrees that tradition is not 'an inert body of propositions and customs passed along intact from one generation to the next'. Tradition is the 'necessary medium' or form of discourse for intellectual and moral debate—'not just a chest of treasures, but also a web of debates'.[12] As Jaroslav Pelikan notes memorably, this is what distinguishes *tradition* as 'the living faith of the dead' from *traditionalism* as 'the dead faith of the living. And it is traditionalism that gives tradition such a bad name'.[13]

While Giddens' cosmopolitan democracy is probably best for global society, its mantra of inclusion or 'emotional democracy' must itself be weighed and tested, as he hints earlier, by the questions tradition puts to it. For Christians this is the tradition of the catholic church across time and space

---

10. Dean Inge, *Possible Recovery?* Cited in *The Oxford Dictionary of Quotations* (Oxford: Oxford University Press, 1979), 270.

11. Alasdair MacIntyre, *Whose Justice? Which Rationality?* (Notre Dame: University of Notre Dame Press, 1988), here chapter XVIII, and *Three Rival Versions of Moral Enquiry: Encyclopaedia, Genealogy, and Tradition* (Notre Dame: University of Notre Dame Press, 1991) chapters VI–IX.

12. Wilfred M McClay, 'Planting Sequoias: Reflections on Tradition and History', *Fides et Historia*, 45/2, (Fall 2002): 44.

13. Jaroslav Pelikan, *The Vindication of Tradition* (New Haven: Yale University Press, 1984), 65.

which is more genuinely pluralist than contemporary 'cosmopolitan' inclusivism because it allows a range of people and communities their own public voice, space and polities, rather than the liberal monotone of a Western secular individualist polity.[14]

The second major reason why tradition is a dirty word today, at least when it comes to the church and sex ethics, is what CS Lewis calls 'chronological snobbery'. This is:

> the uncritical acceptance of the intellectual climate common to our own age and the assumption that whatever has gone out of date is on that account discredited. You must find out why it went out of date. Was it ever refuted (and if so by whom, where, and how conclusively) or did it merely die away as fashions do? If the latter, this tells us nothing about its truth or falsehood. From seeing this, one passes to the realization that our own age is also 'a period', and certainly has, like all periods, its own characteristic illusions. They are likeliest to lurk in those widespread assumptions which are so ingrained in the age that no one dares to attack or feels it necessary to defend them.[15]

Let me illustrate this epistemological privileging of novelty or what Chesterton calls 'the language of innovation'.[16] I once had an argument with former Archbishop of Brisbane (and former Australian Governor General) Peter Hollingworth in his diocesan newspaper. Like several Australian bishops he was bailing out of the 1998 Lambeth Congress resolution against homosexual practice but for pastoral care of and listening to homosexual people. The then Archbishop Hollingworth spoke in more measured and less racist tones than Bishop Spong used at Lambeth 1998 but the cultural

---

14. See Bryden Black, 'Whose Language? Which Grammar?: "Inclusivity" and "Diversity" versus the Crafted Christian Concepts of Catholicity and Created Differentiation', in this volume.

15. CS Lewis, *Surprised by Joy* (San Diego: Harcourt Brace Jovanovich, 1956), 207–8.

16. 'Modern men are not familiar with the rational arguments for tradition, but they are familiar . . . with the rational arguments for change . . . The language which comes most readily to everyone's mind is the language of innovation; but it is a language which is rather exercised than examined'. GK Chesterton, 'The New Groove', in *The Common Man* (London: Sheed and Ward, 1950), 112.

imperialism and Eurocentric logic is similar.[17] Hollingworth said that these were complex interpretive issues that the African bishops, being relatively *new* to the faith, found difficult. Further, *new* discoveries of modern science cast doubt upon the traditional view and so we need to 'keep our minds open to new information and insights'. I'll leave science to David Clarke in this volume, but I asked Archbishop Hollingworth why newness is wrong when referring to the fresh grasp of ancient Scripture and tradition by the African bishops and not when referring to the ambiguous, 'jury's out' findings of modern science.[18]

We are, as Christopher Ash puts it, 'a neophiliac culture', lovers of the new, obsessed with novelty. 'In the early centuries of the Christian era it was the other way around. One of the defences the early Christians had to make against non-Christian Jewish opponents was to prove that Christian faith was not a newfangled religion, the new kid on the religious block'. You needed a pedigree in the past to match it with Plato and Aristotle. 'Whereas wisdom was once perceived to be like a good wine, maturing with age, now it is like perishable goods, to be binned when it passes its sell-by date'.[19] We seek the latest ephemeral experience, but tradition offers us the expanded experience of the people of God through the centuries as they read the Bible and the Bible reads them in their time and place.

When Dean of Ridley Residential College in the University of Melbourne I had to chat to a student about not having overnight guests of the opposite sex. He told me the students thought the College rule was 'Medieval'. I told

---

17. See John Shelby Spong, *The Sins of Scripture* (HarperSanFrancisco: 2005) for examples summed up in the statement 'the new consciousness of today collides with the old and dying definitions of the past. There is no doubt how this debate will come out: The new consciousness will not be defeated'. Cited in John Makujina's review, *Christianity Today*, 50/3, (March 2006): 78.

18. Gordon Preece, 'Sexuality and Authority', *Focus*, November 1998 in response to former Archbishop Hollingworth's Bishop's column in October 1998. Yet science itself, and all theories and technological artifacts are tradition laden as is shown by Edward Shils, *Tradition* (Chicago: University of Chicago Press, 1981).

19. Christopher Ash, 'Leviticus on Sex: It Just Might Matter Today', *Engage: Quarterly Comment from the Jubilee Centre,* Issue 4 (Winter 2003): 1. Newer societies, like Australia, New Zealand and the United States, are probably more susceptible to this infatuation with novelty. In postmodernity we're also suspicious that history and tradition is the domain of 'dead, white males'. See Davis McCaughey, *Tradition and Dissent* (Melbourne: Melbourne University Press, 1997), 53.

Graham Cole the then Principal who said 'oh it's older than that', as old as creation, in fact. The very use of the term Medieval or Middle Ages is hardly a piece of ahistorical, objective labelling. The patronising tone towards the past is a giveaway. Coined during the Renaissance, it was designed to relegate the previous period to be a mere primitive precursor to the time of new birth. Similarly, the use of 'modern' is a way of surreptitiously substituting the *telos* of progress for the *telos* of creation, on the assumption that later must be better.

However, that arrogant assumption is applied to ethics but not aesthetics. Compare our fascination with the ancient architecture of the Greeks, Egyptians and Romans or recently Jane Austen's novels or Tolkein's *Lord of the Rings,* now movies. For Tolkien: 'all that is gold does not glitter/ not all those who wander are lost; the old that is strong does not wither/ deep roots are not reached by the frost'. Deep roots of tradition are not just for fair-weather but survive all sorts of climate change, providing guidance to wanderers and life to all in all seasons, and in ethics as well as aesthetics. Compare Simone Weil's argument from the swiftness of the French tree's fall before the Nazi frost, that a sense of rootedness in a transcendent tradition is an essential need for the soul of the individual and the nation. In condemning the opposition of the future to the past she says 'we possess no other life, no other living sap, than the treasures stored up from the past and digested, assimilated and created afresh by us'.[20]

We can juxtapose Tolkien and Weil's affirmation of tradition with Ralph Waldo Emerson's Romantic rejection of it at the start of his *Nature*. There he contrasted (before their time) their 'party of memory' and his 'party of hope':

> The foregoing generations beheld God and nature face to face; we, though, through their eyes. Why should not we also enjoy an original relation to the universe? Why should we not have a poetry and philosophy of insight and not of tradition, and a religion by revelation to us, and not the history of theirs? . . . The sun shines today also. There is more wool and flax in the fields. There are new lands,

---

20. Simone Weil, *The Need for Roots: Prelude to a Declaration of Duties Toward Mankind* (London: Routledge and Kegan Paul, 1952), 48ff.

new men, new thoughts. Let us demand our own works
and laws and worship.[21]

Emerson's purple prose is worth quoting not only for his huge influence on
the US and thus the world, but also for his Promethean desire to behold God
directly and presently as an equal. He denies in effect, our historical
particularity and dependence, our standing upon the shoulders of giants gone
before. This is not that they are better than us, merely better placed, to
particular events of revelation. Emerson and Romantic modernity's quest for
originality is an attempt to jump out of our own situated skins into some kind
of surreal eternal Now.

Like Emerson, but more prosaic and pragmatic, is Henry Ford's depiction
of history as not only 'one damned thing after another,' but also as 'more or
less bunk. It's tradition. We don't want tradition. We want to live in the
present, and the only history that's worth a tinker's damn is the history we
make today'.[22]

Jaroslav Pelikan shows how Emerson's divorce between 'insight' and
'tradition' is impossible, but also incidentally answers Ford:

> the growth of insight . . . has not come through
> progressively sloughing off more and more of tradition, as
> though insight would be purest and deepest when it has
> finally freed itself of the dead past . . . By including the
> dead in the circle of discourse, we enrich the quality of the
> conversation. Of course, we do not listen only to the dead,
> nor are we a tape recording of the tradition. That really
> would be the dead faith of the living, not the living faith
> of the dead. But we do acquire the insight for which
> Emerson was pleading when we learn to interact creatively
> with the tradition which he was denouncing.[23]

---

21. Brooks Atkinson, editor, *The Essential Writings of Ralph Waldo Emerson* (New
York: Modern Library, 2000), 3.

22. Henry Ford, quoted in the *Chicago Tribune,* 25 May 1916.

23. Pelikan, *Vindication of Tradition,* 81–2.

Pelikan concludes his defence of tradition with a charge from Goethe:

> What you have as heritage,
> Take now as task;
> For thus you will make it your own.[24]

The Romantic naturalism of Emerson and the pragmatic capitalism of Ford seem to have little in common but their worship of the present. However, the co-opting of Romantic imagination by capitalism (think of car ads in sublime surroundings) and the dismantling of all traditional and time barriers to postmodern polymorphous desire, Hollywood's export of 'Californication',[25] the news literally as new or novelty, the fascist dictatorship of fashion, the pink dollar and *Global Sex*[26] are all linked. We face today a conflict between the global economy of ever-demanding desire and the catholicity of tradition. This lies behind our debates about homosexuality.

As Wilfred McClay writes:

> It is the inevitable tendency of consumer capitalism, with its relentless drive toward fluidity and mutability, to encourage the constant erasure of memory to make room for new desires, new markets, new purchases; and that therefore memory itself, always a mutable thing, is lost or debased in the process. Tradition not only cramps the human spirit. Even worse (!), it is bad for the economy.[27]

While Matthew Arnold's 'Sea of Faith' becomes just 'melancholy, long, withdrawing roar,/ Retreating',[28] in secular Europe and Australia, the tide of Zygmunt Bauman's *Liquid Modernity*[29] (the mobile, fluid global economy aptly described by McClay above) and *Liquid Love*[30] has rushed in. It is aptly

---

24. Pelikan, *Vindication of Tradition*, 81–2.
25. The name of a best-selling Red Hot Chilli Peppers' album.
26. As Denis Altman calls it in *Global Sex* (St Leonards, NSW: Allen and Unwin, 2001).
27. Wilfred McClay, 'Planting Sequoias', 42 to whom I owe much of this section including the Emerson and Ford quotes.
28. Matthew Arnold, 'Dover Beach' in *The Oxford Dictionary of Quotations*, 3rd edition, 1979, 12:23. Contrast Alister McGrath, 'The Incoming Sea of Faith', *The Spectator*, 18 September 2004, www.lewrockwell.com/spectator/spec384.html.
29. Zygmunt Bauman, *Liquid Modernity* (Cambridge: Polity, 2000).
30. Zygmunt Bauman, *Liquid Love* (Cambridge: Polity, 2003).

pictured in the latter's cover image of a love heart on the sand about to be washed away. We live in a world of casual work, casual sexual relationships and a casual approach to tradition—useful for aesthetic (or nostalgic) but not ethical purposes. Compare the consumerist aesthetic criteria for work and sex in *Liquid Modernity.*[31] Beauty is in the eye of the buyer; truth too. Christians often carry over these consumeristic attitudes to both their use of Scripture and tradition—in fact all four components of the Wesleyan quadrilateral. In particular, we pick and choose what suits us from the past, not discerningly, but consumeristically.

By contrast, tradition or the weighty voice of the Christian past, based on both the substance and incompleteness of the church's comprehension of Christ, provides the ship of the church with the biblical ballast that prevents us from being like 'infants tossed back and forth by the waves and blown here and there by every wind of teaching and by the cunning and craftiness of people's deceitful scheming' (Eph 4:14 NIV adapted). Tradition is, after Scripture, the church's way of keeping course through being true to Christ.

Much of the reason for the heat over the homosexuality issue, is that it is an authority and *identity* issue, for the church and not only, though most poignantly and pastorally, for homosexual people. The church's identity is in tradition. We, not just old people, live by our memories. Think of the many recent movies about memory: from the trivial, like *50 First Dates* about a girl whose lost her memory and has to be wooed again every day; or *Eternal Sunshine of the Spotless Mind* (based on a William Blake quote) about trying to get rid of painful memories of broken romance; or *Mement*, about a young man with total short-term memory loss who has to write everything down on his own body. Much of the church today is like these movie characters, but it is long-term memory loss, loss of identity we suffer from. Even the church's most future focused theologian, Jürgen Moltmann, the theologian of hope, said the criterion for Christian theology is identity and relevance. But if we rush to relevance alone, we lose our identity, anchored in the Christian tradition.[32] A fellow theologian of hope, Johann-Baptiste Metz, somewhere called this tradition 'dangerous memories', contrary to Emerson's false dichotomy between the radical 'party of hope' and the conservative 'party of memory'.

---

31. See Gordon Preece, 'Vocation in a Post-Vocational World', in *The Bible and the Business of* Life, edited by Simon Carey Holt and Gordon R Preece (Hindmarsh, South Australia: ATF Press, 2004).
32. Jürgen Moltmann, *Theology of Hope* (Minneapolis: Fortress Press, 1991)

We are what we remember. This isn't just nostalgia. It's about knowing who we are, using the past as a platform for self-projection into the future. We are like rowers, facing backwards to get our bearings to row in a straight line, pun intended, forward not backward.[33] By looking in our rear vision mirror we avoid being overtaken by or making the mistakes of the past again. 'There is nothing new under the sun' after all.

Who we are as Christians is 'catholic'. It comes logically after apostolic or scriptural. We trace our heritage, our genealogy, our roots, through catholic tradition. From an Anglican perspective it is not infallible, not primary, but a good, authoritative guide to interpreting Scripture. Catholic tradition, in Vincent of Lerins famous formula is: 'what all Christians in all times and all places have believed'; that is, universality, antiquity and consensus.[34] This catholic tradition is what Cardinal Avery Dulles calls 'catholicity in length' and 'in time'[35] This is no nostalgia about the now, nor parochialism of the present, as in the West today. Other societies and churches with stronger roots in the pas—like the Africans, Asians, Catholics and Orthodox, Orthodox Jews, in fact all the great monotheistic religions—hold that homosexual practice is against the created order of our sexual ecology. They also reminds us that Christianity is not simply Western as the Episcopal Churches of New Westminster Canada and New Hampshire in the US seem to think in their schismatic claims that their time (ironically included in their names) and place has supremacy.

2. Muriel Porter's liberal Anglican and Whig-progressive view of tradition

In this section I will critique Muriel Porter's preceding paper, originally from the Doctrine Panel of the Australian Anglican Church's *Faithfulness in Fellowship,* as a clear representation of both a theologically and politically liberal Anglican position on tradition in relation to homosexual practice. I will also examine and critique her earlier book *Sex, Marriage and the Church,* as together they exemplify that liberal Anglican tradition, which is a selectively anti-tradition stance (pro- ritual, anti- doctrine and sexual ethics). Both writings display a table-like view of equal authorities, not a ladder-like hierarchy headed by scripture, then tradition. Together they also exemplify the

---

33. HW Wolff, *Anthropology of the Old Testament* (London: SCM, 1973).

34. Vincent of Lerins, AD 434, quoted in Reinhold Seeberg, *Textbook of the History of Doctrine*, volume 1 (Grand Rapids: Baker, 1961), 384.

35. Avery Dulles, *The Catholicity of the Church* (Oxford: Oxford University Press, 1985), 86.

liberal individualist imposition of 'emotional democracy' on the church and a parochial progressivist perspective on tradition challenged in my two points under section one above.

While I will disagree strongly with Porter I want to first acknowledge her passionate pastoral concern for homosexual people and women, both inside and outside the church, which I share. However, I do not share her hermeneutic of liberation which assumes a linear development from endorsing women's ordination (which I endorse, against much of church tradition, on the grounds of a development in its direction within Scripture[36]), to endorsing

---

36. At the Ridley College conference from which these papers arose I was asked how I justify women's ordination but not practising homosexual ordination. I do not have space here but see Richard N Longenecker, *New Testament Social Ethics for Today* (Grand Rapids: Eerdmans, 1984) especially chapter 2, 'A Developmental Hermeneutic', with its analogy on page 25 of a seed developing into a tree within Scripture and beyond, which speaks of the movement beyond the Bible, in tradition remains 'both continuity with a foundational core and genuine growth in conceptualization and expression'. 'Real growth always involves genuine innovations of structure . . . yet that growth is always controlled and judged by what is inherent in the seed itself'. Longenecker is following John Henry Newman's *The Development of Doctrine* here. I broadly agree with Longenecker and WJ Webb, *Slaves, Women and Homosexuals: Exploring the Hermeneutics of Cultural Analysis* (Downers Grove, Illinois: IVP, 2001) who on the basis of a 'redemptive movement' in Scripture distinguishes between Scripture's relatively more ameliorating and liberating and counter-cultural approach to slavery and women compared to its relatively stricter approach to homosexual practice compared to the surrounding cultures. See also IH Marshall, *Beyond the Bible: Moving from Scripture to Theology* (especially chapter 2, 'The Development of Theology') including Kevin J Vanhoozer, 'Into the Great "Beyond": A Theologian's Response to the Marshall Plan'. Vanhoozer rightly raises the danger of assuming that we stand at the end of the redemptive trajectory or further along than the authors of Scripture. He notes that 'Webb [like me], for his part, thinks that it leads toward . . . egalitarianism between men and women, but he does not believe it is so inclusive as to permit homosexual relations. And yet others, such as Luke Johnson and Stephen Fowl [*Engaging Scripture: A Model for Theological Interpretation* (Oxford: Blackwell, 1998), chapter 4], appeal to the very same logic of redemptive trajectory in order to legitimate same-sex relations. Just as the early Christians discerned the redemptive trajectory of the Spirit in the Gentiles in Acts 15, so we should detect the Spirit's work in the lives of homosexual Christians, thus leading us to be more inclusive. The redemptive movement of the text is, on this view, the Spirit of truth who sets free by breaking cultural taboos. The Episcopal Church of America has

practicing homosexual marriage and ordination, which I do not endorse, on the grounds of Scripture (moving in a stricter direction than the surrounding culture) and tradition.

The Anglican Bishop of South Sydney, Robert Forsyth, helpfully summarises the argument of Porter's book *Sex, Marriage, and the Church* under four points, yet the summary also applies to her 'Homosexuality in Christian Tradition':

> 1. For most of its life the church has had a very negative attitude to sexual pleasure;
> 2. Yet, in the face of community moral consensus the mainstream churches changed their minds substantially on numerous sexual and other issues like clerical marriage, divorce, contraception and the value of sexual pleasure;
> 3. Today our society displays a growing community consensus approving homosexual and de facto relationships
> 4. Therefore the church should also recognise the moral legitimacy of these relationships.[37]

Forsyth notes that Porter is profoundly negative concerning the church's ability to ever get things right from its own resources and naive about society's ability to do so.[38] This is where her democratic liberalism is dangerous as the criterion for truth and behaviour for all spheres, not just politics.

---

just ordained its first openly gay bishop, and other mainline churches are hoping that this particular "redemptive trajectory" will pick up locomotive momentum . . . can one go beyond Scripture via the redemptive trajectory approach and at the same time prevent one's own view of the trajectory from lording it over the text?' Vanhoozer argues for a 'Christological trajectory' summing up God's wisdom revealed finally in Christ, not going beyond it. Yet he sees the contemporary Church unpacking this from the same redemptive-historical position to the primitive and eschatological church (90–1). I hear his warnings but think Webb and Longenecker have built in sufficient safeguards and criteria. Further, Andrew Goddard has shown that Acts 15's proscribing of fornication for Gentiles includes homosexual relations. See his *God, Gentiles and Gay Christians: Acts 15 and Change in the Church* (Bramcote: Grove, 2001).

37. R Forsyth, 'The Joy of Anglican Sex?', 'Bah Humbug' column, *Southern Cross* (October 1998): 9.
38. Forsyth, 'The Joy of Anglican Sex?', 9.

This doesn't mean that church tradition hasn't made mistakes—witness the treatment of women. Tradition has a 'shadow side', and 'mixed in with the lived experience of wisdom and love in our tradition there is also much unwisdom and unlove'.[39] Yet rather than merely succumbing to a postmodern 'hermeneutics of suspicion' or an utterly uncritical attitude to tradition, that is traditionalism, we should adopt Theodore Adorno's maxim of 'knowing one's tradition so as to hate it properly'.[40] Unfortunately, in our abandonment of any tradition or canon of classic literature, in any field, not just theology, we no longer know our own tradition. [41] Further, as Rene Girard writes: 'the most powerful anti-Christian movement today' is 'the one that takes over and

---

39. Kevin T Kelly, *New Directions in Moral Theology: The Challenge of Being Human* (London: Geoffrey Chapman, 1992), 2. He refers to his own Roman Catholic tradition but it has broader resonance. The quote about the shadow side is a summary of Kelly from Bernard Hoose, *Received Wisdom? Reviewing the Role of Tradition in Christian Ethics*, (London and New York: Geoffrey Chapman, 1994), 153. Hoose goes on to unpack Kelly's use of the medieval metaphor for tradition of us being able to see further being like dwarfs sitting on the shoulders of giants. 'He rightly states that we can easily "find ourselves hanging onto the hem of the giant's coat, thereby seeing even less than our ancestors could see, if we fall into the error of regarding our own age as far superior to any that has gone before and forget where the basis of our presumed superior knowledge is to be found. However, the saying also reminds us that, while it is of immense importance to be aware of our inheritance, it is also important to acknowledge the fact that we too have our own experience and our own capacity to be wise. In other words, to use a different metaphor, we can, and should, build on what previous generations have left us. Only thus will we be able to see from a better vantage point than any they had". If we relinquish the responsibility to build "to return to the previous metaphor, we can too easily slip into the role of little children rather than that of truly adult dwarfs (152–3)'''.

40. Cited unsourced by Simon Cooper, 'Postmodernism-Lite: reflections on the recent VCE English debate', *Arena Magazine*, 79 (October-November 2005): 22.

41. As English author Madeleine Bunting says: 'It becomes harder and harder to explain how two millennia of meditation and reasoning on the human condition may be worthy of consideration. There is an extraordinary arrogance to the modernity that tosses aside so contemptuously the traditions that have sustained generations of our forbears. Are we so different? Are we so superior?' cited by David Kettle, 'Beyond Retrieval' in *The Gospel and our Culture Network Newsletter*, 44 (Autumn 2005): 3.

"radicalizes" the concern for victims in order to paganise it. In Christian history they see nothing but persecution, acts of oppression, inquisitions'.[42]

For instance, on Porter's first point we must admit that the church has been sadly anti-sexual. However, this was largely due to an eschatologically oriented and persecuted minority's understandable over-reaction to the rampant sexual decadence of the late Roman Empire.[43] Further, Richard Price highlights the difficulty many moderns have in understanding the distinctive ecclesiology underlying early Christian asceticism:

> The church sought to preserve the purity of the body of Christ through the purity of the bodies of its members. To maintain her own integrity as a heavenly society that was only sojourning on earth, the Church needed members whose bodies stood apart from the blurring and contamination, the loss of personal integrity and bodily vigour, brought about by easy sexual relations. It was this ecclesial concern that gave the sexual ethic of the early Christians its distinctive edge, its sharp clarity, its reiterated emphases. Modern Christians who feel that traditional Christianity attached undue importance to sexual morality and made it too restrictive need to be aware that their own lack of sympathy with the traditional discipline arises not only from sexual liberation but also from a different ecclesiology, from a lowering of boundaries between the Church and the world. The broad questions of the . . . precise sense in which the Christian should be in the world but not of it, need to be . . . resolved before the sexual ethic of traditional Christianity can be rightly understood and fairly judged.[44]

---

42. Rene Girard, *I See Satan Fall Like Lightning* (Maryknoll, New York: Orbis, 2001), 180.

43. As Roman historians like Livy well recognised and put down partly to decline in worship of the Roman goddess of modesty, *Pudicitia* or Chastity. See Livy, *A History of Rome*, Book 10, 23 and Preface, 6–7 and 9–23 (Loeb edition), *Rome and Italy* (London: Penguin, 1982), 319–20. See also Patrick Riley, *Civilizing Sex: God, Chastity and the Common Good* (Edinburgh: T and T Clark, 2000), chapter 4.

44. Richard M Price, 'The Distinctiveness of Early Christian Sexual Ethics', in *A Thatcher and E Stuart, editor, Christian Perspectives on Sexuality and Gender* (Herefordshire/Grand Rapids: Gracewing/Eerdmans, 1996), 29. See also Peter Brown, *Body and Society,* chapter 1 and the epilogue, especially 428. It should also

Price's point is correct in terms of the origin of Porter's liberal advocacy of accommodation to society and lack of sympathy for the early church. However, the early church in other ways conformed to Greek society's body-soul dualism in its sexual ethic. While Porter abhors the results of this dualism, it is ironically due to this very conformity to society's mores, or rather its intellectual and philosophical elites' mores, that Porter commends.

This leads us to see that Porter's second point concerning the church's changing its position on sexual ethics following society's consensus, is simplistic. Though she bases it on relatively modern examples from the sixteenth and seventeenth centuries on, she treats this as a standard paradigm, not only of what *was* the case (that is church conformity to social consensus) but what *should* be the case. The early church's case shows that it is a much more ambiguous situation involving aspects of both social conformity (to body-soul dualism) and non-conformity (through ascetic sexual practices).

Porter admits that 'Christian tradition has always treated homosexual practices—though not always homosexual love—as sinful. However, the degree of sinfulness . . . has varied, creating a tradition that can best be regarded as ambivalent'.[45] This creation of ambiguity is a common approach by liberal authors in *Faithfulness in Fellowship* concerning the Bible and tradition. The introduction summarises Porter's paper as saying '"the Church's traditional teaching" is in many respects a figment'.[46] This strategy creates what Martin Luther King called the 'paralysis of analysis'—an unwillingness or inability to form convictions or concrete actions in a counter-cultural way.

Porter's third point, that, analogous to earlier society-led church changes to sexual ethics, there is an emerging social consensus concerning the legitimacy of homosexual relations obscures the fact that there isn't much of a contemporary consensus to mimic either. Porter's argument ignores the pluralism of modern/postmodern societies split on such issues. Even the minority gay community is split regarding gay marriage. As one lesbian argues:

---

be added that the Church's confining of the use of sex to procreation was also due to the high value placed upon procreation in a society whose survival was constantly threatened by a high death rate.

45. *Faithfulness in Fellowship*, 5.

46. *Faithfulness in Fellowship*, viii. The chapters by Carnley, Dunham, Thomson and Edwards, and Garrett all create this sense of ambiguity.

> When it comes to same-sex marriages, John Howard has got us
> pretty well summed up. We're not cut out for it …
> [heterosexuals are] welcome to it. 'For life!' It'd be like sitting
> through one of those interminable bloody Indian films but
> when you get to the end it starts all over again and you can't
> leave. Let's leave marriage and other drudgery to
> heterosexuals. They've had millenniums of practice. They're
> good at child-rearing and taking out the rubbish, I never
> wanted to be like them even when I *was* one of them . . .
> Surely we can come up with something better: semi-marriage
> or quarter marriage, which would narrow the field down to
> eight. Or a casual, part-time or temporary marriage. Or even a
> flexible marriage. [47]

Porter's fourth point,[48] that the church should therefore follow society's
moral consensus, is extremely muddled. It is like the cartoon of the
clergyperson running after their flock saying 'I'm their leader I must follow'.
It also repeats, mantra-like, the 1960s and 70s World Council of Churches
slogan for 'prophetic' action, 'let the world set the agenda'. But as a true
prophet, Jacques Ellul, once said 'I'd like to see the church being really
prophetic by saying something *before* the world rather than *after* it'. Porter's
church is hardly an *ek-klesia*, literally called out from the town halls of
worldly kingdoms (including democratic ones) to the town hall of the city of
God, with its constitution in Scripture, and interpretation and enactment of
that constitution in tradition.

Porter's view of tradition is not Chesterton's 'democracy of the dead', but
a Whig revisionist or progressive history that sees the past as little more than
evolutionary stepping stones of progress towards the present panoramic or
privileged perspective that we enjoy. JI Packer is pertinent concerning the
Grand-Canyon-wide difference between historic orthodox acceptance of the
authority of Scripture and the liberal position Porter represents on
homosexuality. This:

> applies to Christianity the Enlightenment's trust in human
> reason, along with the fashionable evolutionary
> assumption that the present is wiser than the past. It

---

47. Amy Lowell, 'Do Lesbians Need Marriage? *MCV*, 4 June 2004: 6.
48. Repeated in 'How our Church Leaders and Politicians are Exploiting Gays', *The Age*, 14 June 2004, Opinion: 14.

concludes that the world has the wisdom, and the church must play intellectual catch-up in each generation in order to survive. From this standpoint, everything in the Bible becomes relative to the Church's evolving insights, which themselves are relative to society's continuing development, and the Holy Spirit's teaching ministry is to help the faithful to see where Bible doctrine shows the cultural limitations of the ancient world and needs adjustment in light of latter-day experience.[49]

Packer shows how reason and contemporary experience surround Scripture and tradition in a pincer movement, with reason used to rationalise experience and relativise Scripture and tradition. Scripture and tradition are treated selectively as authoritative stepping stones towards the *telos* of today's exalted experience.

Let me demonstrate from Porter. She sees such stepping stones in the decisions to allow clergy marriage during the Reformation and contraception at the Lambeth Anglican Bishops Conference of 1958 and the reversal of the priority of procreation in the purposes of marriage from the 1662 Book of Common Prayer to contemporary prayer books' 'mutual society, help and comfort first.'

For Porter, 'the present debate on homosexuality is a logical development from these radical changes that have occurred in the Church's teachings on women, marriage, sexuality, contraception and divorce', opening up recognition of 'non-reproductive sexual activity'.[50] Yet, 'the implications of this historically novel attitude for sexual relationships in general, and homosexual relationship sin particular, so far remain unexplored in official Anglican teaching'.[51] But this is a *non sequitur* or logical leap. This Whiggish /progressive 'inevitability' does not logically follow for the following reasons:

Firstly, for those taking Scripture as primary authority non-procreation is not the only argument used against homosexual practice. More fundamental is the biblical emphasis on our sexual ecology or created order of complementarity (and equality) as male and female. Paul, remarkably for a time when procreation was an urgent imperative of survival, mentions nothing of procreation in Rom 1:24–7, the clearest biblical text against homosexual

---

49. JI Packer, *Christianity Today,* January 2003.

50. Porter, 'Homosexuality in Christian Tradition', 21.

51. Porter, 'Homosexuality in Christian Tradition', 19.

practice. Paul is not merely mimicking the Greco-Roman philosophers' views of nature, as Porter implies,[52] but going back to Gen 1:26–8 about the complementary nature of male and female as the image of God. For all the biological and philosophical baggage the tradition brings, as systematised by Aquinas in the thirteenth century, it fundamentally seeks to interpret Paul's 'against nature' in Romans 1.

Secondly, the Lambeth 1958 resolution 115 led to the modern prayer books' priority on marital 'mutual comfort' by giving 'equal weight to sexual union for relational reasons'.[53] But this refers to opposite sex relationships ('Husbands and wives') in all their complementarity, difference and otherness (to use the latter two postmodern terms), not to same-sex relationships. Each change has to be argued on its merits, not assumed by some Whig logic of inevitable progress.

Thirdly, tradition is not Porter's smooth evolutionary road to progress but has biblical (and unbiblical) bumps in it. The Scriptural signposts led to changes in the traditional direction of the road. Scripture (though not always alone) trumped existing tradition in the Reformation allowing clerical marriage and in Martin Bucer's biblical argument for the at least equal priority of companionship with procreation in marriage.[54] This was belatedly accommodated in our prayer book's marriage priorities and in the Lambeth Conference's justification of contraception in 1958. Resolution 115 refers crucially to the biblical notion of mutual sexual knowledge invalidating the idea that sex is sinful unless procreational.[55] Scripture also had priority at Lambeth 1998 in rejecting homosexual practice, though agreeing with tradition there. This does not fit Porter's neat evolutionary pattern. The

---

52. Porter, 'Homosexuality in Christian Tradition', 8.
53. Porter, 'Homosexuality in Christian Tradition', 8.
54. Porter, *Sex, Marriage and the Church*, 96, 104.
55. See: *Lambeth Conference 1958* (London: SPCK, 1958). Resolutions 13 and 15 of the 1930 Lambeth Conference reached similar conclusions but with less robust biblical and theological argument. It was Karl Barth, writing in 1945, who provided much of this biblical ballast for Protestants showing that the biblical mandate to multiply is no longer unconditional for Christians and showing that divine providence and nature are not antitheses of responsible human intervention and stewardship of sexual and procreative abilities. See Megan Curlis-Gibson, 'Contraception in Protestant Perspective Yesterday and Today', *Zadok Paper*, (forthcoming, Summer 2007) Parts 3 (on Lambeth) and 4 (on Barth citing *Church Dogmatics* III/4 (Edinburgh: T and T Clark, 1961), 265–76 and 459–61). Porter may be sometimes right on Anglicans descriptively, but Barth shows that this is not the way to go prescriptively.

smooth stepping stone has become a biblical boulder blocking the road to change, though of course, she would see this as a merely temporary impediment to the inevitable unfolding of the implication of non-procreational sex allowing homosexual practice.

As Alasdair Macintyre argues in his seminal *After Virtue*,[56] tradition is not set in concrete, it is an ongoing argument. It is an argument about classical, authoritative texts, in the church's case, about the interpretation of Scripture. And while some modification of the anti-sex asceticism of the tradition was needed and was first accomplished by the Puritans interestingly, it was not just a matter of social evolution, but of exegesis and interpretation, the trumping of traditionalism by Scripture.

Porter's 'pattern of change' commits a kind of historical version of the naturalistic fallacy whereby one cannot get an 'ought' or moral imperative from an 'is' or natural descriptive. For her, if 'point two' change *has* happened in the church's sexual ethics in history where society's consensus has led the way; then thirdly where society's consensus is again leading the way it *ought* therefore fourthly to continue to happen.[57] The unspoken assumption here, that covers the logical gap for those who share her assumptions, is that contemporary experience of progressive emotional democracy trumps Scripture and tradition.

But Porter displays some doubt when she wonders whether her argument that the church has to play catch up with society has proved too much? She asks 'does this mean anything goes? That the church should mindlessly endorse any and all sexual behaviour?'.[58] Yet she gives no real answer or

---

56. Alasdair Macintyre, *After Virtue* (Indiana: University of Notre Dame Press, 1981).

57. See Muriel Porter, *The New Puritans: The Rise of Fundamentalism in the Anglican Church* (Carlton: Melbourne University Press, 2006), 135. Porter is right to note inconsistencies in the changes to sexual and gender ethics the church has allowed and the level of seriousness or threat of schism entailed, but some of these changes, for example allowing women's ordination, have a scriptural trajectory allowing changes in tradition whereas homosexual practice, marriage and ordination has a scriptural trajectory stricter than surrounding societies. See Webb, *Slaves, Women and Homosexuals*, 92. There is also a hierarchy of doctrine, as Graham A Cole has shown in lectures, between fundamental, salvific or credal articles of faith (for example, the person and work of Christ), which are worthy of schism, and secondary articles, (for example, the nature of sacraments) and nonfundamental articles (for example, Antichrist's identity). See: RA Muller, *Dictionary of Latin and Greek Theological Terms* (Grand Rapids: Baker, 1985), 45–6.

58. Porter, *Sex, Marriage and the Church,* 134.

criteria for discerning what is normative in society's sexual attitudes and what is not. In her most recent book she does, however, defend herself as a married woman with adult children of more than thirty years against being 'caricatured as a proponent of sexual licence and promiscuity'. She distinguishes this from her endorsing faithful, committed *de facto* and same-sex partnerships.[59]

Yet Porter is rightly worried where her Whiggish argument might lead her. In one of those earlier church controversies, between the Puritans and the Anglicans, John Spenser rightly warns against 'zeal to every man's [and we might add, every woman's] private cause . . . So much the better were it in these our dwellings of peace, to endure any inconvenience whatsoever in the outward frame, than in desire of alteration, thus to set the whole house on fire'.[60] RR Reno wrote a last impassioned plea to his fellow Episcopalians before converting to Roman Catholicism after the consecration of practicing gay bishop Gene Robinson. He writes in response to William Countryman's allegorising interpretation of the accepting of the Gentiles in Peter's vision in Acts 10 as acceptance of not only practicing homosexuals but also 'the end of taboo' *in toto*:

> A surgical change in matters of sexual discipline may be possible. Our inherited tradition is extraordinarily complex, deep, and durable, and someone may find arguments that make sense of a change-in-continuity in this matter. But I think we are kidding ourselves if we do not see that a wide and violent range of revolutionary pressures could easily erupt. There is a very good chance that once unhindered by loyalty to the past, surging forces of ideological revision will be very destructive.[61]

Such forces have been unleashed in the Anglican communion. They are the result of 'zeal to every man's private cause'. This is where the absolutising of democratisation of emotion leads us, without, as Giddens partly understands, traditions that point us to the transcendence of the sacred. Such zeal is apparent in the hyper-Protestant individualism of the liberal Anglo-Catholic Porter's recent *cri de cour* of private conscience. In using her journalistic gifts to bypass the church and go direct to the public to advocate a loosening of the

---

59. Porter, *The New Puritans*, 116.

60. See preface to Richard Hooker's *Laws of Ecclesiastical Polity* (1604).

61. RR Reno, *In the Ruins of the Church: Sustaining Faith in an Age of Diminished Christianity* (Grand Rapids: Brazos Press), 121, 125.

church's traditional stance against homosexual practice, she concluded with her own personal confession of freedom of conscience *à la* Martin Luther's famous cry at the Diet of Worms—'here I stand I can do no other'. However, she didn't cite the preceding sentence of the Luther quote: 'Unless you prove to me by Scripture and plain reason that I am wrong, I cannot and will not recant'; nor the following sentence: 'my conscience is captive to the Word of God', and for Luther, in an important, but secondary sense, to the best of church tradition—'the democracy of the dead'.

5

The Fruit of the Spirit or the Works of the Flesh? : Come Let Us Reason Together[1]

Mark Thiessen Nation

Introduction

'There was once an art critic, I have been told, who had a sure way of identifying ancient Maltese art objects: he found himself crying before them.'[2] So begins the moving wonderful story of Magda and André Trocmé and the parish of Le Chambon in southern France. In the midst of the terrors of World War II, these three thousand or so people, led by a pacifist pastor, saved the lives of thousands of Jews from the Nazis. This opening sentence reflects Philip Hallie's own response when he first read the story of Le Chambon: he found tears streaming down his cheeks.

By opening his book this way Hallie intends to suggest that there are emotions that are appropriate for certain experiences, certain realities. In this case those emotions relate to the excellence and moral goodness that were embodied in Le Chambon. Today many emotions are connected with the varied realities surrounding homosexuality: anger, fear, disgust. Within the church I do not know how we can approach this subject without considerable pain. In fact, as I approach this issue I am reminded of the truth

---

1. This chapter appears by kind permission of the publisher and is a slightly revised version of an essay published, with the same title, in *To Continue the Dialogue: Biblical Interpretation and Homosexuality*, edited by C Norman Kraus (Telford, Pennsylvania: Pandora Press US, 2001), 223–44.
2. Philip P Hallie, *Lest Innocent Blood Be Shed*, (New York, New York: Harper and Row, 1979), 1.

of Walter Brueggemann's statement that 'theology that is "pre-pain" must be treated with suspicion.'[3]

In relation to the issue of homoerotic relations there must be pain, because there are still 'ministers' of the Gospel who attend the funerals of prominent gay people carrying placards saying 'God Hates Fags'. Pain, because adult children tell wrenching stories of how they are disowned by their families when they come out to their parents that they have been gay or lesbian for as long as they can remember. Pain, because of sitting in the presence of someone who has repeatedly wished he was dead because he lives in a world that tells him he must be straight and, yet, after years of yearning to be, of seeking help to be, he isn't. Pain, because those who claim to be brothers and sisters within the church want to know why they cannot be fully a part of this church that is every bit as much a part of their lives as anyone else's. Pain, because this issue of homosexuality continually threatens to divide denominations. Pain, because, in fact, many churches, through more than two decades of struggle, have still not really moved forward on this issue: this 'issue' that is replete with many complicating factors about which various questions have been raised, yet without apparent resolution.

One of the reasons we cannot move forward is because we are polarised, or rather we appear to be polarised, which is not uncommon with emotionally charged matters. Many of us, after some period of agonising, believe we cannot live in mid-air forever. Therefore, we, with considerable discomfort and with an awareness of remaining questions and areas of ambiguity, nonetheless take positions. We are, when all is said and done, for or against homoerotic relations.[4] From that point forward we are mostly identified by our public stance as being 'for' or 'against'.

---

3. Walter Brueggemann, 'The Third World of Evangelical Imagination', in *Interpretation and Obedience: From Faithful Reading to Faithful Living* (Minneapolis, Minnesota: Fortress Press, 1991), 26, n18.

4. One of the issues I have struggled with in this essay is the use of language. It is perhaps impossible to use neutral language. I have usually chosen to use the term *homoerotic relations* as the matter being debated. It is the sexual behaviour of gays and lesbians that, for most people, is *the* issue. *Homoerotic*, a term used by various writers in this debate, seems to be as neutral as any word I can think of to refer easily to the issue at hand. A caution: though I have adopted this language, it is still imperative that we remember that the relationships between people who identify themselves as homosexual cannot and should not be reduced to the erotic

This brief essay is, in part, an attempt to do in essay form what practitioners of conflict resolution do in relation to such polarised issues. It attempts to help people realise that most of us are not at opposite poles. In point of fact, most of us, even after having taken positions, are somewhere along a spectrum. We agree with many others on a variety of closely related issues, even when we have finally taken a different stand on homoerotic relations.

I will attempt to display this spectrum and name what continues to separate us through four steps. First, I will delineate a number of issues about which I believe most of us agree. Second, I will name a few issues I believe cause some in this debate to reach for strong rhetoric. Third, I will provide glosses or annotations on what I have named in the first step. These glosses are an invitation to people who disagree to hear the potential inadequacies in their own positions as well as to hear the views of others. Finally, I will offer some thoughts to keep in mind which, I hope, will help us to move forward in ways that are potentially helpful for the church.

In all of this discussion I am not pretending to be neutral. I have attempted to read widely and listen carefully to many voices in this debate over the last twenty years or so. But I am aware of my own views. However, throughout most of this essay I am attempting to keep my views in the background.

1. What can we agree on?: naming the spectrum

I am under no illusions that *all* of us agree on the following matters. Some of us are at opposite ends of the spectrum. However, we should not assume that the majority are at opposite extremes simply because activists, who are often most visible and vocal, tend to represent the opposite extremes. I suggest that most people within Mennonite Churches (and also the larger church) would agree on the following:

(1) The social and biological sciences have raised a set of complicated questions about how people come to be gay and lesbian, questions that present a set of puzzles we do not pretend fully to understand.

---

or sexual component of their relationships. This is but a reminder that this 'issue' is connected to a variety of complicated matters not adequately reducible to simple terminology.

(2) We affirm that the Bible is centrally authoritative in defining the Christian faith and thus, among other things, provides instruction in what it means to live morally.

(3) There is only a hand full of biblical texts that speak directly to the issue of homoerotic relations. Those texts which do address the subject, taken at face value, speak negatively.

(4) Any adequate discussion of biblical teachings on homoerotic relations must include a more comprehensive biblical framework that would include not only other texts related to sexuality, but also a broader understanding of Christian theology and ethics. Furthermore, this discussion should be placed within an overall framework of what it means to be Christian.

(5) We have something to learn from the various ways the church throughout its history has dealt both with sexuality in general and homoerotic relations in particular, as we seek today to wrestle with these matters.

(6) We believe Christians are commanded to love their neighbours as themselves. This would include repudiating any cruel behaviour toward people (certainly including friends, family members and co-workers) who are engaged in homoerotic relationships. Moreover, it would also include being loving toward gays, lesbians, and people who believe homoerotic behaviours to be wrong.

(7) We believe it is important to support and nurture heterosexual married couples (and their children). Moreover, if the church were to shift positions on homosexual relationships, what is being suggested for adoption is a parallel monogamous arrangement for gays and lesbians.

(8) Homoerotic behaviour is really the issue we are wrestling with. Of course this issue can neither be separated from the lives of the people who are in homoerotic relationships nor disconnected from broader issues related to sexuality.

It is important that we not pass lightly over this list (and perhaps there are other things that should be added). If I am right that most of us would agree on these things then it is important to note this common ground, perhaps more common ground than sometimes appears to be the case amid the strong polarising rhetoric. If I am right that most of us agree about this much, then why do we not only disagree on the issue of homoerotic relations but even have substantial disagreements that are sometimes connected to strong oppositional rhetoric? Let me name, in the next section, three possible reasons.

2. Supercharging the rhetoric

(1) The first reason that may help explain the strong rhetoric connected with homoerotic relations is that this is not just an 'issue' but is connected to people. We are talking about family, friends, and brothers and sisters in Christ—in short, relationships. If anyone fails to understand why parents of gay or lesbian children, for instance—even parents who are theologically very conservative—come to have strong feelings about this issue, then they have a failure of imagination or compassion.[5]

In fact, I would guess that this debate may be more painful within a context like the Mennonite Church than in some other denominations (not to minimise the intensity in other churches) precisely because we are in some ways (including literal) an extended family. Families have a commitment to one another and, of course, have closer relationships to each other than to those outside their families. It is also the case that because they trust each other and have granted power to the other family members, they can cause more pain to each other than anyone else can. As Philip Yancey has said, 'Troublesome issues like divorce and homosexuality take on a different cast when you confront them not in a state legislature but in a family reunion'.[6]

The next two reasons are mirror images of each other and are related to what George Lakoff identifies in his book, *Moral Politics*.[7] Lakoff examines the way in which such issues as gun control, feminism, and abortion are connected to worldviews. Therefore, the issues are symbolically related to larger concerns, to convictions, and moral commitments. In times of significant cultural shifts and transitions, worldviews can be under significant challenge, whether perceived or actual. In such contentious times, specific issues assume important symbolic roles. Fears, heightened concerns, become attached to these issues. They become plugs in the dike. If the plugs do not remain, who knows? The whole dam that is presently holding back a flood of evil may come crashing down. So, how does this specifically relate to homoerotic relations?

---

5. See Roberta Showalter Kreider, editor, *From Wounded Hearts: Faith Stories of Lesbian, Gay, Bisexual and Transgendered People and Those Who Love Them* (Gaithersburg, Maryland: Chi Rho Press Inc, 1998). For a fuller narrative of one life see: Mel White, *Stranger at the Gate: To Be Gay and Christian in America* (New York, New York: Simon and Schuster, 1994).

6. Philip Yancey, 'Why I Don't Go to a Megachurch', *Christianity Today* (29 May 1996): 80.

7. George Lakoff, *Moral Politics: What Conservatives Know That Liberals Don't* (Chicago: University of Chicago Press, 1996).

(2) Some who affirm homoerotic relations have fears about those on the conservative side. Within the church they fear fundamentalists may take over. Something like what happened among Southern Baptists could happen in the Mennonite Church. A rigidly defined orthodoxy would be enforced. Pastors and teachers in colleges and seminaries would have to be constantly looking over their shoulders worrying about whether someone was going to haul them before a disciplinary body for not believing and teaching the right thing. Or perhaps the fear is of a more specific Mennonite variety: we will return to our own earlier days (not that terribly long ago) when a set of beliefs and practices were rigidly enforced.

Furthermore some who affirm changing the church's position on homoerotic relations fear that the Religious Right is already too powerful in North American society. We do not want them taking over more and more of society.[8] In fact, matters of sexual (including homosexual) behaviour should be a private matter, not something the state should monitor and enforce.

And finally, often the affirming folk know that the traditional folk have the bulk of the power. They are in the majority of the positions of power within the church and society. It makes the affirming folk feel rather powerless.

(3) On the other hand, those who endorse the traditional stance of the church believe the debates over this issue demonstrate that there is reason for concern about moral decline. Within the church, there is cause for concern about moral and theological confusion and spiritual sickness. The homosexuality issue is not the first sign of such confusion. However, as a presenting issue, it provides an opportunity. For, if this issue is approached with wisdom and discernment, this may be a way of beginning to address the creeping moral, theological and spiritual confusion within the church.

---

8.   See Judith N Shklar, 'The Liberalism of Fear', in *Liberalism and the Moral Life*, edited by Nancy L Rosenblum (Cambridge, Massachusetts: Harvard University Press, 1989), 21–38. On some of the reasons for the fear on this sort of contentious issue see: James Davison Hunter, *Culture Wars: The Struggle to Define America* (New York, New York: Basic Books, 1991); James Davison Hunter, *Before the Shooting Begins: Searching For Democracy in America's Culture Wars* (New York, New York: Basic Books, 1994); Didi Herman, *The Antigay Agenda: Orthodox Vision and The Christian Right* (Chicago, Illinois: University of Chicago Press, 1997); and as a challenge to some of these see Christian Smith, *Christian America?: What Evangelicals Really Want* (Los Angeles, California: University of California Press, 2000).

Many would argue that in the larger society there is also more moral confusion than there needs to be. And although it is true that it is inappropriate for the state to monitor what are quite appropriately private sexual acts, nonetheless it is acceptable to have certain laws that serve not only to restrain but also to educate. Society, with its diversity, can decide it is appropriate, for instance, only to sanction heterosexual marriages or to forbid curricular materials for schools, intended for young children, that affirm homoerotic relationships.[9]

3. Glosses on areas of agreement

In this section I offer some glosses on the numbered items listed in the section in which I tried to name the things about which most of us agree. In doing this I hope to help us name the differences within the agreement so that, once named, they can perhaps be more accessible as points of discussion/debate. Also I want to call for greater honesty about the nature of the disagreements.

3.1 Social and biological sciences

I list this and discuss it first not because I think it most important. I do not. But in many formal and informal discussions, the science related to how people become gay and lesbian assumes a significant role. In fact it often becomes a trump card, preventing honest conversations about difficult issues.

My central point here is simple: questions have been raised about how people become gay and lesbian which present puzzles no one has really solved.[10] The questions make it clear that sexual identity is complex and

---

9. In addition to most of the references in footnote seven, I would also refer to Ellen G Friedman and Corinne Squire, *Morality USA* (Minneapolis, Minnesota: University of Minnesota Press, 1998) and Andrew Bard Schmookler, *Debating the Good Society: A Quest to Bridge America's Moral Divide* (Cambridge, Massachusetts: MIT Press, 1999).

10. To get an overview of the subject see Chandler Burr, *A Separate Creation: How Biology Makes Us Gay* (New York, New York: Bantam Books, 1997); Jennifer Terry, *An American Obsession: Science, Medicine, and Homosexuality in Modern Society* (Chicago, Illinois: University of Chicago Press, 1999); Vernon A Rosario, *Science and Homosexualities* (New York, New York: Routledge, 1999); Stanton L Jones and Mark A Yarhouse, 'The Use, Misuse, and Abuse of Science in the Ecclesiastical Homosexuality Debates', in *Homosexuality, Science, and the 'Plain Sense' of Scripture*, edited by David L Balch (Grand Rapids, Michigan:

includes the interaction of genetics, familial relations, and the social environment beyond the family. Exactly how these factors interact is complicated, different for different individuals, and, I believe, not fully understood by anyone.

It has been intriguing to me to notice that many who affirm acceptance of homoerotic relations within the church seem to presume an essentialist view of sexual identity, that is, 'they have no choice', 'that is just who they are'). On the other hand, many who affirm the traditional Christian approach to homoerotic relations often assume a social constructionist view of sexual identity. That is to say, they presume a substantial plasticity to our sexual identity. Otherwise, why worry that your children might become gay or lesbian if their social world communicates in multiple ways that homoerotic relations are every bit as legitimate as heteroerotic relations?[11] Much of the public rhetoric that has pulled at people's heartstrings has also been essentialist: How could you raise moral questions when they *cannot* be any other way?[12] Yet the recent trend in much secular writing about gays and lesbians is social constructionist in orientation.[13]

What in my view is disingenuous—or reflective of inadequate reading— is to suggest that science provides clear data that make it impossible for us to raise moral questions about homoerotic relations.[14] Or, similarly, that we

---

Wm B Eerdmans, 2000), 73–120; Stanton L Jones and Mark A Yarhouse, *Homosexuality: The Use of Scientific Research in the Church's Moral Debate* (Downers Grove, Illinois: InterVarsity Press, 2000). Also see: Richard Lewontin, *The Triple Helix: Gene, Organism and Environment* (Cambridge: Harvard University Press, 2000); and Matt Ridley, *The Agile Gene: Genes, Experience, and What Makes Us Human* (New York: Harper Collins, 2005).

11. In using 'essentialist' and 'social constructivist' language, I realise I am using language from the social sciences. Though such language is useful and instructive, it is also important to remember that theological language regarding, for instance, creation, sin, and corruptibility, are more determinative for Christians.

12. In case I have not been clear, let me say that I think it is a complicated mixture, thus the truth, I believe, of my previous paragraph.

13. The literature is vast, but see David F Greenberg, *The Construction of Homosexuality* (Chicago, Illinois: University of Chicago, 1988) and Marjorie Garber, *Vice Versa: Bisexuality and the Eroticism of Everyday Life* (New York, New York: Simon and Schuster, 1995).

14. Among other things, the way in which 'choice' often figures into these conversations is overly simplified in important ways. For some very insightful theological reflections that are relevant to these matters see Michael Banner,

know enough about homosexuality today, through what science has taught us, that we can be confident that what the Bible is talking about in Leviticus or Romans is not what *we* are talking about. It goes without saying that the writers of the Bible did not use modern scientific models to study sexual identity or behaviour. However, it does not follow that this silences the Bible's voice on the subject. Furthermore, we need to be a little more circumspect about our own 'clear' knowledge. Science does not provide those in the know with a trump card in these discussions (which is not the same as saying that it is not a part of the conversation).

3.2 The Bible and Christian theology and ethics
First let me speak to those in the church who are not biblical scholars or theologians. It is important for us all to be honest about the complexities surrounding this issue. There are the scientific complexities just discussed. There is also the complexity of interpreting some of the relevant texts.[15] It is true that Leviticus 18:22 is straightforward in what it says, 'You shall not lie with a male as with a woman; it is an abomination'. But then Leviticus is also straightforward when it says, 'You shall not let your animals breed with a different kind; you shall not sow your field with two kinds of seed; nor shall you put on a garment made of two different materials' (19:19).

'Prolegomena to a Dogmatic Sexual Ethic', in his *Christian Ethics and Contemporary Moral Problems* (Cambridge: Cambridge University Press, 1999), 269–309 and especially on choice, 295ff.

15. Among the many debatable points is the naming of immediately relevant texts. Most would agree that Romans 1:26–7 and Leviticus 18:22 and Leviticus 20:13 are among them. Others would include the lists in 1 Corinthians 6:9–10 and 1 Timothy 1:10. Many would concede that there should at least be discussions of Genesis 19:1–8, Judges 19:16–30, 2 Peter 2:6–7, and Jude 7. Even if one includes all of these, it is a small number of texts. Nonetheless, it is worth noting that until roughly the last twenty-five years these texts have set the moral norm within both Judaism and Christianity. Moreover, the prohibition against homoerotic behaviour seems to be presumed within the many teachings about sexuality within the Scriptures.

Let me also mention one essay that is remarkable for being as clear and neutral (and in brief compass) as any essay I have read in laying out the issues in regard to reading the Scriptures on this topic: Walter Moberly, 'The Use of Scripture in Contemporary Debate About Homosexuality', *Theology*, CIII/814 (July/August 2000): 251–8.

Why is it that one text matters a great deal to us and the other not at all? There are (quite legitimately) complex matters of interpretation here.[16] We should not invoke the complexity simply as a way to dismiss or relativise the texts, but rather to be honest about the need for those who study such matters to help us know how to be honest and consistent in interpreting such texts.[17]

Furthermore, we should be honest in asking why the question of homoerotic relations has assumed such importance. Money—and our temptations to serve it—assumes a much larger role in the Scriptures (and in the wealthy US this has considerable relevance). Why is that not exercising us as much, if what we care about is the authority of the Scriptures?

Now, a word to biblical scholars and theologians. It is important that we not, directly or indirectly, communicate contempt for sincere Christians who seek to take the Bible and the call of Christ to discipleship seriously. We cannot expect most Christians to read the Scriptures in the way scholars would. I am grateful for those Mennonites who have refused to kill enemies during America's wars because of their commitment to take the Bible seriously and faithfully to live out Jesus' teaching to love their enemies. That these same people do not understand the complexities of biblical interpretation related to the wars in Joshua or the violent imagery in

---

16. For one of the most thorough, recent studies, and as a guide to other literature, see Jonathan Klawans, *Impurity and Sin in Ancient Judaism* (New York, New York: Oxford University Press, 2000).

17. The person who has shaped much of the debate within the last twenty years is John Boswell. See his *Christianity, Social Tolerance, and Homosexuality: Gay People in Western Europe from the Beginning of the Christian Era to the Fourth Century* (Chicago, Illinois: University of Chicago Press, 1980). Some of the other writings worth taking seriously that attempt to wrestle with the relevant texts and that come to conclusions that would make those who affirm the Church's traditional stance uncomfortable are: Bernadette J Brooten, *Love Between Women: Early Christian Responses to Female Homoeroticism* (Chicago, Illinois: University of Chicago Press, 1996); L William Countryman, *Dirt, Greed and Sex: Sexual Ethics in the New Testament and Their Implications for Today* (Philadelphia, Pennsylvania: Fortress Press, 1988); Martti Nissinen, *Homoeroticism in the Biblical World* (Minneapolis, Minnesota: Fortress Press, 1998); Robin Scroggs, *The New Testament and Homosexuality* (Philadelphia, Pennsylvania: Fortress Press, 1983); and Michael Vasey, *Strangers and Friends: A New Exploration of Homosexuality and the Bible* (London: Hodder and Stoughton, 1995).

Revelation is not something for which they are blameworthy (as if any of the rest of us fully understand these complicated matters). They are called to be faithful Christians. It is our job as teachers and pastors to provide adequate instruction for members of our churches, even as we accept that they need never be scholars.

Furthermore, it is imperative that we be honest about the complexities and diversity of opinions regarding the issues around homoerotic relations and biblical teaching. I have often heard it implied by theologians (Mennonite and otherwise) that no serious Scripture scholarship supports the traditional view (or that only fundamentalists do). That is simply not true.[18] It is true that for a while in the 1980s many were under the sway of the readings of the Bible provided by John Boswell.[19] However, beginning in

---

18. See, for example, Robert A Gagnon, *The Bible and Homosexual Practice* (Nashville, Tennessee: Abingdon Press, 2001); Richard Hays, 'Homosexuality', in *The Moral Vision of the New Testament* (New York, New York: HarperCollins, 1996), 379–406; Richard Hays, 'Relations Natural and Unnatural: A Response to John Boswell's Exegesis of Romans 1', *The Journal of Religious Ethics*, 14/1 (Spring 1986): 184–215; Thomas Schmidt, *Straight and Narrow?: Compassion and Clarity in the Homosexuality Debate* (Downers Grove, Illinois: InterVarsity Press, 1995); Mark D Smith, 'Ancient Bisexuality and the Interpretation of Romans 1:26–7', *Journal of the American Academy of Religion*, LXIV/2 (Summer 1996): 223–56; and David F Wright, 'Homosexuals or Prostitutes?: The Meaning of ΑΡΣΕΝΟΚΟΙΤΑΙ (1 Cor 6:9, 1 Tim 1:10)', *Vigiliae Christianae*, 38 (1984): 125–53. Gagnon's book is by far the most careful and thorough book that has been published on the subject. (See additional resources on his faculty website.)

Finally, mention should be made of three excellent essays on hermeneutics. Anthony Thiselton, who probably knows as much about hermeneutics as anyone in the world, has written, 'Can Hermeneutics Ease the Deadlock?', in *The Way Forward: Christian Voices on Homosexuality and the Church*, edited by Timothy Bradshaw (London: Hodder and Stoughton, 1997), 145–96 (issued in a revised edition by Eerdmans, 2003). Also see: Kathryn Greene-McCreight, 'The Logic of the Interpretation of Scripture and the Church's Debate Over Sexual Ethics', in *Homosexuality, Science, and the 'Plain Sense' of Scripture*, 242–60 and Walter Brueggemann, 'Biblical Authority: A Personal Reflection', *The Christian Century* (3–10 January 2001): 14–20.

19. As mentioned above, this is Boswell's 1980 book, *Christianity, Social Tolerance, and Homosexuality*. More recently he published John Boswell, *The Marriage of Likeness: Same-Sex Unions in Pre-Modern Europe* (London: HarperCollins, 1995) [published in the US with the titles and subtitles reversed]. For critical responses, in addition to some of the references to Boswell's biblical

the mid-1980s and continuing today, there are serious scholars who come to various conclusions.[20]

Moreover, since there are various academically respectable views, it is important that we as scholars not over-estimate our role. I believe we do have a crucial role in these conversations. Within this role we need to remember the larger theological and moral contexts within which we discuss specific texts and specific issues. But it will not do to imagine that we can invoke the word *scholarship* as a trump card to short-circuit full conversations with contributions by various people, including biblical scholars and theologians.

3.3 Church history

More than a few believe that our central learning from the church on this topic, as with sexuality generally, is a negative learning. That is to say, the church has so often gotten it wrong, been overly negative about the body and preoccupied with sexual behaviour, that—except for learning what not to do and say—we can largely ignore much of what has been done and said in relation to sexual and homosexual behaviour throughout most of the church's history. There is some truth in this. We can find numerous quotations and incidents to support the claim. There is much we need to learn by looking at mistakes of the past.

However, might we also have some other important things to learn from the church on this subject? I believe we do. The stereotype of Christian

---

interpretations mentioned in an earlier footnote, see: Bruce A Williams, OP, 'Homosexuality and Christianity: A Review Discussion', *The Thomist*, 46 (1982): 609–25 and Brent D Shaw, 'A Groom of One's Own?: The Medieval Church and the Question of Gay Marriage', *The New Republic*, 211 (18 and 25 July 1994): 33–41; and Matthew Kuefler, editor, *The Boswell Thesis* (Chicago: University of Chicago Press, 2005).

20. Rather than list more writings here, let me simply mention the bibliographies in two important, recent books (which themselves have very different views and approaches): Stanley J Grenz, *Welcoming But Not Affirming: An Evangelical Response to Homosexuality* (Louisville, Kentucky: Westminster John Knox Press, 1998), 187–201 and Bernadette J Brooten, *Love Between Women: Early Christian Responses to Female Homoeroticism* (Chicago, Illinois: University of Chicago Press, 1996), 363–72.

sexual repressiveness from the outset is at best an exaggeration.[21] As renowned classicist Paul Veyne has said:

> If any aspect of ancient life has been distorted by legend, this is it. It is widely but mistakenly believed that antiquity was a Garden of Eden from which repression was banished, Christianity having yet to insinuate the worm of sin into the forbidden fruit. Actually, the pagans were paralysed by prohibitions.[22]

Similar things could be said about other periods of church history.[23] Again, this is not to say one could not find writings and actions regarding sexuality by church leaders that would be objectionable (though such texts should be read contextually, not anachronistically). This is simply to say that other voices—from the history of the church—can provide guidance, guidance that is much needed in our time.

I believe Linda Woodhead has it just right in saying that 'When "Christianity" and "the Christian tradition" come under attack, it often seems that what detractors have in their targets is not two thousand years of Christian history, but the Christianity of their youth and of the previous

---

21. For one instance of a recent book that helps rescue Paul from this claim see Francis Watson, *Agape, Eros, Gender: Towards a Pauline Sexual Ethic* (Cambridge: Cambridge University Press, 2000). Also see Raymond F Collins, *Sexual Ethics and the New Testament* (New York, New York: Crossroad Publishing Co, 2000).

22. Paul Veyne, 'The Roman Empire', in Philippe Ariès and Georges Duby, editors, *A History of Private Life, I: From Pagan Rome to Byzantium* (Cambridge Massachusetts: Belknap Press, 1987), 202. See also Aline Rousselle, *Porneia: On Desire and the Body in Antiquity*, translated by Felicia Pheasant (Oxford: Basil Blackwell, 1988) and Peter Brown, *The Body and Society* (New York: Columbia University Press, 1988).

23. See, for example, John Behr, *Asceticism and Anthropology in Irenaeus and Clement* (New York, New York: Oxford University Press, 2000) and Margaret R Miles, *Fullness of Life: Historical Foundations for a New Asceticism* (Philadelphia: Westminster Press, 1981). For an overview of much of the history, with substantial bibliographical guidance, see Mary E Wiesner-Hanks, *Christianity and Sexuality in the Early Modern World* (New York, New York: Routledge, 2000).

generation.'[24] For Mennonites this is relevant to much more than the subject of sexuality. Many currently living have memories of overzealous church leaders seeking to enforce codes of conduct on a whole church or an area conference in ways that were experienced as oppressive and may often have been unwise.[25] These memories should provide a caution. And they should counsel us to desire wisdom. But the caution and counsel should not equal moral or doctrinal neutrality. Nor do they negate either the authority of Scripture or the riches that can be gained from drawing on Christian history.

3.4 Love of neighbours

I believe it should be obvious to any Christians that—as people called to love our neighbours as ourselves—we are not to be cruel to anyone. This 'anyone' certainly includes those engaged in homoerotic relationships. Moreover, our love should express itself in tangible, positive ways toward our neighbours. However, it is more than that, is it not? Mennonites (as a group) believe that following Jesus entails, among other things, being peacemakers—being committed to peace, justice, inclusion, welcoming the marginalised as Jesus did. Does this not exclude rejecting those who are engaged in homoerotic relationships?

This question deserves brief exploration. Some have made much of the fact that Jesus said nothing about homosexuality. However, there are many issues to which Jesus never spoke. If, as Martti Nissinen and others have said, the Judaism Jesus knew was rather unequivocally negative on the

---

24. Linda Woodhead, 'Life in the Spirit: Contemporary and Christian Understandings of the Human Person', in *New Soundings: Essays in Developing Tradition*, edited by Stephen Platten, Graham James and Andrew Chandler (London: Darton, Longman and Todd, 1997), 118.

25. One of the subjects that should be revisited in this regard is the Mennonite understanding of church. Paul Hiebert has described what he refers to as three basic approaches to understanding church: the bounded set, the fuzzy set, and the centred set. To oversimplify, the Mennonite Church has often taken a bounded-set approach, one that focuses considerably on boundary issues that define people in or out. The centred-set approach, in contrast, focuses mostly on the centre, what it is that centrally defines the church. See Paul Hiebert, 'The Category *Christian* in the Mission Task', in his *Anthropological Reflections on Missiological Issues* (Grand Rapids, Michigan: Baker Books, 1994), 107–36. This clearly has relevance for the debates about homosexuality, as is shown in Michael A King, *Trackless Wastes and Stars to Steer By* (Scottdale, Pennsylvania: Herald Press, 1990), 115–36.

matter of homoerotic relations, then Jesus had no reason to say anything if he agreed with the consensus.[26] In fact, given the consensus, it might be significant that Jesus didn't challenge convictions and practices firmly in place that denied the legitimacy of homoerotic relationships.

At a more abstract and principled level, one might argue that Jesus welcomed the marginalised; he was inclusive. But stating it this way begs the question. Adulterers (especially women) were marginalised in the world of Jesus and although Jesus (according to John 8) prevented the stoning of a woman caught in adultery, he nonetheless asked her to 'go and sin no more'. As Croatian theologian Miroslav Volf has put it:

> Jesus was no prophet of "inclusion". . . for whom the chief virtue was acceptance and the cardinal vice intolerance. [He did scandalously include many who were normally excluded, but he also] made the "intolerant" demand of repentance and the "condescending" offer of forgiveness.'[27]

In short, an argument either from Jesus' teaching on peacemaking or his silence on the specific issue of homoerotic relationships in no way provides an endorsement of homoerotic relations.

3.5 Support for heterosexual married couples

I do think it is important to note that most of those who want the church to affirm homoerotic relationships do not intend to undermine heterosexual relationships or families. Quite the contrary, they wish them well. However, whether or not the formal affirmation of homoerotic relationships does in fact undermine the future of heterosexual identities and relationships in some

---

26. As Martti Nissinen, who is affirming of homoerotic behaviour, says: 'To the extent that Rabbinic and Hellenistic Jewish literature sheds light on the norms of Jewish society in Jesus' time, it can be assumed that public expressions of homosexuality were regarded as anomalous, idolatrous, and indecent'. (Martti Nissinen, *Homoeroticism in the Biblical* World: *A Historical Perspective* (Minneapolis, Minnesota: Fortress Press, 1998), 118. See also Robin Scroggs, *The New Testament and Homosexuality* (Philadelphia, Pennsylvania: Fortress Press, 1983), 66–84 and Robert AJ Gagnon, *The Bible and Homosexual Practice*, 185–209.

27. Miroslav Volf, *Exclusion and Embrace* (Nashville, Tennessee: Abingdon Press, 1996), 72–3. See also: Gagnon, 210–28.

ways is an open question.[28] It depends on how gays and lesbians come to be gay and lesbian or, put differently, how their gay and lesbian identities are formed (about which, I believe, we are still unsure). And it depends on what specific proposals for affirmation are suggested and accepted.[29]

Moreover, there are two other complicating issues. First, the debate about homosexuality is happening at a time when there is hardly a consensus within society, the church, or the theological world about sexual relationships and monogamous marriages.[30] Second, many who write theological books or essays about homoerotic relations argue for non-traditional ways of structuring relationships, to put it most neutrally.[31] It is not clear to me that most of the relevant parties to these conversations distance themselves from, say, non-monogamous relationships. If that is indeed the case, then it needs to be stated.

---

28. For a theological argument for homosexual marriage, see David Matzko McCarthy, 'Homosexuality and the Practices of Marriage', *Modern Theology* 13/3 (July 1997): 371–97. See also Catherine M Wallace, *For Fidelity: How Intimacy and Commitment Enrich Our Lives* (New York, New York: Vintage Books, 1998) and the critique of Wallace: J Budziszewski, 'Just Friends', *First Things*, 87 (November 1998): 60–3.

29. As least as a way to see what some of the issues are, consult David M Estlund and Martha Nussbaum, editors, *Sex, Preference, and Family* (New York, New York: Oxford University Press, 1997) and Christopher Wolfe, editor, *Homosexuality and American Public Life* (Dallas, Texas: Spence Publishing Company, 1999), especially Part III.

30. For some sense of the diversity within the theological world, see James B Nelson and Sandra P Longfellow, editors, *Sexuality and the Sacred: Sources for Theological Reflection* (Louisville, Kentucky: Westminster John Knox Press, 1994) and Elizabeth Stuart and Adrian Thatcher, editors, *Christian Perspectives on Sexuality and Gender* (Grand Rapids, Minnesota: Wm B Eerdmans, 1996).

31. As examples, see Gary David Comstock, *Gay Theology Without Apology* (Cleveland, Ohio: Pilgrim Press, 1993); Kathy Rudy, *Sex and the Church: Gender, Homosexuality, and the Transformation of Christian Ethics* (Boston, Massachusetts: Beacon Press, 1997); Elizabeth Stuart, *Just Good Friends: Towards a Lesbian and Gay Theology of Relationships* (London: Mowbry, 1995) and Gary David Comstock and Susan E Henking, editors, *Que(e)rying Religion: A Critical Anthology* (New York, New York: Continuum, 1997).

3.6 Homoerotic relations and broader issues of sexuality

I am certainly in agreement with those who say that it is inappropriate to reflect on homoerotic relations without dealing with the contexts within which we discuss such relations, including broader issues related to sexuality. We need to discuss cultural and social contexts within which we live our lives, contexts that cannot help but shape our understandings of sexuality and our concepts regarding appropriate and inappropriate sexual attitudes and behaviour. As Christians we also need to name biblical teachings and Christian convictions rooted in the Scriptures that serve to shape our lives, leading us to embody our convictions faithfully, including the ways in which we conduct ourselves sexually. And in fact contexts and convictions are interrelated for us. But what are the contexts to be named? And what are the convictions?

In 1991 a committee of the Presbyterian Church USA produced a document on human sexuality.[32] Early within this document the relevant contexts related to human sexuality were named as 'patriarchy, heterosexism, and homophobia'. It is important to name abusive patterns of authority and structured forms of injustice. Likewise, it is vital that we acknowledge stereotypes of and hateful attitudes and behaviours toward gays and lesbians. However, only to name this one set of contexts ignores too many other relevant elements of our context. For instance, Walter Brueggemann, hardly conservative, said at the beginning of an insightful recent essay that 'we may as well concede at the outset that we live, all of us, in a promiscuous, self-indulgent society that prizes autonomy'.[33] Might these elements of our context not also be relevant for our deliberations about sexuality?

It is not particularly surprising that, when 'patriarchy, heterosexism, and homophobia' are the only contexts named, then the only substantive moral guidance given by the Presbyterian document is a commitment 'to an

---

32. *Presbyterians and Human Sexuality 1991* (Louisville, Kentucky: The Office of the General Assembly, Presbyterian Church [USA], 1991). A summary was published by the chair of the committee: John J Carey, 'Body and Soul: Presbyterians on Sexuality', *The Christian Century*, 108 (8 May 1991): 516–20. That this approach is still considered an important option for the Church by some see: Marvin M Ellison and Sylvia Thorson-Smith, editors, *Body and Soul: Rethinking Sexuality as Justice-Love* (Cleveland, Ohio: Pilgrim Press, 2003).

33. Walter Brueggemann, 'Duty as Delight and Desire: Preaching Obedience That Is Not Legalism', in his *The Covenanted Self: Explorations in Law and Covenant*, edited by Patrick D Miller (Minneapolis, Minnesota: Fortress Press, 1999), 35.

inclusive, egalitarian ethic of common decency', or what is elsewhere referred to as the criterion of 'justice-love'.[34] Our Scriptures certainly implore us to pursue justice and to embody love. However, there are also admonitions regarding sexual immorality, lust, passions, the works of the flesh, and self-control—concerns more at home with Brueggemann's reminders.

I worry that many of us, because of our reticence to be morally clear about sexuality, have been unwilling to take seriously this latter set of concerns that respond to other dimensions of our context. We have, for instance, allowed the conversations about sexuality to be hostage to the public rhetoric about 'safe sex'. But as Kari Jenson Gold has said, 'Surely the words are ludicrously contradictory! Sex can be many things: dark, mysterious, passionate, wild, gentle, even reassuring, but it is not safe. If it is, it's not likely to be very sexy.'[35]

Camille Paglia, an ex-Catholic, offers some devastating and insightful criticisms of the Presbyterian document just mentioned that I think can instruct us all as we approach sexuality.[36] She—herself approving of all manner of dissident sexual conduct—does not want Christians to be naive about the realities of sexuality. As she put it, the document:

> reduces the complexities and mysteries of eroticism to a clumsy, outmoded social-welfare ideology. The old-style Protestant suppression of the passions, torments, and untidy physicalities of the body is in fact still abundantly evident in the report, which, in its opening premise of 'the basic goodness of sexuality', projects a happy, bouncy vision of human life that would have made Doris Day and Debbie Reynolds—those '50s blond divas—proud . . . 'Eros', says the report's glossary, is 'a zest for life'. Is this a soap commercial? Eros, like Dionysus, is a great and dangerous god. The

---

34. See the excerpt of the Presbyterian document published as 'Sexuality and Justice-Love', *The Christian Century*, 108 (8 May 1991): 519.
35. Kari Jenson Gold, 'Getting Real', *First Things* (January 1994): 6.
36. For other, more measured, critiques of the Presbyterian document, see Gary L Watts, 'An Empty Sexual Ethic', *The Christian Century*, 108 (8 May 1991): 520–1 and Michael Banner, 'Five Churches in Search of Sexual Ethics', in his *Christian Ethics and Contemporary Moral Problems* (Cambridge: Cambridge University Press, 1999), 252–68.

report gives us vanilla sex, smothered with artificial
butterscotch syrup. In its liberal zeal to understand, to
accept, to heal, it reduces the grand tragicomedy of love
and lust to a Hallmark card. Its unctuous normalizing of
dissident sex is imperialistic and oppressive. The gay
world is stripped of its outlaw adventures in toilets,
alleyways, trucks, and orgy rooms. There are no
leathermen, hustlers, or drag queens. Gay love is
reduced to a nice, neat, middle-class couple moving in
next door on 'Father Knows Best' . . . This is censorship
in the name of liberal benevolence . . . [37]

Moreover, given the complex, powerful realities of sexuality, Paglia thinks
Christians make a serious mistake when we strip ourselves of our own best
resources:

The report assails the 'influential tradition of radical
asceticism' in 'Western Christianity' . . . It assumes that
eremites and monks were not contemplatives but killjoys,
neurotics, and misogynists, scowling while the rest of the
world caroused, footloose and fancy free. The report
complains of 'our cultural captivity to a patriarchal model
of sexuality and its ethic of sexual control', as if sexual
rules and taboos were not prevalent in every culture . . .

---

37. Camille Paglia, 'The Joy of Presbyterian Sex', *The New Republic* (2 December
1991): 24–7; reprinted in Camille Paglia, *Sex, Art, and American Culture* (New
York, New York: Vintage Books, 1992), 26–37. Also see Camille Paglia, 'Rebel
Love: Homosexuality', in her *Vamps and Tramps* (New York, New York: Vintage
Books, 1994), 67–92. I have serious disagreements with Camille Paglia's own
views on sexuality and think some of her over-charged rhetoric unnecessary.
However, her response to the Presbyterian document is an important one in at
least three regards. First, she refuses to let us forget the complex emotional,
relational, and physical dimensions of sexuality. Second, if, with the document
she criticises, a church is going to offer an affirmation of sexual (and
homosexual) behaviours without simultaneously offering moral guidance
regarding right and wrong behaviours (other than those connected to oppression
and injustice), then we need to be honest, as Paglia is, as to the range of
behaviours on offer in the larger culture (most of which, incidentally, she
affirms). Third, despite her own, self-proclaimed, pagan views, she wants the
Church to be honestly Christian, in its own views.

> The institutional religions, Catholic and Protestant, carry
> with them the majesty of history. Their theology is
> impressive and coherent. Efforts to revise or dilute that
> theology for present convenience seem to me
> misguided.[38]

Is there something 'impressive' and 'coherent' about our theological
traditions—even in relation to sexuality and homosexuality—that we ignore
at our peril? Are there cautions here that we should heed?

4. Revision for present convenience?: some closing comments

I believe it is reasonable for Christians—simple believers or academics—to
ask, with Paglia, whether or not revisions regarding our approach to
homosexuality (and sexuality), currently underway in many circles, are 'for
present convenience'.[39] Moreover, it seems reasonable to argue that the
burden of proof is on the shoulders of those who would challenge the
historical consensus within the church that the plain sense of Scripture on
this issue is right, that homoerotic behaviour is not to be formally affirmed
within the church.

However, that is not the same as saying that anyone should approach this
subject without humility. Rather, for many of us it seems quite appropriate to
approach it with an openness to learn, with humility, and with significant
pain. I sense this, for instance, in the recent words of Kathryn Greene-
McCreight:

> Let me say for the record that I am among those who wish
> they could be convinced that Scripture and tradition could
> be read to support the revisionist position, which would
> argue for the theological and religious appropriateness of
> homoerotic relationships for Christians who feel drawn to
> them . . . While I have not yet been convinced by the

---

38. Camille Paglia, 'The Joy of Presbyterian Sex', *The New Republic* (2 December
 1991): 24–7. For her general knowledge on the subject of sexuality see: Camille
 Paglia, *Sexual Personae* (New York, New York: Vintage Books, 1990).
39. Wendell Berry insightfully shows how well many contemporary approaches to
 sexuality fit with the general, consumerist *Zeitgeist*: Wendell Berry, *Sex,
 Economy, Freedom and Community* (New York, New York: Pantheon Books,
 1993), 117–73.

revisionist position, I keep listening in hopes that someone
will come up with something new.[40]

Furthermore, though I hope this essay has communicated that I want people
at various places along a spectrum to hear each other, I nonetheless think it
is a mistake to minimise the potential importance of the issues at stake in
relation to this matter. No less a voice than that of the major German
Protestant theologian, Wolfhart Pannenberg, has said that:

> if a church were to let itself be pushed to the point where
> it ceased to treat homosexual activity as a departure from
> the biblical norm, and recognized homosexual unions as a
> personal partnership of love equivalent to marriage, such a
> church would stand no longer on biblical ground but
> against the unequivocal witness of Scripture. A church
> that took this step would cease to be the one, holy,
> catholic, and apostolic Church.[41]

Lest someone imagine that strong theological claims are made only by
theologians who affirm the tradition which stands against homoerotic
relations, we should listen to Eugene Rogers Jr, another theologian. Rogers
argues that if straight Christians do not move to affirm monogamous gay and
lesbian marriages, then they are in danger of losing their salvation!

In his substantial recent work, *Sexuality and the Christian Body*, Rogers
makes the argument, offered also by others in recent years, that homosexuals
are analogous to Gentiles in the New Testament.[42]

---

40. Kathryn Greene-McCreight, 'The Logic of the Interpretation of Scripture and the
    Church's Debate Over Sexual Ethics', in *Homosexuality, Science, and the 'Plain
    Sense' of Scripture*, 245. On the other hand, read within the context of her whole
    essay, her words hardly represent a cavalier approach.

41. Quoted in Gilbert Meilander, 'What Sex Is—And Is For,' *First Things*, 102 (April
    2000): 44.

42. Eugene Rogers Jr, *Sexuality and the Christian Body* (Oxford: Blackwell
    Publishers, 1999), 28–66. It should perhaps be noted that this is only one
    component of Rogers' argument. For an interesting use of Rogers' book see:
    Stout, Jeffrey, 'How Charity Transcends the Culture Wars: Eugene Rogers and
    Others on Same-Sex Marriage', *Journal of Religious Ethics*, 31 (Summer 2003):
    169–80.

If there is anything that is central to many of Paul's theological arguments, it is that in Christ, Jews and Gentiles have been made one. Paul went to great effort and used strong rhetoric to indicate that Gentiles (which now includes almost all of us) are, in Christ, equal members of the people of God. Paul proclaimed this despite how offensive this was to many of those who, like himself, were Jews. In fact, to deny the inclusion of the Gentiles, said Paul, is to deny the Gospel and the work of the Holy Spirit. Likewise, so this argument runs, in Christ, gay and straight have been made one.[43] If this is right, says Rogers, then 'failing to accept faithful, monogamous gay and lesbian marriages may deny the work of the Spirit and put Gentile Christians [who are in the present denying what some Jews were then denying] in danger of their salvation'.[44]

I think we do no one any favours if we forget that more than a few share the views of either Pannenberg or Rogers. Each side can claim that profound theological issues are at stake—that the gospel and the future of the church are in the balance. And even if the theological stakes are not this high, we are still left with what seem irresolvable issues. We still need help moving forward when many tell us the stakes are this high. Thus this discussion should be taken seriously. We err if we take the questions related to homoerotic relationships with less seriousness than they deserve.

Whether Rogers' argument is convincing or not, he is at least attempting to do what needs to be done. That is to say, he is attempting to give solid, compelling theological reasons for his position, a position that seeks to overturn the consensus within the church.[45] Kathryn Greene-McCreight contends that:

---

43. For other proponents of this argument, see Jeffrey S Siker, 'Homosexual Christians, the Bible, and Gentile Inclusion: Confessions of a Repenting Heterosexist', in *Homosexuality in the Church: Both Sides of the Debate*, edited by Jeffrey S Siker (Louisville, Kentucky: Westminster John Knox Press, 1994), 178–94 and Stephen E Fowl, *Engaging Scripture* (Oxford: Blackwell, 1998), 119–27. See also arguments against this approach: Richard Hays, 'Homosexuality,' in *The Moral Vision of the New Testament*, 395–7, 399–400; Kathryn Greene-McCreight, 'The Logic of the Interpretation of Scripture and the Church's Debate Over Sexual Ethics', 253–60; and Gagnon, 460–6.

44. Rogers, *Sexuality and the Christian Body*, 52.

45. Rogers' book represents the most serious attempt I have seen to make a theological argument, on traditional grounds, for the affirmation of homoerotic relationships. This is not to say he is successful. For a review that suggests he is not successful see Gilbert Meilander, 'What Sex Is—And Is For', *First Things*,

for traditional readers to be convinced of the righteousness
before God of homoerotic relationships, they would need to
be convinced on "traditionalist" grounds . . . Or the
revisionist side must convincingly show how and why the
rules must be changed.[46]

It will not do simply to invoke words like tolerance, inclusion, or 'our
commitment to peace and justice'. Properly understood, all of these are a
part of the discussion. However, they must be situated in a broader
theological framework that includes the centrality of Jesus, the teachings of
the Scriptures on homosexuality, sexuality, and what it means to be
embodied persons while being faithfully Christian.[47]

---

102 (April 2000): 44–9. Also see the reviews of his book in *Modern Theology*
(July 2000) and the review essay: Douglas Farrow, 'Beyond Nature, Shy of
Grace', *International Journal of Systematic Theology*, 5 (November 2003).

46. Greene-McCreight, 'The Logic of the Interpretation of Scripture and the Church's
Debate', 246–7. This is similar, formally, to what Luke Timothy Johnson
suggests. See Luke Timothy Johnson, *Scripture and Discernment: Decision
Making in the Church* (Nashville, Tennessee: Abingdon Press, 1996), 144–8. One
could say that what Greene-McCreight is saying is vital for the ongoing integrity
of the Church.

47. There are many resources I would consult to wrestle with these issues. Along with
writings listed in other footnotes, they would include William J Abraham, 'United
Methodists at the End of the Mainline', *First Things*, 84 (June/July 1998): 28–33;
Banner, 'Prolegomena to a Dogmatic Sexual Ethic'; Rodney Clapp, 'Tacit
Holiness: The Importance of Bodies and Habits in Doing Church', in *Border
Crossings: Christian Trespasses on Popular Culture and Public Affairs* (Grand
Rapids, Michigan: Brazos Press, 2000), 63–74; Marva Dawn, *Sexual Character*
(Grand Rapids, Michigan: Wm B Eerdmans, 1993); Robert W Jenson, *Systematic
Theology, volume 2: The Works of God* (New York, New York: Oxford
University Press, 1999), 53–111; Gilbert Meilander, 'The First of Institutions',
Pro Ecclesia, VI/4 (Fall 1997): 444–55; Oliver O'Donovan, 'Homosexuality in
the Church: Can There Be a Fruitful Theological Debate?', in *The Way
Forward?*, edited by Timothy Bradshaw (London Hodder and Stroughton, 1997)
20–36; Ronald Rolheiser, *Seeking Spirituality* (London: Hodder and Stoughton,
1998); David Matzko McCarthy, *Sex and Love in the Home* (London: SCM
Press, 2001); 'St Andrew's Day Statement: An Examination of the Theological
Principles Affecting the Homosexuality Debate', in *The Way Forward?*, edited by
Bradshaw, 5–11; Kiernan Scott and Michael Warren, editors, *Perspectives on
Marriage*, 2nd edition (New York, New York: Oxford University Press, 2001);

As we continue to wrestle with these matters, we need to listen to each other. We need to speak honestly and humbly, with an openness to learn.[48] And we would do well to live with the Apostle Paul's admonitions regarding 'the works of the flesh' and 'the fruit of the spirit' (Gal 5:16–26).[49] We should not allow categorisations (for instance, liberal or conservative) to prevent any of us from taking seriously Paul's admonitions regarding fornication, impurity, licentiousness, carousing, faithfulness, self-control, and 'things like these' (Gal 5:19–23). Nor, if we need to remind ourselves, should we allow these categorisations to prevent any of us from hearing Paul's admonitions regarding enmities, strife, anger, quarrels, dissensions, factions, love, patience, kindness, and gentleness (Gal 5:19–23).[50]

Rowan Williams, 'The Body's Grace', in *Our Selves, Our Souls and Bodies*, edited by Charles Hefling (Cambridge, Massachusetts: Cowley Publications, 1996), 58–68; Linda Woodhead, 'Sex in a Wider Context', in *Sex These Days: Essays on Theology, Sexuality and Society*, edited by Jon Davies and Gerard Loughlin (Sheffield: Sheffield Academic Press, 1997), 98–120; and Sara Butler, 'Sex or Gender?', *First Things*, 154 (June/July 2005): 43–7.

48. We could do worse than heed Luke Timothy Johnson's admonitions: 'The church should not, cannot, define itself in response to political pressure or popularity polls. But it is called to discern the work of God in human lives and adapt its self-understanding in response to that work of God. Inclusivity must follow from evidence of holiness; are there narratives of homosexual *holiness* to which we must begin to listen?' (Johnson, *Scripture and Discernment*, 148.)

49. On the fruit of the spirit see Philip D Kenneson, *Life On the Vine* (Downers Grove, Illinois: InterVarsity Press, 1999).

50. I must thank the many friends who read and commented on an earlier draft of this essay: Jeremy Brooks, Alan and Eleanor Kreider, Phil Kenneson, Wayne and Leabell Miller, Martin Shupack, JR Burkholder, Margo Houts, Ted Grimsrud, Jeremy Thomson, Tim Foley, Willard Swartley, Nik Ansell, Gordon Preece, Brian Haymes, John D Roth, Alastair McKay, Stanley Hauerwas, Fran Porter, Michael A King, C Norman Kraus and Mary Thiessen Nation. I hope I haven't forgotten anyone. Of course, they have varying opinions about my essay. They are certainly not to be held responsible for my approach to this issue. However, all of them have improved the essay through their comments. Thanks.

6

Scientific Reason and Homosexuality

David M Clarke

Writing from the viewpoint of reason, within the framework of the Wesleyan quadrilateral, might suggest that those writing from other perspectives do not use reason. This would be an incorrect assumption indeed. In this chapter, we deal with what useful information, with the use of reason, can be known from sources other than scripture and tradition; more specifically, how do the sciences—biological, psychological and social—inform our consideration of homosexuality. In conclusion a brief consideration will be given to the goals and philosophy of science and its limitation, and to the sociopolitical forces within which science operates. These last factors are critical in informing how we use science to answer the questions before us.

Recently an Australian children's television program filmed an episode depicting two presumably lesbian women with their daughter, with the voice of the daughter announcing 'I'm Brenna. That's me in the blue. My mums are taking me and my friend Meryn to an amusement park.'[1] This caused an immediate strong reaction with a spokesperson for the Australian Family Association claiming that, '*Play School*, and other shows featuring homosexuals, could influence children's sexuality.'[2] In reply, a letter was published saying, ' I was raised on a solid diet of heterosexual television and I have to say that all those years of *The Sullivans, The Restless Years, The Brady Brunch* etc. I was exposed to in the 1970s had absolutely no effect on my inborn (homo)sexuality.'[3]

These two reactions exemplify two common and opposing views. The one saying that sexual orientation is innate, fixed or hard-wired; the other, that it develops over time—especially in the early years of life—due to environmental influences. Nature versus nurture. Both these views imply

---

1. The programme, *Play School*, was shown on ABC television on 31 May 2004.
2. K Nguyen, '"Two mums" episode sparks the mother of all rows', *The Age*, 4 June 2004.
3. Wayne Murdoch, 'Letter to the editor', *The Age*, 5 June 2004.

determinism—the view that human behaviour is pre-determined by influences such as biology or early upbringing. There is of course a third view; that it is a choice.[4] This chapter will take a quick look at the evidence of nature versus nurture and of biological and psychosocial determinants of sexual orientation.

1. Genetics

Although anatomy and hormone studies are interesting, and will be reviewed later, the most informative area that potentially quantifies the contribution of biology to homosexuality is that of genetics. Despite media attention given in the past to the possibility of there being a 'gay gene', there are no contemporary researchers encouraging such a view—that is, that a single gene will explain homosexuality. Human sexual orientation is patently complex and best considered along a number of dimensions including attitudes, beliefs, identity and behaviour. These are not all-or-nothing phenomena but spectrums. Therefore, there is unlikely to be a single responsible gene as found in Huntington's disease or phenylketonuria. Genetics of human behaviour is built on a polygenic model which assumes many genes involved, each with a small effect, some perhaps directly and some indirectly. Behavioural genetics measures the degree of genetic effect (heritability) by studying family inheritance. A confounder in this research is the effect of environment, such as early home-life and other influences. Twin and adoption studies help to differentiate these contributions (see Figure 1). Identical twins (also called monozygotic or MZ twins) share one hundred per cent genetic material (as if cloned); children, siblings and fraternal twins (the latter called dizygotic or DZ twins) share fifty per cent genetic material. Both MZ and DZ twins share significant environmental influences. A comparison of MZ twins and DZ twins will indicate the degree of genetic contribution; a comparison of MZ twins reared together and those reared apart would be able to differentiate genetic effects from those of shared environment, although there are few such studies.

---

4. Many homosexual people maintain that it is a choice—perhaps a political choice. For instance, see 'Letter to the editor' by Belinda Sweeney, *The Age*, 20 April 2004.

David M Clarke

Figure 1: The role of gene and environment

- ■ Siblings: share 50% genes + shared environment
- ■ DZ twins: share 50% genes + shared environment
- ■ MZ twins: share 100% genes + shared environment
- ■ MZ twins adopted out: share 100% genes, no shared environment
- ■ Siblings 'adopted in': no genes + shared environment.

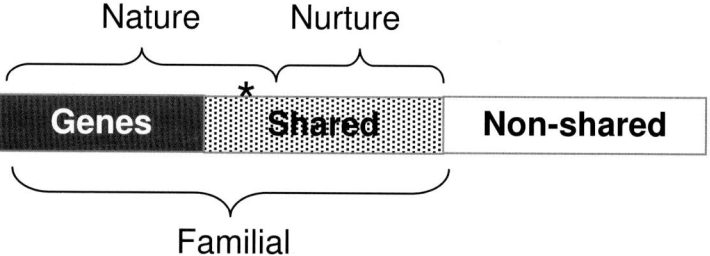

* pre-natal environment would commonly be considered nature, not nurture, although is clearly shared environment, not genes.

If genes contribute to homosexuality, one would expect to find increased prevalence of homosexuality in siblings in families with one identified homosexual person. This is more or less true when the results in Table 1 are compared with a prevalence of homosexuality in the community, estimated to be between one and four per cent.[5] It is impossible, of course, to separate out here the effect of genes from the effect of the social environment and upbringing. Twin studies begin to untangle genes and environmental effects.

---

5. M Diamond, 'Homosexuality and Bisexuality in Different Populations', *Archives of Sexual Behaviour*, 32 (1993): 291–310.

Table 1: Family studies: prevalence of homosexuality in brothers and sisters of homosexual men and women respectively (concordance):

	Brothers	Sisters
Male homosexuality		
Pillard and Weinrich, 1986[6]	22%	8%
Bailey *et al*, 1991[7]	10%	2%
Bailey and Pillard, 1991[8]	9%	6%
Bailey and Bell, 1993[9]	9%	3%
Bailey *et al*, 1999[10]	7.3%	3.8%
Female homosexuality		
Pillard, 1990[11]	13%	25%
Bailey and Bell, 1993[12]	12%	6%
Bailey and Benishay, 1993[13]	7%	12%
Bailey *et al*, 1993[14]	5%	14%
Patatucci and Hamer, 1995[15]	6%	12%
Bailey *et al* 1999[16]	9.7%	2.8%

6. RC Pillard and JD Weinrich, 'Evidence of familial nature of male homosexuality', *Archives of General Psychiatry*, 43 (1986): 808–12.

7. JM Bailey, L Willerman and C Parks, 'A test of the maternal stress hypothesis of human male homosexuality', *Archives of Sexual Behavior*, 20 (1991): 277–93.

8. JM Bailey and RC Pillard, ' A genetic study of male sexual orientation', *Archives of General Psychiatry*, 48 (1991): 1089–96.

9. JM Bailey and AP Bell, 'Familiality of female and male homosexuality', *Behavior Genetics*, 23 (1993): 313–22.

10. JM Bailey, RC Pillard, K Dawood, MB Miller, LA Farrer, S Trivedi and RL Murphy, 'A family history study of male sexual orientation using three independent samples', *Behavior Genetics*, 29, (1999): 79–86.

11. RC Pillard, 'The Kinsey Scale: is it familial?' in *Homosexuality/Heterosexuality: Concepts of Sexual Orientation*, edited by DP McWhirter, SA Sanders, JM Reinisch (New York: Oxford University Press, 1990) 88–100.

12. Bailey and Bell, 'Familiality of female and male homosexuality'.

13. JM Bailey and D Benishay, 'Familial aggregation of female sexual orientation', *American Journal of Psychiatry*, 150 (1993): 272–7.

14. JM Bailey, RC Pillard, M Neale and Y Agyei, 'Heritable factors influence sexual orientation in women', *Archives of General Psychiatry*, 50 (1993): 217–223.

15. AML Pattatucci and DH Hamer, 'Development and familiality of sexual orientation in females', *Behavior Genetics*, 25 (1995): 407–20.

If twins were examined, we would expect that identical twins, who share one hundred per cent genetic material, would be more likely to have the same sexual orientation than DZ twins or siblings (see Table 2). The first study, by Bailey and Pillard, supported this, finding a concordance of homosexuality in identical twins of fifty-two, in fraternal twins of twenty-two per cent and in brothers of nine per cent.[17] However, they found a concordance rate in adopted-in brothers of eleven per cent—essentially the same as for non-twin brothers— and the concordance for non-twin brothers was unexpectedly lower than for DZ twins, suggesting a strong environmental effect of upbringing.

On balance however, these studies, summarised in Table 2, do show concordance in MZ twins consistently greater than in DZ twins, suggesting a genetic effect. There are, however, potential biases introduced in the sampling for some of these studies, particularly in recruitment by advertisement, when contrasted to methods of systematic population sampling. It may be that twins or siblings who share a trait are more or less likely to volunteer; or that MZ twins are more likely to volunteer than non-twin siblings. When sampling from a group of homosexuals, twin or sibling pairs with concordance will have twice the chance of being recruited as a discordant pair. Finally, we do not know how much of the environment of twins is truly shared and how much is distinct.

16. Bailey, Pillard, Dawood *et al*, 'A family history study'.
17. Bailey and Pillard, 'A genetic study of male sexual orientation'.

Table 2: Summary of studies reporting concordance for MZ and DZ twins, siblings and unrelated (adopted-in) siblings. The concordance is the number of instances (given in percent) when, if one sibling or twin displays the trait (in this case homosexuality), so does the other.

		MZ	DZ	Siblings	Adopted-in
Bailey and Pillard, 1991[18]	male	52%	22%	9%	11%
Buhrich *et al*, 1991[19]	male	47%	0%		
King and McDonald, 1992[20]	male and female	25%	12%		
Whitam *et al*, 1993[21]	male and female	66%	30%		
Bailey *et al*, 1993[22]	female	48%	16%	14%	6%
Bailey *et al*, 2000[23]	male	20%	0–10%		
	female	24%	10–17%		
Kendler *et al*, 2000[24]	male and female	32%	8%	17%	

18. Bailey and Pillard, 'A genetic study of male sexual orientation'.

19. NJ Buhrich, JM Bailey and NG Martin, 'Sexual orientation, sexual identity, and sexual dimorphic behaviours in male twins', *Behavior Genetics*, 21 (1991): 75–96.

20. M King and E McDonald, 'Homosexuals who are twins: a study of 46 probands', *British Journal of Psychiatry*, 160 (1992): 407–9.

21. FL Whitam, M Diamond and J Martin, 'Homosexual orientation in twins: a report of 61 pairs and three triplet sets', *Archives of Sexual Behavior*, 22 (1993): 187–206.

22. Bailey, Pillard, Neale, *et al*, 'Heritable factors'.

David M Clarke

New methods of behavioural genetics are now more able to estimate the relative genetic (nature) and environmental (nurture) components of individual differences observed in human behaviour. The statistical method involves the use of correlations, from which are derived measures of heritability. Correlations range from zero when there is no agreement, to one when there is absolute agreement. Heritability is a measure of genetic contribution (again, zero being no genetic contribution, one being totally genetically determined). Heritability (H) is calculated as the difference between the correlations for MZ and DZ twins multiplied by two (H=[MZ-DZ]x2). The remaining contribution is environment. Environment may be shared (as for siblings living together) or unshared (as for people living apart). Because MZ twins share genes and shared environment, the non-shared environment (NSE) can be calculated as what is left over once the concordance for the MZ twins is accounted for (NSE=1-MZ). Shared environment can then be estimated from what remains (SE=1-[H+NSE]). A number of studies have made these calculations and report estimates for heritability and shared and non-shared environment (see Table 3). These data are reviewed well by Mustanski *et al* 2002.[25]

---

23. JM Bailey, MP Dunne and NG Martin, 'Genetic and environmental influences on sexual orientation and its correlates in an Australian twin sample', *Journal of Personality and Social Psychology*, 78 (2000): 524–36.

24. KS Kendler, LM Thornton, SE Gilman and RC Kessler, Sexual orientation in a US national sample of twin and non-twin sibling pairs', *American Journal of Psychiatry*, 157 (2000): 1843–6.

25. BS Mustanski, ML Chivers and JM Bailey, 'A critical review of recent biological research on human sexual orientation', *Annual Review of Sex Research*, 13 (2002): 89–140.

Table 3: Estimates of heritability (H), shared environment (SE) and non-shared environment (NSE). Ranges reflect the 95% confidence intervals.

		Sample size pairs	H	SE	NSE
Bailey and Pillard, 1991[26]	male	161	0.31–0.74	0.00–0.23	0.17–0.73
Buhrich *et al*, 1991[27]	male	161	0.14–0.67	0.01–0.38	0.14–0.46
Bailey *et al*, 1993[28]	female	147	0.27–0.76	0.00–0.23	0.15–0.73
Bailey *et al*, 2000[29]	male	1538	0.45 (0.00–0.71)	0.00 (0.00–0.41)	0.55 (0.18–0.85)
	female		0.08 (0.00–0.67)	0.41 (0.00–0.64)	0.51 (0.30–0.69)
Kendler *et al*, 2000[30]	male and female	564	0.62	0.05	0.33

It can be seen that there is a range of estimates. The study by Bailey *et al* (2000) is of particular importance, being based on a large population-based sample of Australian twins. In that study, the ninety-five per cent confidence interval ranges from zero to 0.71. That is, from those data, the statisticians can be ninety-five per cent confident that the true result lies somewhere between zero and 0.71! In the words of the authors writing elsewhere, 'our confidence

26. Bailey and Pillard. 'A genetic study of male sexual orientation.'
27. Buhrich, Bailey and Martin, ' Sexual orientation'.
28. Bailey, Pillard, Neale *et al*, 'Heritable factors'.
29. Bailey, Dunne and Martin, 'Genetic and environmental influences'.
30. Kendler, Thornton, Gilman *et al*, 'Sexual orientation in a US national sample'.

intervals for heritability estimates were so wide that we could not reject the null hypothesis of no genetic influence'.[31]

The idea that homosexuality is genetically determined is attractive to many. The data suggest that genes do play a part, but it is difficult to know how much. The results, in particular of the study by Bailey *et al* (2000), suggest that science is not going to be able to answer the question definitively. The inability of a large study to find a clear result suggests that there is great variability in the determination of homosexuality and that it is unlikely that further studies will clarify this.

But we do need to be asking also, what is it, if anything, that is inherited? Could it be various personality traits? Many complex human behaviours have been shown to have significant genetic heritability, including cognitive abilities (for example: spatial reasoning, verbal reasoning), self esteem and social attitudes,[32] novelty-seeking and harm-avoidance.[33] The Australian Twin Study showed significant heritability for childhood gender non-conformity (0.50 for men, 95% CI 0.28–0.62) and gender identity (0.31 for men, 95% CI 0.00–0.44).[34] Once inherited, what other forces come into play to determine the outcome of sexual orientation. In behavioural research, it is now recognised that it is not just genes or environment, but the way the two interact that is important in determining outcome.[35] The likely social and psychological contributions to this will be considered shortly.

2. Neuroanatomy

Biological theories of homosexuality have particularly focused on neuroanatomy and hormone studies. Unlike the genetic studies described above, this research is unable to give quantitative measurement of the biological contributions. But they do offer the potential of opening windows of understanding into *how* genes and biology work.

Anatomical research has focused particularly on the hypothalamus, an area of the brain intimately involved in hormone regulation. In rodents, some groups of nerve cells in this region of the brain have been found to be larger in

31. MP Dunne, JM Bailey, KM Kirk and NG Martin, 'The subtlety of sex-atypicality', *Archives of Sexual Behaviour*, 29 (2000): 549–65 (here, page 562).
32. R Plomin, MJ Owen and P McGuffin, 'The genetics of complex human behaviours', *Science*, 264 (1994): 1733–9.
33. Dunne, Bailey, Kirk, *et al*, 'The subtlety of sex-atypicality'.
34. Bailey, Dunne and Martin, 'Genetic and environmental influences'.
35. MT Tsung, JL Blar, WS Stone and SV Faraone, 'Gene-environment interaction in mental disorders', *World Psychiatry*, 3 (2004): 73–83.

males, while other groups are larger in females.[36] It has also been suggested (though the finding has not been reproduced) that there is a sex difference in the anatomy of the hypothalamus of humans.[37] Following on from this research, Simon Le Vay and colleagues examined the post-mortem brains of nineteen homosexual and sixteen heterosexual men.[38] They reported that a group of cells, perhaps analogous to the identified group in rodents, was smaller in homosexual men than in heterosexual men, whilst being the same size as in heterosexual women. This study has been criticised on the basis of small sample size; that all the homosexual men and some of the heterosexual men had AIDS, a disease known to affect the brain; that the sexual histories of the 'heterosexual' men were in fact unknown; and the difficulty of making comparisons between the rodent and human brain.[39] There have been no significant developments of this line of work in the past ten years.[40]

3. Hormones

The dominant hormonal explanation for the development of sexual orientation has been termed the 'prenatal hormonal hypothesis.' This is also based on animal studies, where male mating behaviour (mounting) can occur in female rats exposed to androgens at a critical stage of prenatal development, and female sexual behaviour (lordosis) can occur in male rats experimentally deprived of androgens in early development. There is of course great difficulty in equating this simple animal model to the complex motivated sexual behaviour of humans. Nevertheless, it does provide a crude model and raises the interesting proposition of whether a similar hormonal influence can be responsible for human sexual orientation.

---

36. See W Byrne and B Parsons, 'Human sexual orientation: the biological theories reappraised', *Archives of General Psychiatry*, 50 (1993): 228–39 for a review of these studies.

37. DF Swaab and E Fliers, 'A sexually dimorphic nucleus in the human brain', *Science*, 228 (1985): 1112–14.

38. S LeVay, 'A difference in hypothalamic structure between heterosexual and homosexual men', *Science*, 253 (1991): 1034–7.

39. W Byrne and B Parsons, 'Human sexual orientation: the biological theories reappraised', *Archives of General Psychiatry*, 50 (1993): 228–39.

40. For a recent summary of this area, see DF Swaab, WCJ Chung, FPM Kruijver, MA Hofman and TA Ishunina, 'Structural and functional sex differences in the human hypothalamus', *Hormones and Behaviour*, 40 (2002): 93–8.

There is one report of a 'natural' human experiment that supports the idea of a prenatal influence of hormones on later sexual orientation. Congenital adrenal hyperplasia is a genetically recessive condition that leads to virilisation of females—that is, genetically female children are born with masculinised genitalia. One study[41] has reported an increased incidence of homosexuality in women with this disorder which the authors have attributed to prenatal masculinisation of the brain. However, this conclusion ignores the important social and psychological effects of being born with male genitalia whilst being told you are a girl. Such a situation might be expected to lead to some gender confusion.[42] It is very difficult, therefore, to tease out environmental from biological effects. Nevertheless, the animal studies, though not being directly applicable to the human experience, do leave open the possibility that the intra-uterine hormonal environment may determine some aspects of later sexual behaviour.

4. Sociological science

The genetics research described above highlighted the variability in estimates of genetic contribution to sexual orientation, and the importance of, in particular, non-shared environment—that is individual environmental experiences. Kinsey's studies of 1948 reported a wide variety of sexual practices in the community.[43] In western cultures, there are examples of 'institutional' homosexuality, in prisons and the military, where it is considered that the behaviour is driven not so much by orientation as by other factors such as convenience, peer pressure or an expression of dominance. It is not known how enduring is the influence of such practices.

An important twentieth-century social development has been the focus on sexual identity, rather than behaviour. This has brought a preoccupation with categorisation and labelling whereby a homosexual exchanges an aspect of behaviour for a total identity. This has led, on the one hand, to the formation of a 'minority group', with group identity and feelings of victimisation, and on

---

41. J Money, M Schwartz and VG Lewis, 'Adult erotosexual status and fetal masculinization and demasculinization; 46 XX congenital virilizing adrenal hyperplasia and 46 XY androgen-insensitivity syndrome compared'. *Psychneuroendocrinology*, 9 (1984): 405–14.

42. For a comprehensive review of hormonal aspects of sexual identity see L Gooren, 'The endocrinology of transsexualism: a review and commentary', *Psychoneuroendocrinology*, 15 (1990): 3–14.

43. A Kinsey, WB Pomeroy and CE Martin, *Sexual Behavior in the Human Male* (Philadelphia: WB Saunders, 1948).

the other hand to stigmatisation of homosexuality. The effect is to make it harder for people to talk and deal with homosexual feelings in a constructive way. Rather than deal with the unique experience of the individual there is a rush to label. This leads to pressure for people to 'come out' and claim an homosexual identity and express it publicly. Because of stigma, coming out may be hard, but paradoxically, so too is abandoning the lifestyle once attained. In other words, there is a range of social forces that might contribute to a person affirming homosexuality or maintaining a homosexual lifestyle, just as there is contributing to the denial of homosexuality in others.

5. Psychological theories of sexual orientation

A helpful way to understand psychosexual development is in the context of human development generally and in particular the processes of bonding and attachment, separation/individuation and identification. Whether, and with whom, a person develops strong dyadic attachments as an adult, and the nature of that relationship, will depend very much on these factors.

Clearly, a newborn infant is totally dependent on others for needed physical and emotional care. Without physical and emotional care the infant dies. The development of the infant depends therefore on him or her being loved and being able to receive love. This requires the development of a relationship, called bonding or attachment. The quality of this attachment will determine the extent to which these early needs are met and also becomes the prototype for future relationships. This process of attachment, however, involves another important developmental process—the recognition of the other as being different from the self. This process is called separation /individuation.

It is understood at birth that the child does not have a sense of itself being different from any other. Indeed, that is the physical reality of the *in utero* experience. The birth is the first observable event of the infant becoming separate from the mother. The psychic awareness of this, however, takes longer than the physical event. 'Attachment' to a person—mother in the first instance—can only occur when some level of self-other differentiation has occurred. This is observed at about six months of age when the non-discriminating social smile changes to a specific and preferential smile in response to the mother, and we see the first evidence of differentiation occurring and bonding becoming established. Margaret Mahler describes, following this early differentiation, the processes of practice, rapprochement and consolidation.[44] Practicing is seen in the infant moving away from the mother, first by crawling, but soon by walking. The sense of self is still primitive. Rapprochement occurs as the child becomes more aware of their separateness and so, despite having the ability and the desire to move away and explore, has a need to be near, to share experiences and to be affirmed and loved. Ambivalence and separation anxiety are the hallmarks of this stage. Associated with the development of object constancy—that ability whereby the infant knows that an object exists even though it has moved out of sight—consolidation occurs, and the child can function separately, albeit with discomfort. This final stage occurs during the third year of life and is when a stable sense of identity, including a primitive consolidation of sexual identity, is attained.

Although these stages can be neatly described we know that they are not perfectly distinct. Neither are the tasks fully completed and of course they are repeated, particularly in adolescence. Disturbances at the very earliest stages lead to profound impairment of differentiation of self and other, narcissistic behaviour, and a failure to make meaningful attachments. The ambivalence in relationship (the desire for both separateness and closeness, distance and intimacy) seen in the rapprochement phase persists into later childhood and even adulthood. The development of the capacity to trust people, occurring during this process, also is variable. Important to note in relation to the development of specific sexual identifications is that a child will make a number of attachments with people of both sexes, most notably mother and father, and that these relationships will be tinged with ambivalence.

Identification, the third of these important early developments, is a psychological process whereby a person 'assimilates an aspect, property or attribute of another person and is transformed, wholly or partially, after the model the other provides. It is by means of a series of identifications that a personality is constituted and specified.'[45] This process involves idealisation of a person or attribute and then an internalisation of that attribute. Although degrees of identification occur throughout life, it especially occurs early in life when differentiation of self is occurring and incorporation of aspects of the other into the self occurs readily. The main focus for identifications will, of course, be the parents, and a child can be expected to identify with various aspects of both, and in some special ways, with the parent of the same sex. As

---

44. M Mahler, F Pine and A Bergman, *The Psychological Birth of the Infant: Symbiosis and Individuation* (London: Karnac, 1975).

45. J La Planche and JB Pontalis, *The Language of Psychoanalysis* (London: Hogarth Press, 1985), 205.

well as identifying with some aspects of mother and father, the child will not identify with other aspects, and perhaps because of some break in relationship that makes idealisation impossible or painful, will actively dis-identify with a parent or with particular aspects of that parent. Again, ambivalence is involved.

The final stage in psychosexual development is the eroticisation that occurs in adolescence under the influence of an hormonal surge, with increased sexual desire and interest in sexual expression. To some extent patterns of relating are already developed and sexual activity simply becomes a mode of expression of these. Pre-existing patterns become sexualised. On the other hand, personality and relating style is not fully developed by adolescence, and much of what has been described before gets repeated. Issues of separation and individuation get reworked with the drive to separate from parents and to develop new attachments and intimate relationships. The process of identification continues as the adolescent finds new role models to idealise (and values to internalise) and struggles with issues fundamental to identity formation—work, self-image, relationships. These 'reworkings' of the early developmental processes make adolescence an important, yet vulnerable, stage. Attachments, individuation and identifications set the scene for the consolidation of sexual identity and the development of sexual relationships.

It is likely that there is not one dynamic leading to one particular sexual pattern. An explanation for the homosexual male is that there is a fear of women arising from a difficulty breaking away from the mother. For a female, homosexuality can be seen as an attempt to find her own femininity. Freud particularly focused on the idea of homosexuality as a regression to narcissism,[46] involving identification with the mother, taking 'themselves as the sexual object. That is to say, they . . . look for a young man who resembles themselves and whom they may love as their mother loved them.'[47] Another explanation has focused on problems of identification with the parent of the same sex.[48] Where there has been some (perhaps unnoticeable) breach in

---

46. Narcissism is an early developmental stage of differentiation of the self in which there is a preoccupation with the self for gratification.

47. S Freud, *Three Essays on the Theory of Sexuality* (1905). See, Standard Edition of the Complete Psychological Works of Sigmund Freud, volume VII, edited by J Strachey (London: Hogarth Press, 1953), 145. Freud mostly considered male homosexuality.

48. ER Moberly, *Homosexuality: a New Christian Ethic* (Cambridge: James Clarke 1983).

relationship between the child and the same-sex parent, the child emotionally withdraws, in a sense deciding that this is a 'safer' thing to do. The result is that the important early needs for love are not met and there is increased difficulty in idealisation and identification with that parent. This markedly increases the ambivalence—the ambivalence being maintained by, on the one hand the unfulfilled longings for love and affirmation, and on the other hand the emotional withdrawal and dis-identification. The struggle of this ambivalence is so strong that one or both sides of it are often denied and not recognised.

The result of this dynamic is variable. Mild dis-identification is observed in effeminate behaviour in men. Stronger dis-identification may lead to homosexuality or trans-sexualism.[49] However, if the denial of the need for same-sex love is strong there will be a retreat into heterosexual behaviour, and because of the fear that 'latent homosexuality' may break through, homophobia. Alternatively, the emotional withdrawal may lead to avoidance of sexual intimacy altogether or to a dissociation of sex from meaningful human contact. Underpinning these specific dynamics are the more general attributes of trust, security and self-esteem that a person brings to any relationship, and further, the wider social and cultural environment.

6. Can sexual orientation change?

The above discussion has looked at the determinant of sexual orientation, considering nature and nurture, and the sciences of biology, psychology and sociology. An important remaining question, which immediately tackles the issue of 'determinism' head on, is whether sexual orientation can change. In the scientific literature this question has been posed in relation to the effectiveness of reparative therapies. Needless to say, this has been a controversial area, with scientific opinions being coloured by the politics of the situation. Early attempts to change sexual orientation used aversive therapy and for a long time there was little strong evidence for their effectiveness. In 2000, the American Psychiatric Association published a summary report stating, 'To date, there are no scientifically rigorous outcome studies to determine either the actual efficacy or harm of reparative

---

49. For instance, JRB Ball found that transsexuals as a group tested more feminine on psychological testing than would have been expected for a group of women. They interpreted this to represent some degree of active rejection of masculine attributes. See JRB Ball, 'Transsexualism and transvestitism', *Australian and New Zealand Journal of Psychiatry*, 1 (1967): 188–95.

treatments'.[50] In 2003 a study was published by Spitzer with results from 200 subjects who had undergone therapy. There was substantial though incomplete change reported, with females describing more change than men, suggesting that reparative therapies are effective.[51] A whole issue of the journal was devoted to commentaries on this study, and these made it clear that not all his professional peers were ready to accept his conclusion. Nevertheless, from this and other anecdotal reports, it is clear that some people can and do change, though in the light of our complex understanding of the formation of sexual orientation—the variable contributions of nature and nurture, motivation and choice, and the role of politics—we cannot expect that any one intervention will be uniformly effective in all situations.

The reaction that this study drew reminds us of the politics within which this science operates. It is often cited that the American Psychiatric Association (APA) removed homosexuality from its list of mental disorders (DSM-III) in 1973 as evidence that science has now determined that homosexuality is not a mental disorder. The first part of this statement is true, though DSM-III did include a category of 'ego-dystonic homosexuality' to allow for people who were uncomfortable with their homosexual orientation and sought help. However, this was not a decision based on any new scientific discoveries but rather a result of a political process—a process that has been documented in a number of places[52] [53] [54]—and a reconsideration of the function and purpose of diagnostic categories. The authors of DSM-III very reasonably decided that preferential homosexuality was not a mental disorder because it did not cause subjective distress or significant impairment in functioning.[55] This reminds us that the giving of a diagnosis, particularly in

50. American Psychiatric Association, 'Therapies focussed on attempts to change sexual orientation (reparative or conversion therapies)', COPP position statement (APA Document Reference Number 200001, 2000). (Accessed on the web 11 Nov 2004).

51. RL Spitzer, 'Can some gay men and lesbians change their sexual orientation? 200 participants reporting a change from homosexual to heterosexual orientation', *Archives of Sexual Behaviour*, 32 (2003): 403–17.

52. RL Spitzer, 'The diagnostic status of homosexuality in DSM-III: a reformulation of the issues', *American Journal of Psychiatry*, 138 (1981): 210–15.

53. R Bayer and RL Spitzer, 'Edited correspondence on the status of homosexuality in DSM-III', *Journal of the History of the Behavioural Sciences*, 18 (1982): 32–2.

54. G Mendelson, 'Homosexuality and psychiatric nosology', *Australian and New Zealand Journal of Psychiatry*, 37 (2003): 678–83.

55. Spitzer, 'The diagnostic status'.

psychiatry, is not a completely objective process and serves a number of purposes, some determined by social and cultural values.

7. Conclusion

The present chapter summarises the role and contribution of science to the issue of homosexuality. Readers hoping for evidence to support a deterministic view of homosexuality, either psychological or biological, will be disappointed, as will those believing that homosexuality is simply a matter of behavioural choice. The evidence, particularly the heritability evidence, shows that there is great variability in the mix of genetic and environmental influence. It is therefore likely that for some people genes are particularly important and others for whom social and psychological factors are more important in determining sexual orientation. In any case, science can never give an answer to the moral question of the good or otherwise of any behaviour. That must be sought elsewhere. But science can provide the knowledge and understanding to inform our responses to people with sexual orientation different from our own. Homosexuality is not simply a choice, or at least not an easy choice. But neither is it determined. Sexual orientation develops in a person, 'shaped and reshaped by a cascade of choices'[56] made in a maelstrom of a biological and social environment. Understanding a person's sexuality must involve understanding that person's unique history and, at the same time, those dynamics common to every woman and man—the need in every heart for intimacy and respect, and a degree of ambivalence in all relationships.

---

56. Byrne and Parsons, 'Human sexual orientation'.

7

On Being a 'Gay Anglican'

Peter Sherlock

Early in 2005, on the day I was moving house, a reporter from Melbourne's *Age* newspaper telephoned and asked for my reaction to the latest seizure in the Anglican Church's long-running drama over sexuality. I gave my usual line: 'It's certainly not the end of debate, and I'm certainly not about to leave my church'. Then the reporter asked if he could describe me as 'Gay Anglican Peter Sherlock, a Melbourne University lecturer'. I was a bit shocked. Can my whole existence be summed up in only eight words? Are these really the defining elemental pieces of my life? I suggested that perhaps a preferable phrase might be 'Peter Sherlock, an Anglican who happens to be gay and who lectures in history at the University Melbourne', before conceding that no editor worth their salt would let such verbosity into a daily paper. 'Gay Anglican' it was. I resigned myself to the fact that anyone who didn't know before, certainly did now.

On reflection, I'm not so uncomfortable with the description. It's good for gay and lesbian people to stand up and be counted. More importantly, however, is the space for dialogue that being identified as gay and Christian can create. The most interesting and—dare I say it—evangelistic conversations I have ever had have been about my sexuality and its relationship to my Christian faith. They happen quite regularly. Although most people don't blink an eyelid these days when someone reveals that they have a partner of the same gender, they almost always demand an explanation when they find out that my partner is a priest. People variously express surprise, shock, or pleasure, ask which church we belong to, and then want to know how this came to pass. While there are some parts of my story I'm not prepared to share with casual acquaintances, I enjoy talking about sexuality and faith with people who never had or no longer have a connection with the church. Here is a chance to engage with another human being about issues that matter deeply to us, issues of life, love and God. Here is a chance to reflect on human experience, and to suggest gently that the church, the Scriptures, even

God might be larger, more challenging, and more inclusive than any one of us imagines.

Within the church, however, I suspect I am like a lot of Anglicans and am sick of talking about sexuality. On this issue, the church does not provide a safe space in which to express doubt, or to share experience; it is more common to rehearse isolated Bible verses or half-remembered sermons rather than discuss the bloody reality of both Scripture and life. It would be much easier to be silent, to go back to the relative comfort of my parish, and get on with singing in the choir, worshipping God, cooking up a storm and providing hospitality to all who come in search of God. But this is no longer sufficient. Even if I wanted to retreat to the shelter in a parish that is supportive of gay and lesbian people and ignore the diocese, the communion, the wider church, there is no guarantee in the current climate that my parish could remain that way. Too much is at stake. This essay, therefore, attempts three things: first, to show why I think this issue is important, second, to examine how I react to the way the church speaks about gay people, and third, to offer a positive, alternative vision for the church and its mission in the world.

1. Why sexuality matters

I find it faintly ridiculous that the Anglican Communion might be about to split, or send some of its member churches packing, just because some of us believe that we are both gay and Anglican. How could the sexual identity of a handful of the world's population be such a threat to a worldwide church encompassing millions of people in every part of the globe? Some of you will agree with me, but remain upset by the concept of gay weddings, or think that a gay bishop is definitely going too far. Well, I happen to think gay bishops are a great idea. Not long after Gene Robinson was consecrated, he was named as the person of the year by one of America's leading gay magazines. I know so many people who were drawn to reconsider their antipathy towards the churches in general as a result. When was the last time the church had such positive press in one of the communities it has systematically marginalised? I found it liberating, even pleasantly shocking, to see a relatively happy bishop grace the front cover of a gay magazine.

The current debate is crucial to the Anglican Church as I know it for a number of reasons. Perhaps most obviously, I have a number of friends and acquaintances who are being called by the church to a particular ministry, and are unable to test whether that call should result in ordination as deacons, priests, and, yes, even as bishops. What are they supposed to do? Wait for a better time and that 'courageous bishop' we are told is always just around the corner? Find a church that will test their vocation? Leave their partners and break their vows so they can comply with current thinking? I consider myself blessed indeed that I do not have a calling to ordained ministry. The Anglican Church of Australia is a stony place at the moment for homosexual people who do. Why would anyone go and see the bishop and his or her chaplains, when everyone knows that the answer will either be, I wish I could ordain you but it is too politically sensitive just now, or, more directly, your kind is not wanted in our church?

The debate is not only important for gays and lesbians, either. Melbourne's largest Anglican parish recently asked all its ministers and leaders, lay and ordained, to sign statements affirming that homosexual activity was wrong, and guaranteeing that they would uphold this belief in their representation of the faith to others. I was heartened to learn that at least some of the leadership team refused to sign this statement. For it was designed precisely to close down any conversation and, quite frankly, it aimed to stop people reading the Scriptures for themselves. Sadly, as a result of this and other debates on the issue of sexuality, one congregation has parted ways with the rest of the parish. Even a relatively conservative and very successful evangelical parish is divided by beliefs about sexuality.

The debate is not just about homosexuality. I know of a priest who recently had his licence suspended and was brought before a church tribunal because he had had a consenting sexual relationship with his long-term girlfriend. As is usual in these kinds of cases, no one asked her what she thought, and I know the church has done a pretty good job of alienating more people within its own membership and the wider community in this situation.

But the question of human sexuality reaches beyond the level of the person and the parish. I believe it has now become the key metaphor in the Anglican Church for revealing what we think about human salvation, the interpretation of Scripture, and the whole reason for existing as a church. This is why sexuality is such a battleground. When we pass synod motions, commission reports and sign petitions we punish those who differ from us in identity, belief or behaviour.

In this time and place, I perceive the way a church treats gay and lesbian people as an index to how anyone is ultimately to be treated within the household of faith—whether those people are children, people without anywhere to sleep, people who live alone—anyone who does not fit the dominant, twentieth-century Western stereotype of the family of mum, dad, and two children.

For several decades both the church and society at large have discussed sex and human relationships in an atmosphere characterised by fear. John Howard, the Australian Prime Minister, believes that gay marriage poses a fundamental threat to our way of life that will ultimately undermine civil society. The Archbishop of Sydney, Peter Jensen, wrote in his diocesan magazine that marriage is a 'bedrock institution' which must be defended from invasion by gays and lesbians (*Southern Cross*, June 2004). A recent *Play School* episode featuring a child being raised by a lesbian couple was highly controversial. The lack of proportion in that debate was neatly captured in a fake newspaper article someone pinned up at work headlined 'Toddler lesbianism up by 79%'.

I find it hard to understand why these politicians and churchmen get so worked up. After all, Jesus specifically commanded us to leave our families and follow him. Even on a purely rational basis, how could a handful of same-sex couples overturn law and order in Australia just by getting married? Surely the basis of civil society as we know it is found not in marriage, but in land title (remembering that Indigenous Australians cannot get access to their traditional lands), in generosity of spirit (although refugees can barely step foot on this continent), and the protection of the weak and disadvantaged (even while some of our children continue to be sexually abused and raped by their parents, teachers, counsellors and priests).

It is right and natural to be afraid of God. But why must we be so afraid of each other's behaviours and beliefs? Are we to share our lives as they are actually lived with each other, are we to reject other people because we think we know better, or, worst of all, are we to put on our church faces and Sunday best, and pretend that we conform to the standard of purity currently in vogue, whether that is the scones-and-jam school of church fetes, or the Arian heresy espoused by the Jensen brothers in Sydney?

2. What the Anglican Church says

The Anglican Church has been obsessed with moral issues surrounding the family, marriage, contraception, divorce, the role of women, homosexuality and polygamy for the last one hundred years or so. If you're in any doubt, have a look at the hundreds of resolutions passed by the Anglican bishops as they have met at the decanal Lambeth conferences since 1867. For the present, I wish to respond to some of these resolutions by asking, what is it like as a gay Christian to listen to what the church says in its official pronouncements on sexuality?

At Lambeth 1988, resolution 26 was on the contentious question of polygamy, relating largely to the Anglican Church in African nations. It reads as follows:

> This Conference upholds monogamy as God's plan, and as the ideal relationship of love between husband and wife; nevertheless recommends that a polygamist who responds to the Gospel and wishes to join the Anglican Church may be baptized and confirmed with his believing wives and children on the following conditions . . .

This is a very charitable statement. The conditions simply ask the polygamist—assumed to be male—to refrain from taking further wives, and to keep his wives after conversion to avoid economic deprivation. What I find interesting is the assertion that 'monogamy is God's plan': where's the scriptural evidence? There is only one monogamous couple about whom we have any significant information in the whole biblical narrative. In contrast to the bishops, I always thought that polygamy was absolutely necessary to the fulfilment of God's plan. How else could the twelve tribes of Israel have appeared, if Jacob had not had first one then two wives, not to mention the two recognised concubines? And surely, according to Paul's letters to Timothy, it is perfectly acceptable to have multiple partners, for we are only told that it is bishops who must have one wife each. How would this statement read if the category of 'polygamist' were replaced with 'person in a same-sex committed relationship'?

On the topic of homosexuality, Lambeth 1988 passed resolution 64:

> This Conference:
> 1. Reaffirms the statement of the Lambeth Conference of 1978 on homosexuality, recognising the continuing need in the next decade for 'deep and dispassionate study of the question of homosexuality, which would take seriously both the teaching of Scripture and the results of scientific and medical research'.
> 2. Urges such study and reflection to take account of biological, genetic and psychological research being undertaken by other agencies, and the socio-cultural factors that lead to the different attitudes in the provinces of our Communion.

> 3. Calls each province to reassess, in the light of such
> study and because of our concern for human rights, its
> care for and attitude towards persons of homosexual
> orientation.

There are two problems I have with this seemingly harmless statement. First, how can those of us who identify as homosexual possibly study this issue in a dispassionate way? Jesus was never, in my opinion, a dispassionate student; rather, he was consistently a model of compassion. Second, the resolution suggests that the 'us' of the Anglican Church does not include homosexual people. Instead, we are to be located externally as subjects of the church's attention and interest.

The most frequently circulated statement of the Lambeth conferences on sexuality is presently the infamous resolution I.10 of 1998, which has become something of a litmus test for church groups who wish to force people to subscribe to one set of articles or another. The content actually isn't quite as bad as some resolutions. For example, the statement:

> recognises that there are among us persons who experience
> themselves as having a homosexual orientation. Many of
> these are members of the Church and are seeking the
> pastoral care, moral direction of the Church, and God's
> transforming power for the living of their lives and the
> ordering of relationships.

It immediately proceeds, however, to rule out same-gender marriage or the ordination of people in same-sex relationships, ensuring that those of us who are homosexual and are truly seeking the church's moral direction for our lives don't misbehave.

This theme of listening to homosexual people was introduced into the Australian General Synod in 2004 when it passed a series of four resolutions on sexuality, the first time it had pronounced on this issue beyond receiving or recommending a report. The synod has requested 'Dioceses to commit themselves to listen as the church develops a Christian response to the contemporary experience of human sexuality.' Unfortunately it doesn't say to what persons or institutions the dioceses are supposed to listen. The key resolutions passed by the General Synod read as follows:

1. Recognising that this is a matter of ongoing debate and conversation in this church and that we all have an obligation to listen to each other with respect, this General Synod does not condone the liturgical blessing of same sex relationships.

2. Recognising that this is a matter of ongoing debate and conversation in this church and that we all have an obligation to listen to each other with respect, this General Synod does not condone the ordination of people in open committed same sex relationships.

I had three reactions when these were passed. First, to whom is the church listening with respect? It sounds to me as if gays and lesbians aren't included; it's about straight Anglicans with power who can talk to each other about sexuality and make decisions about other people's lives. Second, as much as I might I love the General Synod speaker but not the General Synod speech, I am in a committed same-sex relationship, and my partner is an ordained priest. By telling me that it does not condone some of the central planks of my life, I feel like the General Synod has respectfully told me that I'm not an Anglican, that my whole way of life is sinful, and that I'm not to be considered a child of God.

What makes matters worse for my experience of the institutional church, is that statements such as Lambeth I.10 or the General Synod resolutions are seen as moderate. The debate can go on, these statements assert, but the line has been drawn in the sand. At a recent meeting about the forthcoming election of a new archbishop of Melbourne, the sexuality debate was mentioned, and all agreed that the best that liberal Anglicans could hope for was an archbishop who did not actively persecute homosexual people. That's not exactly comforting, in my book.

So what's the net effect of the current debate on people like me? In delivering the Windsor Report to the Anglican primates in 2004, Archbishop Robin Eames summed up the current crisis by posing the following question: 'Do we want to remain in communion and can we do so in ways where deep differences can be addressed without fracturing what is essential in communion?' He went on to ask, with the commission, 'how high a price we are willing to pay for unity?' Well, I'm willing to lay bets that Gene Robinson won't be invited to Lambeth 2008, and if all of the bishops of Canada and the United States are excluded, then there probably won't be any women there either.

I pay the price for unity pretty much every time I receive communion. Each Sunday no matter where I am, no matter the gender, age, race or beliefs of the vicar, there is just the tiniest thought in the back of my mind that this will be the Sunday when the priest says no, you are not fit to receive the bread and wine, because you're an unrepentant homosexual. This has been my experience ever since I was living in England and witnessed the bitter fights between Anglican bishops at Lambeth 1998. But, before you get too worried about the state of my spiritual ego, I suspect that, actually, deep down, most of us have profound doubts about our worthiness to stand or kneel at the lord's table and receive the sacrament—fortunately, the liturgical invitations to come forward are powerful and compelling, as is the communal movement to share the lord's supper together.

3. An alternative vision

For me, the way out of this mess is to encourage gay and lesbian people to stand up and offer their visions for the church, and to encourage other Christians to help make that vision a reality. So here are some of the elements of my vision.

First, let us stop reading Scripture as a book of rules or a list of statutes, and instead seek the continuing inspiration of the Holy Spirit to open the Scriptures to us afresh. Let us see the fractured and fractious lives recorded in the Bible as true reflections of the craziness of human experience. Let us celebrate that God took on that very human form completely in the person of Jesus Christ, and understands us completely, far more than we understand ourselves or our sexuality.

Perhaps we need to re-examine what our guiding passages of Scripture are. Must we take the 'seven texts' referring to homosexuality? Why should we begin with the model of man and wife offered by Genesis? What would happen if we used, say, Ezekiel 23:19–20 as our dominant hermeneutic for interpreting difficult texts—if you haven't read it, I strongly recommend trying a few different translations.

Second, we must stop looking for the rules that might get us across the line into heaven. Instead we should focus on the life that we will lead there in the presence of God and the company of angels. That is something to get excited about. And as part of that, I would really like the church to help me celebrate my relationships, not just with my partner, but with all manner of people. We ought to rejoice in the joy and despair brought by human companionship, so well revealed in the gospel narratives of Jesus and his disciples.

It breaks my heart to watch the Anglican communion at the moment. For the tendency seems increasingly towards division, towards separating the elect from the damned and determining who is worthy of sacramental grace whether in the form of holy orders, or marriage. This tendency impacts upon us all; to those who would draw lines in the sand, the gospels offer a punishing discipline. When Jesus drew a line in the sand in front of the woman accused of adultery, he silenced everyone in his presence. When confronted by the rich man in search of salvation, Jesus set us the standard of a camel passing through the eye of a needle. Yet the Christ also embraced the whole world when he ascended the cross and ultimately that is where we will all find ourselves, within Christ's embrace.

Finally, I wish we could trust God a bit more. I think we should consider the vocation of all people who are baptised, and that we should ordain those homosexual men and women, whether or not they are in relationships, who are called by the people of God to ordained ministry. I believe that we need to re-think the whole area of human relationships, especially marriage and household, and their significance within the life of church communities, their liturgical recognition—and especially their idolatrous place as a defining metaphor of church organisation, despite the diversity of the biblical witness. I trust that God can sort out all of our mistakes along the way. I hope that you can too.

8

The Least of These . . .

Debra Hirsch

Over the years I have been privileged to be involved in a ministry supporting Christian individuals experiencing varying levels of same-sex attraction. For reasons of sexual orientation these people have found themselves on a path that has that has required them to go up against the flow of what is considered the norm in society and in some sectors of the church. What this has meant is that they have had to choose to live in a way that sometimes goes contrary to how they may *feel* and what is generally accepted and this has required a unique sacrifice of them in their following of Jesus Christ. As a result their discipleship has been both uniquely costly and as well rewarding—I have to say that some of these people are the bravest people I know. They have shown me a different side of the face of God, a side that many in the church would prefer to keep hidden.

It was through a variety of factors that I became involved in supporting Christians who experienced unwanted homosexual desires. Homosexuality was not something I was unfamiliar with. Before 'finding God' I had lived openly as a lesbian woman. This lifestyle fulfilled many of my social and emotional needs, however my existential longings and questioning remained unfulfilled until I was introduced to Jesus. In finding God I soon realised that one search had ended but another deeply enriching one had begun. So began my story, one story among many.

In the limited space I have I'd like to share with you snippets of these stories, stories of real people who for better or worse are endeavouring to live with choices they have made. And whatever one might make of these choices, they are theirs to make, and it is this fact alone that many forget in all the controversy and debate and even hostility that is so often present when the issue of homosexuality in the church is raised. We need to be attentive to hearing the stories of real people and refrain from making judgments removed from the concrete human situation.

I also want to share with you something of the context of where these stories were 'heard' or more importantly 'lived out'. Over twenty years ago a number of really good, compassionate, people, themselves from a gay and lesbian background, formed an organisation called Exodus. Exodus' core task, as it was conceived then, was to focus on helping people who struggled with sexuality and also to help educate and equip the church in relation to the problematic issues of homosexuality and Christianity. As the ministry developed and matured, it became quite controversial and was taken to task by the media and the gay community at large. I have to say upfront that I believe that Exodus, at least in its earlier expressions, has for the most part been misunderstood by both church and non-Christian audiences alike but I believe that it has been a blessing to many people and was in fact birthed from the heart of God. Exodus was birthed in North America through passionate individuals dedicated to helping people walk free from their homosexual desires and behaviours.

1. Ministry years

In the early years of our ministry we decided to affiliate with Exodus when it went International. The ministry we set up in Melbourne was seen as one of the largest ministries of its kind in the Australian context. We had a ministry team that included trained psychologists and counsellors, many with theological training. We had a board of management, individual and group supervisors as well as a number of other professional people associated with us on a variety of levels. We ran support groups, offered individual counselling and spoke frequently at conferences and church services. We were also running annual conferences and being invited to speak nationally. Our profile was growing and we were being run off our feet with referrals.

By all outward appearances we were a successful, thriving, ministry. People were being supported, churches and counsellors were becoming more aware of the needs and issues surrounding people with sexual identity problems and we were seeing individuals grow and change in a variety of ways that were positive and life giving for them. All involved were hopeful and trusting of God that he would meet each person where they were at and help them in their journey towards wholeness. This I have no doubt that he did. However, I must confess, what we then understood as wholeness and what I now understand of sexual wholeness are not quite the same thing. Let me explain.

Many of the ministries that make up Exodus North America were at that time, presenting a view of wholeness for the homosexual as heterosexuality. Much of the literature and testimonies circulating at that time seemed to emphasise that true freedom in Christ for the homosexual meant embracing heterosexuality. While as a team none of us would have wholeheartedly agreed with this we were to some degree unwittingly communicating this view through much of the literature and teachings that we were utilising. If you had asked any of our team individually what we believed we would have said that some people may experience heterosexual response but certainly this would not be a possibility for all individuals. In fact, our teaching was quite clear that an individual's goal should be to grow in their relationship with God, it was about discipleship, not a pursuit of heterosexuality which, for many, we knew wasn't attainable or even desired. This view ultimately led us to a place where we became increasingly uncomfortable with much of the Exodus literature and teachings. Eventually after much discussion with all parties we decided, as a ministry it was best to forge our own path and formally disaffiliated with Exodus International.[1]

While we were experiencing a shift in some of our methodology, for most of us our theological position hadn't really altered. The majority of the team would have held the view that a homosexual lifestyle was not part of God's original intention for humanity and was just one expression of the 'brokenness' that humans experience. We believed that God's original design for humankind was heterosexuality, and that in a perfect, ideal world, homosexuality wouldn't exist and neither would all the other various expressions of brokenness that beset heterosexuals. Through much reflection we began to articulate more clearly what we really believed and what God had called us to do, thus Purple Heart ministry was birthed.

2. Stories

Over the years of being involved with Purple Heart I have heard many, many stories. Stories of individuals who have struggled at some level with their sexual identity. Men and women who have tried to make sense of their faith in light of their sexual orientation. Following you will read some snippets of the stories of some of these people. Real stories, real people. A friend of mine once said our stories are the most authoritative things we can say because they are *our* stories.

2.1 Rick's story
Rick is a man who is in his mid 30s who has experienced homosexual desire for as long as he can remember, he reports never having a heterosexual

---

1.   While we decided to forgo our affiliation I want to affirm the work of Exodus International.

response. Rick chooses to live as a celibate man. He has had homosexual sex in the past but feels that to pursue a same-sex partnership would be against what God wants for him. He realises the cost of his choice and has expressed that at times 'sorrow is his companion'. Rick endeavours to live within the context of community where his social/relational needs are on some levels satisfied. Rick lives a full and active life and chooses to invest his identity in his Christianity, not his homosexuality.

2.2 Steve's story

As a younger man Steve lived as a homosexual and even dabbled in prostitution. He had a pretty radical conversion to Jesus as an early adult and ended up attending a Pentecostal Church with a strong, triumphalistic theology. Steve believed that with God all things were possible and ardently pursued a heterosexual relationship knowing up to that point he had experienced minimal heterosexual response. He eventually met a woman, fell in love, got married, and over time had two children. Steve would say that in the early years he had to learn how to be 'heterosexual' and spent time investing in a 'heterosexual' identity rather than his homosexual identity which was very familiar to him, and up to that point all he knew. He would acknowledge that it had been a difficult path to walk down and says if he wasn't so young and idealistic he's not sure whether it would have been possible. But he *is* living a life that he, at one time never thought possible. He loves his life as a husband and father. Life for Steve and his family, as with all of us, continues to bring with it many challenges. There are times when Steve experiences various insecurities that can bring with them homosexual needs and desires. At these times Steve and his wife journey through them together knowing that to deny these things is unhealthy and unhelpful. They choose to face the insecurities head on and discover that when they are honest and open then it is much easier to go through the rough patches that life inevitably brings.

2.3 Mandy's story

Mandy spent much of her earlier years hungering after female affection and love. Throughout high school she had a few boyfriends but it never really seemed to work out. As she got older the realisation came to her that she was more attracted to the same sex. After several years of trying to deny this she decided to embrace it and for the next few years became a regular in the gay social scene. While Mandy hadn't 'come out' to her immediate family she did live a rather open life and identified quite easily with her gay friends and associates. Unexpectedly a few of Mandy's friends found faith in Jesus and shared their story with her. Over time she also came to love and follow Jesus. In her first years as a Christian Mandy had moved away from her same-sex partnerships because she felt it wasn't what God wanted from her, but many years later Mandy came to a place where she thinks that it's not such a big deal to God. She is currently in a partnership and has been for many years.

2.4 Mike's story

Mike was always a fairly sensitive boy who didn't really cut it with the other little boys in the playground. Mike had grown up in a predominantly female household. He had a dad but due to his father's work commitments he wasn't really much of a presence in the house. When Mike did get to spend time with his father he reported that he always felt different and uncomfortable with his dad. Mike's father was what you would classically call a 'macho male' fulfilling many of the stereotypes of what our culture designates as 'masculine'. When Mike's dad tried to teach him football or how to handle tools Mike showed little interest which further isolated him from his dad. Over time Mike and dad grew further and further apart, their differences only becoming more highlighted. While Mike increasingly became alienated from the world of the 'masculine' his security and comfort was found more in the world of the 'feminine'. Throughout, Mike had been called all sorts of names including 'sissy', 'fag' and 'homosexual'. He knew he didn't fit into the 'stereotypical' male world and began to realise that he was drawn emotionally and sexually to men. Mike's awareness to his own homosexual longings came slowly but steadily. As a teenager Mike had his first homosexual encounter, and gradually became part of the homosexual community.

At the age of twenty-one Mike had an encounter with God. As Mike grew in his faith and love of God he recalls having an increasing awareness that his homosexual lifestyle wasn't consistent with his Christian walk. As Mike had yet to find a spiritual home or 'church' he feels that this awareness was due to the Holy Spirit's leading rather that anyone in particular telling him that it was 'wrong'. Mike continues to live his Christianity today choosing a lifestyle of celibacy. He is comfortable with acknowledging his homosexual orientation but says that his identity is derived from his relationship with God, not his sexual orientation, and that it is this that determines the life that he chooses to live.

2.5 Some common elements

These stories, while only a handful, can be seen as representative of many other stories too numerous to mention. While there are differences, let me make some comments that would be true for all these stories including my own. Each of the people mentioned have in all integrity tried to understand the issues that surround homosexuality both generally and personally. Each are aware of the theological issues that divide some churches. Each have conducted their own research and looked at the issue from theological /psychological and sociological perspectives. They are aware and have made themselves aware because they have had to. For most of the people mentioned their 'homosexuality' has not been experienced as something life giving and fulfilling. The embracing of the homosexual lifestyle has ultimately been contrary to what many would see as God's will for them.

While there are many things common to the above stories there are also some differences, one being that some have been able to experience heterosexual response and others haven't. Some now are married while others seek to live as celibate followers of Jesus. More often than not the debate that rages within the church is about the 'fairness' of the church insisting on homosexually oriented people to remain celibate. For those who seemingly have 'changed' their orientations, or at least are able to experience hetero-sexual response, another whole argument arises.[2] For the purposes here I will comment briefly on the former: homosexuality and celibacy.

3. Celibacy

The classic response to the evangelical church regarding its view on homosexuality is the claim that 'it isn't fair to deny the homosexual person any possibility of fulfilment of their genital sexuality'. Marva Dawn, an insightful theologian and author, makes two helpful comments when dealing with this. Firstly, she makes the observation that the statement points to the fact that genital sex is not only overrated but also idolised in our Western culture. Secondly, this highlights the need for the church to be asked the question as to why the church is not more supportive of 'social sexual'[3]

---

2. One of the key arguments around the issue of a former homosexual now expressing himself/herself as a heterosexual is that the individual was never really a homosexual in the first place. The point being, like the old slogan that gets bandied around, 'once gay always gay'. While this is tending to lose favour with some people who hold to a more 'fluid' view of sexuality it is still an issue that is argued quite strongly.

3. Marva Dawn, *Sexual Character*, (Grand Rapid: Eerdmans, 1993). Dawn comments on Joyce Hugget's terms 'social' and 'genital' sexuality where a divide is made

relationships. In other words, why are we not better friends and more intimate with one another, because if we were the need for 'genital' sexual fulfilment wouldn't be so strong. [4]

I have had many discussions with people who have questioned the classic orthodox position on celibacy in relation to homosexually oriented people. One of the most common arguments claims that to enforce celibacy on people inevitably causes them to repress their sexuality which then ends up coming out in other, often harmful, ways. The number of incidences of sexual abuse from those within the priesthood is often cited as a powerful argument against the 'repression of one's genital sexuality'.

I do believe that celibacy is a gift and not all who choose a path of celibacy have that gift. So how can we call some to walk the road of celibacy if not all have the gift? We need to distinguish, I believe, between the *gift of celibacy* and the *choice to be celibate*. And *both*, as far as I can see, are biblical options in relation to our sexuality and both apply in situations of dealing with issues of homosexuality. Perhaps we can call the latter situation 'situational celibacy': that is, an option for a lifestyle of celibacy based on a situation of singleness (heterosexual or homosexual) that requires an ongoing choice to live in a way consistent with the revealed will of God regarding genital sexual expression. In a sense I believe that all single followers of Jesus are called to situational celibacy and only some might *also* have the gift of celibacy. But in my opinion and experience, it is largely out of this situational form of celibacy that the person with same-sex attraction is called to live.

Jean Vanier, author and founder of L'Arche Communities says:

> Celibacy remains a mystery. It is found as a vocation in many religions, even in the religion of ancient Rome; thus it has been shown as a special way of uniting oneself with God and preparing oneself to receive a new and more intimate union with him . . . Celibacy, for the sake of the Kingdom, answering the call of Jesus, has always been lived in the Church by those who were able to welcome it and to choose it.[5]

---

between our needs for intimacy and our needs or genital connection—suggesting that the two don't always have to go hand in hand.

4. Dawn, *Sexual Character*, 105–9.
5. Jean Vanier, *Man and Women He Made Them*, (Homebush: St Paul Publication, 1986) 115–16.

Therefore celibacy becomes an issue of sacrificial discipleship because it flows out of a relationship and commitment to follow Jesus, no matter what.

I realise that given the prevailing cultural understandings of sexuality this perspective is not politically correct, but I for one simply cannot see an orthodox understanding of the biblical revelation permitting genital sexual expression outside of covenantal relationships, be they homosexual or heterosexual. If this is considered a seedbed for repression then so be it, but then we have to consider Jesus himself to be a profoundly repressed individual, and few would venture to suggest that this is the case. In fact he profoundly demonstrates that one can live a full and complete human life without having sex.

Thankfully, sexuality is a much larger affair than mere genital contact and therefore celibacy need not end up in repression, although in many cases it can and clearly does. But voluntarily refraining from sex does not necessarily equate to dysfunction. In fact the opposite might well be true. If the opposite of repression is considered to be unbounded sexual *expression*, then it can easily be argued that this can lead to a whole other set of sexual dysfunctions and disorders. The ability to have sex does not make one moral or whole. Moral frameworks for our choices, sexual or otherwise, always limit individual human freedom in order to preserve general human relationships and interpersonal health.

The real question remains: can celibate singles attain high levels of intimacy without genital contact? The answer must surely be in the affirmative.

4. Intimacy

Benedict Groeschel says that the great question that faces the single person is intimacy. He goes on to ask 'must the single person be a loner, someone with repressed emotions and bottled-up feelings, expressing little warmth and affection?'[6] The need for affection and personal intimacy is complex, but however we configure it, it has to be admitted that these real human needs for affection and intimacy can be met outside of genital sexual expression. The question as to whether single people can develop loving relationships and personal intimacy with others must be answered in the affirmative. In fact, human wholeness can only be found in these. We can surely be whole without having sex. Besides, many, perhaps most of those who engage merely on the

---

6.   Benedict Groeschl, *The Courage to be Chaste*, (New Jersey: Paulist Press, 1985) 36–7.

sexual level manage very well to avoid meaningful relationships and tend to confuse orgasms with intimacy. Pornography and sexual lust (as opposed to genuine eros) is a clear case in point. Love is found in mutuality and I–Thou relationships. Sexuality divorced from a covenantal morality readily results in I–It relationships that dehumanise the other, and ends up using people as objects of lust and power. The ability to have sex certainly does not ensure intimacy and healthy relationships—that much is sure. Sex can only enhance love and intimacy where these already occur. We must therefore conclude that love and human mutuality is not based in genital sex and is therefore available to the sexual celibate, be they situationally celibate or gifted for that calling.

6. Sacrifice

There is no doubting the fact that to choose a life of celibacy as a response to one's faith in God and his word is to embrace a life of sacrifice as regards one's genital sexual expression. In the West we are captivated by a culture that elevates the individual needs, wants and desires above all else. Within a culture that is riddled with consumerism and is slowly drowning in its own overindulgence, sacrifice can be considered anathema, or at the very least an odd curiosity. Yet sacrifice is an essential element of love. In some of the stories mentioned above 'sacrifice' has been a key motif at the heart of the walk of faith, the walk of love. We do well to heed the words ascribed to Carl Jung that neurosis is the substitute for legitimate suffering. To follow Christ and walk in obedience to his commands requires sacrifice, the type that is willing, ultimately, to lay down one's own life for another. The gospel is all about sacrifice, it's about laying down your life, it is about taking up your cross daily for the cause of Jesus. This is a strong call and one that demands our all, not just of our sexuality but our total personhood. It is sacrificing what is temporal for that which is eternal. At the very heart of the gospel is placed the suffering Christ who sacrificed his life in order that we may gain life. That is the heart of the gospel and whether one is homosexually oriented or not, to be a Christian is to embrace a life of sacrifice.

7. Wounded healers

Henri Nouwen coined the phrase 'wounded healer' in his book of the same name. [7] This 'wounded healer' was lived by Nouwen himself, who for many years struggled with his sexual orientation. Unable to speak about it publicly he kept it hidden and revealed it to only a few fearing that his ministry would

---

7.   Henri Nouwen, *The Wounded Healer*, (New York: Doubleday, 1986)

be damaged if people were to discover his particular 'wounding'. There is no doubt that when you read his writings you are aware that he understands pain, that his own journey was seasoned with 'dark night of the soul' experiences that led him to a deeper exploration of the heart of God and sufferings of Christ. Nouwen's ability to deeply reflect on his own personal suffering and allow his wounding to be the very place that God's grace ministered out from to others has rightly given him a place among the modern day heroes of the faith.

When followers of Jesus sacrifice much to follow him they can become significant models of Christ-likeness to those around them. They may still remain wounded but in their wounds, and perhaps even because of them, they have an ability to minister in a way that they never would have without their wounding. When these individuals develop self-awareness they actually become a significant gift to others. They are themselves a gift because their story validates the suffering of those who come into their orbit. In a strange and mysterious way they extend the Messianic ministry of Jesus—by their stripes others are healed.

8. Conclusion

When dealing with sexuality and spirituality we are dealing with not only complex issues but sacred ones. These issues affect us at the very core of our beings because we are indeed very much sexual and very much spiritual. When we tread into these areas we do so carefully and with respect.

We each have to journey through this life and make sense of our faith and our sexuality, a very arduous journey indeed. We need to tread carefully, for our own sakes as well as others. We need to remember that we are all different—no matter who we are, we will never fit neatly into a box. Sexuality is a very powerful and pervasive part of who we are, not only as gendered beings but as socially and genitally motivated individuals.

Some of the stories mentioned highlight some of these differences. Each of us has our own story and what makes them authentic is that they are indeed *ours*. When we make choices, choices based around our faith and sexuality, then ultimately we are the ones that need to live with those choices. Others may or may not agree but they remain *our* choices nonetheless. For many these decisions have been hard won and involved significant personal struggle. When we respond to these stories, whether we agree with them or not, we must exercise grace, dignity, and respect precisely because they are *their* stories.

Over the years we have tried to respect each individual's choice and while at times this has meant that they no longer continue to journey with us in quite the same way, we have rarely excluded anyone from our community who may have held a different view. While the majority of the individuals who our ministry has sought to serve and support would adhere to the historic, orthodox position on homosexuality, I continue to have many friends both within and outside the Christian faith who are actively involved in the homosexual lifestyle. The differences in our theological positions or lifestyle choices, while being cause for great discussion at times, do not stop us from ongoing relationship—and nor should it.

Life is indeed a complex phenomenon. All without exception are drawn into its flux; but authentic followers of Jesus find that life takes on even more complex tones—the pursuit of a distinctly Christ-like humanity. This is no small task, especially for the same-sex attracted person who, for reasons stated above, has a uniquely difficult journey towards Christ-likeness. But as an old Swahili song puts it, life has meaning only in the struggle. It's what makes us uniquely human. And at least as followers of Christ, we are joined in this journey by other wounded healers who together comprise the body of Christ. We might well add that life really only has meaning in the journey.

> Two roads diverged in a yellow wood,
> And sorry I could not travel both
> And be one traveler, long I stood
> And looked down one as far as I could
> To where it bent in the undergrowth;
>
> Then took the other, as just as fair
> And having perhaps the better claim,
> Because it was grassy and wanted wear;
> Though as for that, the passing there
> Had worn them really about the same,
>
> And both that morning equally lay
> In leaves no step had trodden black.
> Oh, I kept the first for another day!
> Yet knowing how way leads on to way,
> I doubted if I should ever come back.
>
> I shall be telling this with a sigh
> Somewhere ages and ages hence:
> two roads diverged in a wood, and I —
> I took the one less traveled by,
> And that has made all the difference.

Robert Frost, *The Road Not Taken* (1916).

9

Sexuality, the Image of God and the Doctrine of the Trinity

Brian Edgar

Although it is not my usual approach to commence with personal experiences, please allow me to begin by making reference to a situation which illustrates some of the central theological issues involved in the present debate about sexuality, homosexuality and the church. Some time ago I wrote a letter to *Crosslight*—the Uniting Church newspaper in Victoria—in which I took issue with several previous contributors who I felt had been very paternalistic towards gay and lesbian people. My comment was that they were using the fact that there is a genetic basis to homosexual tendencies in such a way that they were suggesting that gay and lesbian people really have no choice at all in the expression of their sexuality. I believe that everyone has some level of choice in how their sexuality is expressed and respect the fact that gay and lesbian people are often very deliberate and clear about what they are doing and why they are doing it. These commentators had been reflecting what was a very common fallacy at the time. An editorial in the Melbourne *Age*, for example, had spoken repeatedly of biologically or genetically 'determined' homosexuality and also of the possibility of finding 'the gene which causes homosexuality'. It compared the genetic cause of homosexuality with the genetic cause of baldness and suggested that 'what has always been considered a sin by Judaism, Christianity and Islam will surely no longer be sinful: science will have changed the moral universe.' [1]

The writers to *Crosslight* had made some similar claims concerning genetic determination and the elimination of the traditional attitude that homosexual behaviour is sinful. In response I expressed my view that while the precise causes of homosexual orientation will continue to be debated it is quite clear that, just as with heterosexual orientation, it involves some combination of three dimensions of human nature: (a) pre-natal disposition;

---

1. Editorial, *The Age*, 'Science and Morality', (22 July 2004)

(b) post-natal socialisation and (c) personal affirmation. These have to be understood in dynamic relationship. The idea that there is a physical component to human sexuality cannot be denied and the suggestion that there is a connection ought to come as no surprise. People have been aware for some time of the genital, reproductive and hormonal aspects of sexuality. But recent genetic research was the cause of a burst of unjustified speculation which thoroughly exaggerated the connection. There is a huge and unjustifiable leap in any argument which assumes that a biological *connection* involves a biological *determination* of sexuality. Human sexuality is a complex phenomenon which involves mind, will, emotion and action. A comparison with something like baldness is naive and unhelpful. Biological predisposition acts in a very complex way, along with family and community socialisation and personal choice, to produce sexual tendencies and behaviours. The enthusiasm of those who want to defend homosexuality by reference to genetic factors is badly mis-placed. Those who undertake to argue in such a way should realise that one can only have an understanding of genetically determined homosexuality at the expense of the freedom which most would consider to be essential to authentic humanity. This is *not* to minimise or eliminate a (debatable) degree of 'given-ness' in sexual orientation or the difficulty involved in any change, it is simply to say that each of us continually affirm or deny (and thus modify) our sexuality and no one has an un-modifiable, irresistible, 'determined' nature or set of actions. We are responsible for, and able to control, the expression of our sexuality.

The ultimate incompatibility of positions

The result of my contribution to this debate was another letter in the following edition of the paper from David, an ordained minister of the Uniting Church who was a self-declared, practicing homosexual. He thanked me for my contribution and, although I had argued against the ordination of self-declared practicing homosexual people, he strongly supported what I said about treating gay and lesbian people with integrity—as agents able to determine significant aspects of their behaviour. He certainly did not want to be seen as a kind of puppet whose whole sexual identity was completely imposed and who was just swept along by irresistible force. 'We could get on well' he wrote in his letter and he then proposed that we have a public dialogue on the matter. He concluded the letter by asking when and where I thought it should take place. I did wish that he had talked with me *before* he had made this proposal very public by putting it in the paper! But seeing that it was there I thought that it would be helpful and so contacted him and we agreed to talk together. We met on a number of occasions prior to the public meeting and we designed it to be as much of an interactive dialogue as we could. This meant we discussed in advance what each of us was going to say. This had several very positive aspects to it including (a) a significant lesson about the incompatibility of our ethical approaches and (b) the value of exploring one's own weakest points. These can be used to clarify the theological situation.

Firstly, the complete incompatibility of theological and biblical approaches became clear as we prepared the program. David was very helpful in explaining the variety of positions held by the gay, lesbian and bi-sexual people he associated with. In particular though, he was very clear that it was quite inappropriate to characterise the situation in such a way that it could be suggested that changes to the traditional ethical stance of the church could satisfactorily be made by the simple addition of homosexual relationships alongside heterosexual ones. The changes that were required to the church's ethic to accommodate active homosexuality would inevitably have far greater implications than that. The principles that are employed in this process of change are such that they will necessarily bring about other changes as well, relating to, for example, bi-sexuality and other multiple sexual relationships. The logic that leads to the acceptance of active homosexual relationships cannot easily be separated from support for other closely related groups with varying forms of sexual behaviour. From his point of view a gay/lesbian/homosexual ethic was simply *not* a straight/traditional/heterosexual ethic with the genders switched around. It is an ethic of a completely different order altogether which involves a total re-evaluation of the form and expression of relationships. What might be called a minimalist approach to change—which involves approving long-term, faithful, committed homosexual relationships while retaining all the other, associated ethical principles inherent in a traditional view (including two-people relationships, lifetime faithfulness and a family orientation)—is an impractical, halfway house. Indeed, David argued, if this half-way house situation is reached and then maintained then it will become a new state of oppression and restriction for those who have yet other sexual ethics. It will become a repeat of the present situation where some sexual relationships are seen as inappropriate. In fact, if that position is achieved, it is more likely that the arguments used to switch the view of active, committed homosexual relationships from 'sinful' to 'saintly' will actually become a Trojan horse argument used for opening the door for further changes. This is what David sought as he could not see the logic in affirming committed, monogamous relationships while denying bi-sexual, multiple loving relationships.

The minimalist approach (that the church should approve faithful, committed homosexual relationships as a parallel to marriage and go no further than that) certainly exists—it is the position most commonly presented in public discussions about sexuality—but it is by no means the only approach and ultimately not the dominant one in the wider movement relating to sexual liberation which is essentially gay, lesbian and bi-sexual (and therefore, by definition, multi-sexual in approach). Some of those who seek the minimalist changes may well do so deliberately as a first step towards radical change. Others may do so thinking that this one change will be an end to the matter. Often those committed to the minimalist approach and no more, are themselves heterosexual people of a more liberal theological orientation who view this issue as a matter of social justice. But they can find themselves in a very awkward situation, as the logic of their arguments can often be used against them to move towards a more radical position. What must be recognised is that the issue as a whole is not a minor one. The present debate represents fundamentally different approaches to faith and ethics as a whole.

Interpreting the biblical text

The second theological point that was emphasised in our discussion was the importance of exploring ones' weaknesses. As well as sharing in advance the best and most positive arguments that we wanted to make (so that the other could prepare to comment on them) we were also determined to ask ourselves the much harder question about *the weaknesses we perceived in our own positions.*

Where did we think our argument was weakest? At what point were we least confident? We both asked this question, trying to honestly test the strength of what we said. This is a question that is not answered quickly or easily. Nor is it a question often asked in debate where the intention is to defeat ones' opponent rather than find the truth. In a purely debating situation it is not usually thought wise to bring out one's weakest arguments. But truth is best served in this way.

David admitted that his greatest problem was with the biblical material. He used it, interpreted and re-interpreted it, but had a lack of enthusiasm about it. It was difficult to get it to say what he thought it *ought* to say, what he *wanted* and *hoped* it would say. This was an honest approach and, unsurprisingly perhaps, we found ourselves in agreement that this was a problem for those who wanted to change the traditional ethic. The revisionist interpretations—of, for example, Sherwin Bailey, Robin Scroggs, John Shelby Spong and John Boswell—over a period of years produced a flurry of interest, but once they all seemed stronger than they do today. Everyone has to make a judgment on how they perceive the situation as a whole, but my view is that the various attempts to reads specific passages of Scripture in such a way that active homosexuality is seen to be justified have failed and those seeking to justify homosexual practice have, in fact, tended to move on to other forms of argument. David, for one, felt that the biblical case was the weakest part of his argument. The overall difficulties involved in making the Scripture support homosexuality are seen quite clearly in Spong's discussion of sexuality in *Living in Sin* where the implications of Ephesians, 1 and 2 Timothy and Hebrews are simply discounted as a whole: 'Since we know these books not to be apostolic, their argument will not suffice today.'[2] When the individual texts do not support one's position the approach is to discount them as a whole. This approach is simply not acceptable from a canonical point of view. It also illustrates from a different perspective the ultimate incompatibility of theological viewpoints. But not everyone is as dismissive of the text as Spong and some comments need to be made on particular texts. However, in an article such as this it is impossible to be comprehensive and so the comments which follow can only be illustrations of the way the situation has developed. Two of the critical New Testament texts are 1 Corinthians 6:9 and 1 Timothy 1:10. These have been subject to debated interpretations. The texts read this way:

> Do you not know that wrongdoers will not inherit the kingdom of God? Do not be deceived! Fornicators (*pornoi*), idolaters, adulterers, male prostitutes (*malakoi*), sodomites (*arsenokoitai*), thieves, the greedy, drunkards, revilers, robbers—none of these will inherit the kingdom of God (1 Cor 6:9–10).

> Law is made for . . . fornicators (*pornois*), sodomites (*arsenokoitais*) . . . and whatever else is contrary to sound doctrine (1 Tim1:9–10).

John Boswell has, among other things, claimed that *arsenokoitai* has an unambiguous reference to 'male sexual activity, that is, active male prostitution' and therefore, with respect to 1 Cor 6:9 and 1 Tim 1:10, it is argued that *prostitution* was what was of concern rather than any sort of

---

2.   John Shelby Spong, *Living in Sin?: A Bishop Rethinks Human Sexuality* (New York: HarperSanFrancisco, 1990) 107.

homosexual behaviour.[3] Boswell's view is continued more recently by Spong. Spong has to concede that the argument is, at least, not perfect and admits that Paul did not like homosexuality. He concludes though that this is Paul's 'ill-informed, culturally biased prejudice' and possibly related to his own incipient homosexuality.[4] Boswell sees no connection between the early Christian use of *arsenokoitai* and the Levitical (18:22, 20:7, 10, 13, 15) prohibitions against homosexuality. The Levitical laws against homosexuality were not, he argues, utilised by early Christians as an argument against homosexuality because they were interpreted as relating to the distinctive Jewish heritage and associated with idolatry and were not seen as part of the law regarding sexuality and marriage. Boswell also claims that the associated term *malakos* should be interpreted as masturbation[5] rather than as a reference to passive male homosexual activity. In this way the Pauline references are not seen as referring to homosexuality and the Levitical passages are disconnected from early Christian thought. The general conclusion which is reached is that the church did not condemn homosexuality.

While this conclusion and the various elements which go towards it have frequently been reproduced by advocates of homosexual practice this argument has been severely criticised. Many of those who have used Boswell do not appear to be aware that the argument is no longer tenable. DF Wright shows how Boswell has overlooked significant historical evidence with respect to the attitude of the early church with respect to the connection of the Levitical law and early Christian attitudes towards homosexuality. Apart from Clement of Alexandria and the Apostolic Constitutions which Boswell cited as the only instances of any connection, Wright shows how Boswell simply missed references to significant sources in Tertullian and Origen connecting Leviticus with the early Christian understanding of homosexuality and how Boswell reads John Chyrsostom inaccurately and how he again overlooks relevant passages, misinterpreting what Chrysostom wrote.[6] Perhaps more importantly, Boswell utilises inadequate lexigraphical methods. The *arsenokoitai* of 1 Cor 6:9 and 1 Tim 1:10 is a new term not found before Paul,

---

3. John Boswell, *Christianity, Social Tolerance and Homosexuality,* (Chicago and London: University of Chicago Press, 1980).
4. Spong, *Living in Sin*, 151–2.
5. Boswell, *Christianity,* 107.
6. David F Wright, 'Homosexuals or Prostitutes? The Meaning of *arsenokoitai* (1 Cor 6:9, 1 Tim1:10)' *Vigiliae Christianae*, 38 (1984): 125–53, here 128. Also see David F Wright, 'Translating *arsenokoitai* (1 Cor 6:9, 1 Tim1:10)' in *Vigiliae Christianae*, 41 (1987): 396–8.

coined by him (or a source of his) and based on the LXX version of the Levitical prohibitions which refers to *arsenos ou koimethese koiten* (Lev 18:22) and *arsenos koiten* (Lev 20:13). This is confirmed by evidence from early Latin, Syriac and Coptic versions of the Pauline texts all of which preserve the sense of 'those lying with men'. The references are clearly references to male homosexual activity in general and without qualification and not simply active male prostitution. Wright[7] has also criticised Boswell's 'grossly inadequate account of the meaning of *pornos* and its cognates in the New Testament and contemporary literature.' Nor can *malakos* be taken as masturbation. It has the basic meaning of 'soft' and refers to the passive partner in homosexual activity.[8] Others have concluded that:

> Boswell is an assiduous historian, but leaves something to be desired in accuracy when it comes to linguistic matters . . . and heavy handed in dealing with specifically religious and theological implications in his sources, and tends to draw conclusions that are wholly unwarranted by the sources . . . It is irresponsible for Boswell to conclude that 'sexuality appears to have been a matter of indifference to Jesus' and that 'the New Testament takes no demonstrable position on homosexuality'.[9]

While there are other passages which could well be reviewed the overall thrust is clear: there are strong biblical prohibitions against active homosexual behaviour. In short, I think it is obvious why David's main difficulty was with the meaning of the biblical text. Revisionist interpretations have not held up and Scripture simply does not support homosexual practice. As Dan Via concedes, 'Christians who want to take an open, nontraditional position on this [homosexual practice] should be able to find biblical support for it. Of course, the few biblical texts that deal explicitly with the subject offer no such support.' Via (who is 'open' in this regard) and Robert Gagnon (who takes the traditional position) agree (in Via's words) that they are 'in substantial agreement that the biblical texts that deal specifically with homosexual

---

7. Wright, *Homosexuals,* 126.
8. Hans Conzelmann: 'Pervert (effeminate)' in *1 Corinthians, Hermeneia* (Philadelphia: Fortress, 1975) 106.
9. General Assembly of the Presbyterian Church (USA) *Presbyterians and Human Sexuality* (Office of the General Assembly, 1991) 112.

practice condemn it unconditionally'.[10] This means that Via and others have to move to other grounds to attempt to demonstrate the validity of homosexual practice. It should be no surprise that many have moved to do that. There have been signs for a long time that the authority of Scripture is understood differently by the advocates of those positions which are in conflict.

However, it is important to bear in mind that this is only part of the story. Both of us were prepared to explore our weakest argument. What, I asked myself, was the weakest point of my own conviction that homosexual practice is not theologically appropriate?

The problem of theological justification

David's problem related to *what* Scripture actually said. He could not, with integrity, see that it supported homosexual practice. My problem was not with what Scripture said, that seemed perfectly clear to me, my problem was with *why* Scripture says what it does. Why does God forbid sexual relationships between people of the same sex? What is actually wrong with two men or two women having sex together? What difference does it make what gender they are? Particularly given my overall conviction that God does not say things for no reason. God is free to determine all things in accordance with his own will but his will is also always for our own ultimate good. He is not some kind of divine kill-joy who just makes up rules as though he wanted to stop people enjoying themselves. There must be a reason. What is not good in homosexual practice?

This question is tied up with Romans 1:26–7, which, in one sense, aggravates my problem in that it describes homosexual practice as 'un-natural'. I find it difficult to talk about it in that way. It can sound so offensive and I instinctively shy away from that part of the life of the church which has isolated homosexuals as being particularly sinful and as deviants. My reading of the gospel is that we are *all* sinners, so why should homosexual people be separated out as being particularly un-natural? Where can I find an answer to this? The first place to go is the text in Romans which reads as follows:

> For this reason God gave them up to degrading passions.
> Their women exchanged natural intercourse for un-natural,
> and in the same way also the men, giving up natural
> intercourse with women, were consumed with passion for
> one another. Men committed shameless acts with men and

---

10. Dan Via and Robert Gagnon, *Homosexuality and the Bible: Two Views* (Minneapolis: Fortress, 2003) 29 and 93.

received in their own persons the due penalty for their
error. (Rom 1: 26–7)

There are two issues involved with this text. The second is more important for
my purposes as it deals with the meaning and significance of 'un-natural'. But
it is not possible to deal with that without making reference to a preliminary
matter relating to the particular form of homosexuality that Paul had in mind.
This is because the traditional view, that Paul is simply referring to homosexuality, has been challenged by another of the revisionist interpretations
referred to above. The question has been raised as to whether Paul was in fact
condemning pederasty rather than homosexuality *per se*? Scroggs says that
Paul 'must have had, could only have had, pederasty in mind'.[11] To claim this
allows one to argue that this condemnation does not address the question of
faithful, monogamous, homosexual relationships because the only form of
homosexuality known was pederasty. This, however, overlooks the fact that
Paul expresses homosexuality in terms of the more general 'men (*arsenes*–
males) with men' (1:27) rather than as 'men with boys' (as Plato *Laws* 836a–
c). It should also be remembered that it is placed alongside lesbianism which
was usually between adults in a mutual relationship. Scroggs also makes the
unjustifiable assumption that the only form of homosexuality was pederasty
and that adult-to-adult homosexuality, with varying degrees of monogamy and
faithfulness, was not in existence. Do we assume that we now have in history
a new situation which has never occurred before? I think not. As Coleman
says, 'it is unlikely that nothing of its kind existed.'[12]

So, if the text is referring to homosexual activity then it is possible to turn
to the second issue concerning the meaning of 'natural'. It seems to some to
be an injustice to define a person with a homosexual orientation as 'un-
natural'. To those who argue that homosexuality is a biological 'given', an
unavoidable state in which loving action is 'natural' and 'normal', then Paul's
treatment of it seems unfairly condemnatory and less than Christian. However,
as I have argued above, biological influences do not make for biological
determination. It is necessary to look further for the answer.

First of all, it is important to point out that to say that homosexuality is
'un-natural' is not to define a person as 'abnormal' or even 'un-natural' in the
general sense often used in contemporary popular language. Apart from the

---

11. Robin Scroggs, *The New Testament and Homosexuality* (Philadelphia: Fortress,
    1983), 16, 116–17.
12. P Coleman, *Gay Christians: A Moral Dilemma* (London: SCM, 1988), 88.

important distinction that the biblical prohibition pertains to homosexual activity, the action is 'un-natural' only in a fairly specific and theological way, very similar to the way that we might say that it is not 'normal' for people not to worship.

We must remember that the term 'natural' is used today in many ways that derive from conversational, scientific and moral as well as theological sources and the failure to distinguish between the various meanings leads to confusion and disagreement. 'Natural' as it is commonly used refers to some activity or state (whether it be making love, laughing, weeping or whatever) which occurs simply as a part of being human. There is the implication that it is an appropriate, approved, and even unavoidable human activity. It is seen as a 'given' which cannot be condemned or judged without destroying the humanity of the person. Whatever is, is natural. From a biblical point of view though, nature (*phusis*) refers to the constitution of the person, the being which is derived from the Creator. The 'natural' is not whatever actions seems natural to people. It is not something related to personal disposition or orientation.[13] It is determined by God. That which is not part of God's purposes is unnatural.

Other forms of behaviour, apart from homosexuality, may be seen as 'unnatural' in the biblical sense. A Christian is (presumably) convinced of the need to worship, to appropriately recognise the nature, worth and majesty of God and the consequent claims upon their life. Those who are not Christian, not even theist, not believers in God at all and therefore not worshippers, might well be described as 'unnatural' or even 'not normal' in the sense that they are not fulfilling that calling to which the believer believes all people have been called and which completes and fulfils life. However, this is not to say that one would expect to be able to notice in empirical research that such non-believers are inherently 'abnormal' according to the standard of psychological or social research. The same can be said of those who engage in homosexual activity. It is not necessarily to be expected that empirical research will reveal them all to be psychologically deficient or disturbed in some other way. Whether or not they are 'normal' or 'abnormal' by any psychological standard is as relevant or as irrelevant as the psychological (ab)normality of unbelievers. It is thus irrelevant to a biblical description of the action as 'un-natural'.

---

13. For a discussion of the term natural see James B DeYoung 'The Meaning of "Nature" in Romans 1 and its Implications for Biblical Proscriptions of Homosexual Behaviour', *Journal of the Evangelical Theological Society*, 31/4 (1988): 429–41.

A proper recognition of the biblical notion of 'natural' is very helpful because it clarifies what God is *not* saying in this regard. The Bible is not saying that those who engage in homosexual activity are somehow psychologically disturbed or deviant in a way that is fundamentally different to the rest of the population.

This helps, but it still leaves the question open: what then *is* the problem with homosexual practice that makes it 'un-natural' in the biblical sense? The best answer to that question comes from an examination of two important theological concepts. The first relates to humanity being made in the image of God, and the second is the fact that God is described as being Trinitarian.

The image of God and the Trinity

The important description of humanity as being made in the image of God is closely associated with being male and female and thus is connected with sexuality.

> Then God said, 'Let us make humankind in our image, according to our likeness; and let them have dominion over the fish of the sea, and over the birds of the air, and over the cattle, and over all the wild animals of the earth, and over every creeping thing that creeps upon the earth.' So God created humankind in his image, in the image of God he created them; male and female he created them (Gen 1:26–7).

The image of God is itself related Christologically to the doctrine of the Trinity.

> He is the image of the invisible God, the firstborn of all creation; for in him all things in heaven and on earth were created, things visible and invisible, whether thrones or dominions or rulers or powers—all things have been created through him and for him. He himself is before all things, and in him all things hold together (Col 1:15–17).

Sexuality is thus not something God has determined to create which is unconnected with the divine nature. It is an aspect of creation which reflects something of the essence of God. It must be said that God is neither male nor female, but this does not mean that God is 'sexless' as long as sexuality is understood primarily as the expression and form of relationship. God is neither male nor female, but God *is* love. Human sexual relationships (in the broadest sense) are reflective of the intra-Trinitarian love of God—a love which reaches out specifically to the other, rather than to the self or to that which is the same as the self. God demonstrates this by reaching out from within the love of the divine trinity to love the world and to love people. This was a radical demonstration of love of that which is other than self. People demonstrate this love by loving others rather than themselves; it is particularly symbolised in the differentiation of male-female relationships; and this love of other is at its most loving when people love their enemies (those who are least like self and furthest away from them). The Christian notion of love as '*agape-love*' is a special, divine love of the one that is different. This is extremely important, as Ray Anderson puts it:

> The differentiation between Creator and creature is not a barrier to relation: indeed, that which is totally 'other' *constitutes* the basis of relation of persons and is the source of true intimacy.[14]

The polarity of the male-female marriage relationship (as in Ephesians 5:25– 33: for example, 'love your wives just as Christ loved the church and gave himself up for her') is thus able to be seen as a special sign of the essential nature of the love of God: ' . . . the two will become one flesh. This is a great mystery and I am applying it to Christ and the church.' This critical dimension of love of that which is different to self is not seen as clearly when it is love of same gender. This is not to say that love between people of the same gender cannot exist but it does not have the character of the love of 'the other'.

Those who interpret Christian ethics exclusively (and therefore inadequately) as the application of the principle of 'love' (where love is defined in terms of that which contributes towards personal expression without harm to others) will probably conclude that there are no special relationships and that every form of love relationship has equal potential and validity. Obviously, this runs counter to the theo-logic of this paper. If a Christian ethic centres on love as the measure of all relations then there is a tendency for 'love' to become a broad catch-all term which loses all precision and which can be taken to mean almost anything. It certainly opens the way,

---

14. R Anderson, *On Being Human: Essays in Theological Anthropology* (Grand Rapids: Eerdmans, 1982) 105–6.

for example, for 'homosexual marriages' of two committed, loving and faithful people. However, as should be clear given the discussion above about the impossibility of the minimalist approach to changing the church's ethic on sexuality, it also does much more than this. It is not only a justification of committed, monogamous, homosexual relationships it actually become a justification of *any* form of relationship which is deemed to be 'loving'.

If 'love' is the only determinant of a relationship then the monogamous heterosexual or homosexual cannot say anything to the multiple sexual heterosexual or homosexual who says, 'I love them all'. Nor is there any real argument against the one who wants to leave their husband or wife in order to take up a relationship with someone else. The polygamist and the adulterer all have their defense. It is effectively an antinomian position.[15] But, as Mott puts it: 'our ethic is not an "ethic of love" but an ethic of adherence to Jesus Christ' and this, of course, returns us to the particularity of the Trinity.[16] Some forms of sexual (and other) ethics fail to make this distinction and seek to re-create God and divine purposes in the form in which it is believed that 'love' would involve, rather than defining love in terms of the nature and purposes of God. But love is only understood by reference to God and divine purposes. A problem emerges when people believe that it is appropriate for them to be an arbiter of what 'the loving thing to do' is and disregard ordered relationships and biblical prohibitions on sexual activity outside marriage: fornication, adultery and homosexuality. But God is a God of holy love and there is such a thing as sexual sin. Human sexuality is not a playground for self-gratification or an arena in which its forms and significance can be constantly re-molded to fit human desires.

The answer to my question as to *why* Scripture says what it does, is to be found in the fact that human sexuality, as part of the *imago dei*, is clearly a reflection of the relational tri-unity of God. Human sexuality, as intrinsic to

---

15. This point is made by J Stott in *Issues Facing Christians Today* (Basingstoke: Marshalls, 1984) 314–16. Stott points out that N Pittenger's six characteristics of a loving relationship ((1) commitment, (2) mutuality, (3) tenderness, (4) faithfulness, (5) hopefulness, (6) a desire for union) which are intended to outline the possibility of a homosexual union, can, in fact, be fulfilled by polygamists and adulterers. I share with Stott the experience of counselling in the situation where one partner in a marriage is determined to end the marriage in order to live with another out of a conviction that it is alright simply because it is 'loving'.

16. S Mott, *Biblical Ethics and Social Change*, part 1, 'A Biblical Theology of Social Involvement' (New York: Oxford University Press, 1982), 39. Also 1 John 4:19 and Ephesians 5:1.

the image of God, is ontological in character and not merely a social phenomenon. The Christian ethic of sexuality is not rooted in culture to be manipulated as desired,[17] but is to be firmly grounded in this Trinitarian theology. This requires a specific concept of love that is expressed in marriage in the male-female polarity. This is an answer to the question of sexual love that is grounded in a theological understanding of God as Trinity. A full and complete answer to the question of *why* sexuality should be expressed this way requires a full and complete answer to the question of why God is a Trinity. But that is unlikely to be known this side of eternity and so, for the present, we must be content with an answer of faith which grounds our understanding of human sexual relationships in the particularities of the image of God and the relationships of the Trinity which is clearly expressed in the words of Scripture.

---

17. The erotic is not an end in itself. As Markus Barth comments, 'The specific sexual union between a man and a woman which Paul mentions in 5:31 excludes the idea of homosexual marriages as much as the notion that human sexuality is either a playground to be used without obligations, or some piece of machinery whose use and perfection must be learned from technical experts and the methods and tools prescribed (or sold) by them.' Markus Barth, *Ephesians 4–6* (New York: Doubleday, 1974) 718.

10

Whose Language? Which Grammar? :
'Inclusivity' and 'Diversity' versus the Crafted Christian Concepts of Catholicity and Created Differentiation

Bryden Black

Introduction

It has become commonplace in our contemporary global village with its cosmopolitan, multicultural ethos to hear the words 'diversity' and 'inclusivity' used frequently to describe this world. Nor should we be too quick to hear these two words as simply an echo of a presumed 'political correctness'—although, to be sure, on some people's tongues that is exactly the way they *are* being used, especially as a justification for certain forms of attitude and behaviour deemed 'desirable' over against their opposites. Yet can this mode of discourse really perform all that its proponents seek for it to do? For example, in our regional newspaper a while ago, a journalist, in commenting upon a Member of Parliament's sponsorship of Islam in a school setting according to 'the doctrine of diversity', concluded:

> As a concept [diversity] floats free of any fixed reference
> points that a religious or moral ethic could provide. It
> condemns absolute or exclusive truth while making itself
> an absolute.[1]

It is the position of this paper that the language of 'inclusiveness' and 'diversity' has its most natural soil in the discourse of the emancipatory agenda of autonomous human reason, namely the Enlightenment and now postmodernity.[2] However, there is available from a Christian perspective

---

1. This very trap has shown itself again and again: in the demise of the Vienna Circle and logical positivism's 'verification principle', which itself could not be 'verified'; and now the so-called postmodern claim that there are no metanarratives—which is itself a metanarrational claim!

2. For a succinct overview, see especially Alister McGrath, *The Twilight of Atheism: The Rise and Fall of Disbelief in the Modern World* (New York: Doubleday, 2004).

another form of discourse which enables a richer and more stable appreciation of these kinds of observations on our world, both the 'natural' world and human 'cultural' worlds. In addition, we shall take the worldwide Anglican Communion's current 'dilemmas', regarding the consecration of an openly practising gay bishop in the USA, as a crucial 'test case' or example. For when this alternative form of discourse is duly appreciated, these 'dilemmas' take on a very different light—appeals to 'inclusiveness' and such things notwithstanding. In other words, this paper seeks to address the matrix/matrices of human belief systems and ideas, with their associated forms of moral evaluation and behavioural ethics, via their respective forms of discourse.

1

To begin a due *exposé* of our contemporary Western view on these matters, we need an appraisal of pluralism in general, distinguishing at least three aspects to the theme of diversity from the perspective of pluralism.

1.1 As a sheer description of the state of affairs. At this level things are pretty obvious and don't need much comment perhaps. Sheer phenomenological variety is before us all. But what are we to make of it?

1.2 Diversity is good: pluralism as a preferential doctrine. With this category we begin to enter new, albeit perhaps slippery, territory. For on the one hand, there is much to commend: tastes in food, clothing, music, architecture. And creation itself is pretty stunningly diverse: 'If God cannot even make two snow flakes the same!' Moreover, this diversity interacts, and healthily so, at an ecological level; indeed, ecosystems demand diversity. The more so, it is said, at the cultural level as well. So we are all perceived winners. This is prescriptive pluralism.

But on the other hand there is quite quickly another observation to make: that while we (liberal Westerners) are mostly pluralistic in some matters, there are clearly others where we strongly draw the line and demur—'I decline!' This leads to the most problematic question, about which we need to be most circumspect.

1.3 Pluralism as relativism. This seems to be the working assumption of nearly everyone one meets these days—with the exception that, when pushed, most will also wish to 'draw the line somewhere' (as above, and see below) despite the inconsistency that this brings to their overall stance. For there are a number of variants to be considered at this stage.

1.3.1   All expressions of diversity are equally good and beautiful and true.
Superficially this appears a win-win situation for all. Yet as a *modus operandi*
it comes unstuck the moment one asks: But would you also include Adolf
Hitler or Josef Stalin or Pol Pot or Mao's widow, in your 'band of brothers'?
The moment one tries to disentangle the shades of grey by alluding to the
extremes of black and white 'something gets triggered'. And what gets
triggered is the 'awkwardness' of any supposed stance or means of evaluation:
here I stand—but 'should' I do so?! The awkwardness becomes acute when
we not only demur ourselves, but try to insist that 'others' should do so as
well: see the present 'rage' at 'pedophiles'.

1.3.2   This 'awkwardness' leads to the second variant to highlight. *Pluralism*
as moral relativism: there is no way to tell good or evil. Given our popular
postmodern condition, and the denial of *les grands récits*, each
perspective/point of view/opinion is as good as the other on the grounds that
each and all are deemed to emanate from contingent social constructions.

   (We should note though such 'weak' liberal stances/exceptions like: 'as
long as it does not hurt anyone . . . ', 'consenting adults in private' and such
like, which seem currently 'plausible'—despite the fact that even these two
cited examples have enormous inherent contradictions: for example: the
necessary connections between private morality and public justice.)

1.3.3   The most extreme position—or is it merely the most logical expression
(*sic*) of pluralism? —is *nihilism: there is no good or evil, or truth/falsehood.*
Ask many a young person in an inner city, scratch below their skin, and this is
tragically much of what one encounters.[3] There is, as Durkheim claimed
decades ago, a connection between *anomie* and suicide.

---

3. My own personal ministry in an inner city parish focusing especially upon youth
    convinces me of this too.

2

A little circumspection leaves us then in an apparent impasse.[4] Is it indeed a cultural *cul de sac*; or might there be a way through this contemporary morass? Three counterpointing steps lead us much of the way forward.

2.1 The issue of the One and the Many (or, variously, commonality and diverse particularity) has been with us since Heraclitus and Parmenides seemed to oppose each other; another version of the debate would pit atomism against monism. The medievals similarly encountered a variant of the matter in Aquinas' realism and Ockham's nominalism. There is nothing so *passé* as the trendy! In other words, as we try to disentangle our present experience of this fundamental concern, past insights and false leads should assist us. Unless we succumb to Herbert Butterfield's dictum, 'Those who are ignorant of history are doomed to repeat it!'.

2.2 Colin Gunton has provided us with a delightful series of proposals in his 1992 Bampton Lectures, *The One, The Three and The Many: God, Creation and the Culture of Modernity*.[5] Here we have a specific engagement with an Incarnational and Trinitarian view of the world, which permits us to embrace both a form of diversity and a clear set of prescriptive boundaries, both rational and moral. Yet this engagement, it has to be said, is firmly historical, firmly within a specific tradition of practices, both intellectual and ethical; there is an explicit institutional embodiment of 'truth' and 'virtue', no less, which also permits an openness to God's Spirit in the future. This observation leads to the third and final step.

2.3 In Alister McGrath's recent three-volume project, *A Scientific Theology*,[6] he provides the legitimate means both of remaining within a given tradition—

---

4. Although not directly on our chosen topic, nevertheless the related case for the non viability of 'religious pluralism' as customarily construed is even more devastating: see for example *Christian Uniqueness Reconsidered: The Myth of a Pluralistic Theology of Religions*, edited by Gavin D'Costa, (Maryknoll: Orbis, 1990), and most trenchantly, Gavin D'Costa, *The Meeting of Religions and the Trinity* (Maryknoll: Orbis, 2000).

5. CE Gunton, *The One, The Three and The Many: God, Creation and the Culture of Modernity—The Bampton Lectures 1992* (Cambridge: CUP, 1993).

6. AE McGrath, *A Scientific Theology: volume 1 Nature, volume 2 Reality, volume 3 Theory* (London: T and T Clark/Grand Rapids: Eerdmans, 2001/2/3).

which necessarily we all need to be as created human beings (which very comment is itself 'traditional'!)—and of evaluating other traditions via a specific trans-traditional form of engagement. That is, while presenting one's own 'perspective', its particular ethos and world-view, as we encounter 'reality' with all its particulars, can this very 'perspective' be such that it offers sufficient explanatory power of those differences its encounters both between and within the perspectives of others? And granted too that all such explanatory 'theorising' is provisional; yet the very human search for meaning and identity requires formal degrees of settled 'closure'. McGrath is offering his renewed version of 'natural theology' as just such a claimant, with sufficient power and creativity.

3

In other words, steps one to three of sections one and two, taken together, enable us to discriminate between two kinds of difference, two versions of apprehending and dealing with phenomenal diversity. While initially, plausibly similar, these two approaches are in fact hugely different—in basis and outcome. For the more we contemplate them, the more we have to conclude that it is absolutely necessary to discriminate between these two fundamentally opposed forms of discourse, two modes of rationality no less.[7] On the one hand, we have the results of the last three hundred years' project we term the Enlightenment, now eliding into the potpourri of postmodernism. On the other hand, a Christian theology of creation, as applied generally to the cosmological and in particular to the social and the cultural worlds, would fashion a rather different outlook, albeit naturally focused on the same or similar phenomena.

3.1 Re the first, the history is reasonably well known. I for one use Paul Hazard's classic text *La Crise de la Conscience Européenne*[8] to demarcate the

---

7. Oliver O'Donovan in *The Desire of the Nations: Rediscovering the Roots of Political Theology* (Cambridge: CUP, 1996) enjoins upon us to be 'alert to the signs of the times (as) a Gospel requirement', 273, the context being decisive. That is, all this paper seeks to do: to be 'wise' (Matt 10:16, 5:13) about 'the redemption of society' (chapter 7) and the church's role as 'salt' (Matt 5) in such a mission under God—given our Western history.
8. ET Paul Hazard, *The European Mind 1680–1715*, translated and abridged (Harmondsworth: Penguin, 1973).

start, the French revolution to express the mass cultural face (*liberté, égalité, fraternité*), and the collapse of the Berlin Wall exactly 200 years later to delimit the close. Of course that is too neat. But the rise and development of these traits demand attention and evaluation: 'tolerant' 'pluralistic' societies, where a fundamental chasm between the 'private' and the 'public' is 'assumed' (Marx in his *Early Writings* deemed this long before Newbigin),[9] where 'values' and 'facts' respectively reside, and where pluralistic description gives way to 'pluralism' as a prescriptive *modus operandi*, arbitrated by a so-called 'neutral' ratio-legal bureaucracy[10] among the citizenry of a sovereign nation-state: all this is merely the cultural pond of the West, 'assumed' and 'obvious'. But the last creature to ask questions of the water is the fish, as I am fond of saying. We Christian Westerners need to be 'discriminate' about this 'pond' in which we swim so 'naturally'.[11]

3.2 The results of at least my own attempts at such discrimination have produced the following alternatives, amplifying those three steps above. On the one hand, the language of 'inclusiveness' and 'diversity' resonates most naturally within the discourse of the emancipatory agenda of autonomous human reason: namely the Enlightenment and now postmodernity, whose ethos is the self-positing human subject. On the other hand, the Gospel's 'social project' (John Milbank) is precisely the one holy catholic and apostolic church. While all comers are invited (so Galatians 3–4),[12] the 'form of life'

---

9. The reference is to Lesslie Newbigin, *Foolishness to the Greeks: The Gospel and Western Culture* (Grand Rapids: Eerdmans, 1986); Lesslie Newbigin, *The Gospel in a Pluralist Society* (Grand Rapids: Eerdmans, 1989); Lesslie Newbigin, *Truth to Tell: The Gospel as Public Truth* (Grand Rapids: Eerdmans, 1991). O'Donovan has his own set of 'traits' and their 'evaluation' in *Desire*.

10. Just so Weber, whose own distinction between *Gemeinschaft* and *Gesellschaft* is still pertinent re legitimating forms of human sociality.

11. The most comprehensive religious history is MJ Buckley's *At the Origins of Modern Atheism* (New Haven: YUP, 1987), a required complement to the likes of Owen Chadwick, *The Secularization of the European Mind in the Nineteenth Century. The Gifford Lectures, 1973–4* (Cambridge: CUP, 1975), ably if briefly summarised in McGrath, *Twilight*.

12. The Episcopal Church of the United States of America (ECUSA) 'Koinonia Statement', August 1994, drafted by Bishop John Spong, attempts just such a baptismal universality towards homosexual people. This is surely correct. Where they are on slippery ground however is in *not* seeing that very baptism into Christ Jesus as a dying to their old identity and its 'order', to be transformed, in the power

and its corresponding 'virtues' (Gal 5–6), would once again discriminate between certain 'practices' as embodying the Gospel and its freedom-in-faith and others not. Those that do, 'reflect' that redeemed order after the image of the redeemer, whose reclaimed creation is the goal of the Gospel. Those that do not, remain 'under the powers' (Gal 4:8–9, however construed) and are 'reflections' of that tragedy which continues the irony of sin, which need not hold sway given the Christ of Israel's God's 'new creation' (Gal 6:15).

3.3 Having sketched these alternatives, we must elaborate especially on those features of the created order that excite all the talk of 'diversity' and 'unity', 'differentiation' and 'wholeness'—all those terms that depend greatly upon which grammar and/or form of discourse one is employing.

4

4.1 Fascinatingly, the Gospel is both inclusive and exclusive all at once. Once we realise this, then perhaps we need to explore why such opposites can both apply to the same reality. Perhaps because the very terms are simply based on false common assumptions or couched from within an inadequate framework? For this is often the case when presented with a perceived polarity (like the fabled socialism versus capitalism: perhaps both systems as systems are profoundly ambiguous, as expressions of mere human economic practice without a theology of creation). Contrariwise, the church would be comprehensive in its scope, catholic in its goal, and this mission based on the singular and particular event of the *One* human being, Jesus of Nazareth, whose destiny as *totus Christus* (Augustine, after the vision of the church in Ephesians and Colossians) embraces those aspirations—but only aspirations, and as such unfulfilled—evident in the terms 'inclusive' and 'exclusive'.

4.2 'Diversity' and 'unity' have been the talk one way or another ever since Hobbes' *Leviathan* or Locke's essays on, for example, *Toleration*, or *Civil Government*. For what will enable any 'commonwealth' to have a 'commonweal'? This is intensely practical stuff. For once the fractions of European denominationalism have crippled any possibilities from among the religions, other 'contracts' simply have to be found, and/or other sources of

---

of the Spirit of Jesus' resurrection, unto the true image of God. In other words, a *full* baptismal theology is a double-edged sword for such ECUSA folk.

sovereign legitimacy devised, especially after we're too exhausted from all the blood-letting.[13] Once again, the story is well known—or should be![14] But whose story precisely is it?! That's the point. This question, once it arises forcibly via the likes of Alasdair MacIntyre and John Milbank,[15] as well as Oliver O'Donovan, demands an explicit Christian answer. Yet we contemporary Western church folk often avoid the issue by trying to keep a (rational, discursive) foot in both/all camps; after all, such a stance seems so 'obvious', possible and desirable! However, after the long performance(s) of the Enlightenment's story and its ensuing aftermath, including the history of the nation-state, and especially the extraordinary violence of the twentieth century, caused to a large extent by the competing claims of such clashing states and their ideologies,[16] this is simply dishonest: the respective 'logics' and 'grammars' are just *too* different. Karl Barth for one saw this after World War I so clearly. And whatever we think of his particular 'scheme', this lesson remains paramount: his 'fresh attempt to learn [his] theological ABCs all over

---

13. Which is why Ephraim Radner's diagnosis, *The End of the Church: A Pneumatology of Christian Division in the West* (Grand Rapids: Eerdmans, 1998), and *Hope among the Fragments: The Broken Church and Its Engagement of Scripture* (Grand Rapids: Eerdmans, 2004), is absolutely essential—even if it needs to be supplemented by the likes of William Cavanaugh's *Theopolitical Imagination: Discovering the Liturgy as a Political Act in an Age of Global Consumerism* (London: T and T Clark, 2002), which details more broadly the rise of the nation-state as its *own* self-seeking search for singular sovereignty, irrespective of the church's failures (like the religious wars) and precisely over against its successes.

14. See also William Cavanaugh, 'Killing for the Telephone Company: Why the Nation-State is Not the Keeper of the Common Good', *Modern Theology*, 20/2 (2004): 243–74 for a brilliant summary of the story—one which furthermore undermines precisely Christopher Insole's article seeking to defend political liberalism in the same edition, 213–41, even as the latter does seriously qualify the Radical Orthodoxy movement.

15. Alasdair MacIntyre's trilogy is: *After Virtue: A Study in Moral Theory* (Notre Dame: UNDP, 1984), *Whose Justice? Which Rationality?* (Notre Dame: UNDP, 1988) and *Three Rival Versions of Moral Enquiry: Encyclopedia, Genealogy and Tradition* (London: Duckworth, 1990). See also *Theology and Social Theory: Beyond Secular Reason* (Oxford: Blackwell, 1990), and John Milbank, *The Word Made Strange: Theology, Language, Culture* (Oxford: Blackwell, 1997).

16. McGrath, *Twilight*, duly highlights this element of violence in a number of key places.

again' is our task too; to 'begin again at the beginning,'[17] with the Christian Gospel *per se*, the heart of which is the Living Person of Jesus Christ, in our new global millennium demands nothing less.

4.3 This logic (or grammar, or ABC) addresses, among other things, the manner in which we construe the variety of the world in which we live and which we yet try to cohere meaningfully into a whole or a unity. The issue is quite simply as old as Parmenides' monistic solution. Nor is this merely a case of taxonomy. It has huge implications socially and morally - not least for those living after Auschwitz or Apartheid. To once again cut a long story short, I refer to steps *2.2* and *2.3* above, especially to Colin Gunton's *The One, The Three and The Many: God, Creation and the Culture of Modernity*. It is striking just how different (sic) his perspective really is, and if genuinely so, we need to amplify it and apply it to our case in point.

5

5.1 It would appear that only a Christian theology of creation by the triune God has sufficient explanatory power to render intelligible what euphemistically others aspire to (that key word 'aspire' again) via 'diversity' and 'inclusion'. Clearly the historical record of the Enlightenment's key children may not. Either capitalism's individualism or socialism's collectivism reigns (note the ideological 'isms' here),[18] even as the nation-state seeks a monopoly to subsume all within its grasp, at worst, or attempts an ongoing balancing act among competing rights claimants, at best. In which case none of these renders the human adequately, nor truly establishes that 'shalom' or 'commonweal' most 'desire' (O'Donovan). Added to which, post 1989, or

---

17. Barth's lectures at Göttingen, Winter Semester, 1923/24, published in translation as *The Theology of Schleiermacher* (Edinburgh: T and T Clark, 1982), contain an essay or *Nachwort* first published in 1968, 'Concluding Unscientific Postscript on Schleiermacher', 261–79, from which this first clause comes, 264; the second encapsulates much of his 'method': so *Church Dogmatics, I.2* (Edinburgh: T and T Clark, 1956), 868, and *Evangelical Theology: An Introduction* (T and T Clark, 1963), 165. They furthermore crystalise his response to those 'Ninety-three German intellectuals (whose) . . . support for the war policy of Kaiser Wilhelm II' in 1914 precipitated Barth's break with nineteenth-century liberalism.

18. Edmund Wilson's *To the Finland Station: A Study in the Writing and Acting of History*, first published in 1940, remains the English classic re Socialism.

whenever one demarcates 'modernity's' last failure, and the emergence of the postmodern, a major feature has become in fact homogenisation in the face once again of that aspiration for particularity and difference/différance—or however one wants to spell it (*pace* Derrida's 'preference'). Yet such is the tendency too for fragmentation under the 'gods' of the postmodern that frankly we appear set for another titanic struggle between these two features, homogenisation and the fragmentary,[19] parallel to the previous face off between socialism and capitalism. *Plus ça change, rien ne change pas.* (One could also signal the tensions between globalisation and what the sociologists fondly term 'glocalisation'.[20])

5.2 Again contrariwise, Colin Gunton's three posited additional 'open transcendentals', predicated upon an explicitly Trinitarian reading of the history of the created order, of *perichoresis*, substantiality (*haecceitas*), and sociality (relationality), enable a far richer appraisal of the observed differentiation of the world, 'natural' and 'cultural', while offering also a unified vision of 'recapitulation' (Irenaeus). That is, the descriptive and so-called prescriptive aspects of pluralism's aspirations (another ideology after all)—which under the aegis of autonomous human reason only eventuates finally in illogicality and instability (the suggestion above, section 1)—are permitted their legitimate 'space', once given a severe 'twist' of perspective, that is, within prescribed boundaries or parameters. On the one hand,ʼ *différance* may indeed be the endless play of semiotic possibilities, performed by those whose discourse is ever trapped immanently within their own self-referent, linguistic world.[21] The worship of the triune Creator, on the other hand, by a *variety* of creatures bespeaks both an infinity of creativity and an order after the Logos's image alike, opened up by that 'field' established through the redemption of the unique God-man—which 'field' (Pannenberg) is none other than God's very own triune life and love in sovereign freedom

---

19. The literature on postmodernity is as varied as the phenomenon itself; but see for example, David Harvey, *The Condition of Postmodernity: An Enquiry into the Origins of Cultural Change* (Oxford: Blackwell, 1990).

20. A helpful analysis (even if a little 'modernist') of all such matters, via a model of deliberative democracy and a linguistic-philosophical notion of culture, is Seyla Benhabib's *The Claims of Culture: Equality and Diversity in the Global Era* (Princeton: PUP, 2002).

21. Other forms of immanent reaction to the loss of the sense of the transcendent are not only possible but have occurred; Derrida's is not the only one, even as it is currently fashionable.

and fulness, into whom the church is baptised, 'for the praise of his glorious grace' (Eph 1).[22]

5.3 In other words, these very words, 'unity' and 'diversity' *may* be construed as means of groping after a genuine reality—indeed, the very Reality and Actuality of the triune God, in the end, let alone the created reality of this One. But in the light of the biblical story, the better alternative, I suggest, views in the first place that essential difference between the self-existing and self-determined and determining Triune Creator and that Creator's contingent creation.[23] Then secondly, given this creation's 'reflection' of its Creator, created items 'after their kind' (Gen 1) are duly differentiated on the one hand (and so distinctively concrete and particular), with their *all* being *authored* on the other hand by and from and through the *one* divine source. (There is simply not the space here to indulge in an analysis of Aquinas' view of the Divine Being's simplicity versus created beings' composite natures, for example). Yet this revised perspective should not result in either fragmentation or homogenisation, notably in the human case—to select only these two contemporary diseases—especially the political homogenisation of the nation-state. For those 'open transcendentals' (Gunton, as above) ensure not merely a due integration of those otherwise problematic features of creation but precisely a relational *perichoresis* that ensures also a complex view of the world across diverse species and across multiple levels of reality (Polanyi and Bhaskar),[24] which nonetheless cohere into a whole—even if that whole is provisional and partial from any human theoretical or practical, especially political point of view, synchronically and/or diachronically. (That

---

22. This paragraph and the subsequent one echo deliberately the likes of Pannenberg and Jüngel, Jenson and Gunton, but also Catherine Pickstock's *After Writing: On the Liturgical Consummation of Philosophy* (Oxford: Blackwell, 1998). Climaxing with the Eph 1 doxology also echoes that magisterial New Testament treatment of the church in its entirety, referencing baptismal initiation, the church's nature and its destiny.

23. See especially McGrath, A *Scientific Theology: Nature*, chapter 3, 81–133, for the crucial significance of 'nature' as a 'socially mediated' perception *viewed as* such and so, which sets up chapter 4 and 'the Christian doctrine of creation'—*how* Christian theology *views* reality.

24. For the former, see Michael Polanyi, *The Tacit Dimension* (London: RKP, 1966); the latter is basic to McGrath's *Scientific Theology* project, for example volume 2 *Reality*, chapter 10.

is, there is no Archimedean God's eye view *pace* either Plato or Idealism, or modern forms of the secular state, tending towards totalitarianism.) The church's project of being one holy catholic and apostolic too remains under what we may term an 'eschatological reserve', due to the manner and timing in the economy of salvation—which results necessarily in due patience and humility (one hopes!). Just so, Augustine's *City of God* is repeated, with the ongoing tension between the two Cities in real history: the divine is acknowledged and expressed and sought after in the church versus lesser, 'uncertain' versions of 'justice' and 'peace' perpetrated by ambiguous human endeavours, at best, and, at worst, by 'robbers' (Book XIX, chapter 12).

6

6.1 Summary: what this paper has been arguing for is a far more nuanced and considered vocabulary, grammar and syntax—an overall discourse—when we Christians, or anyone else for that matter, try to engage in our present social and cultural 'dilemmas'. Frankly, much of the perceived impasse—mostly felt rather than articulated, or if attempted to be articulated, then usually in the form of diatribe or the odd spiritual RPG (rocket-propelled grenade)—is due to the failure to see that our customary, basic 'furniture of the mind' (DM MacKinnon) just isn't up to the task in hand. Just so, this attempt to refashion the furniture more discerningly, based on a fresh reading of the Christian story in context, a reading prompted by a wrestling with those 'powers', embodied especially in language, which have been displayed in a variety of world views and ethoses over the past centuries. Nor is this merely an academic exercise; social and political consequences follow. Yet Christian faith's seeking understanding is only the counterpoint to the required exposé of alternative forms of faith and life—like the secular humanist or atheistic in post-Christendom societies, no less a religion than others. Their forms of faith and rationalities, and corresponding praxes, are equally under the gun—especially within any postmodern, global ethos, which extols the 'difference' of the 'Other'.[25]

6.2 So where to from here? Back to the example mentioned in the Introduction, of Gene Robinson and the Episcopal Church of the United

---

25. With extraordinary irony, it has to be pointed out that the frequent denial of the possibility of a Christian discourse based on an explicit theology of Creation precisely *fails* to acknowledge the Other, so beloved of the postmodern! So what *is* happening here?!

States of America (ECUSA) and the 'dilemmas' they have provoked, which serve as a vital illustration of the principles of this paper. From within the one scheme of discourse, homosexuality is as 'natural' and 'obvious' as the nose on your face or mine. So too are bisexuality, transsexuality—and of course heterosexuality. All are 'equal'. Added to which, homoeroticism is simply the expression of 'autonomous existential fulfilment', a key form of 'loving communion'. One would 'expect' nothing less! 'Denial' therefore precipitates a version of 'injustice',[26] as gays and lesbians seek their 'rights'. Such is the metanarrative of the last three hundred and more years of the European story as it impinges upon a construal of pluralism; such are the assumed plausibility structures via a sociology of knowledge applied to human sexual behaviour sanctioned by a politically plural state predicated upon a perceived autonomous humanity.

6.3 Yet there *is* another version of the story available, the one I have tried to portray, albeit briefly. By means of a Christian theology of creation (construed via the likes of Colin Gunton,[27] Alasdair MacIntyre, John Milbank to some extent, and Alister McGrath), differences in our world, 'natural' as well as 'cultural', have a different perspective, generating a different language. In particular, homosexuality is a 'tragic irony' viewed from the stance of a fallen-yet-redeemed-in-process world; and homosexual people (while the jury is still out regarding their 'formation')[28] are necessarily to be related to as to any others, any fallen-yet-redeemed/ redeemable human beings, called to become members of the Body of Christ, the Community of the Church, whose destiny is the Son's Spouse[29]: with due patience and humility and care, considering that eschatological reserve mentioned before. For homosexual people, both gay men and lesbian women, are just another, particular sign of our universal

---

26. Alasdair MacIntyre and Alister McGrath are vital at this point re 'versions' of 'justice', and their 'evaluation' via different forms of 'moral enquiry'.

27. See also CE Gunton, *Christ and Creation* (Carlisle: Paternoster, 1992), and CE Gunton, *The Triune Creator: A Historical and Systematic Study* (Grand Rapids: Eerdmans, 1998).

28. As with all things 'human', the 'cause' will be multifactorial: genes, hormones, parental care, siblings, peers, wider society-culture and others—all in combination.

29. See especially, chapter 7, 'The Nuptial Figure', in Radner's *Hope among the Fragments* for how this sacrament (Eph 5:32) providentially orders human history and life.

human fallen condition, of false desire, gone awry, no less or more tragic than anyone else's—though duly awaiting both acknowledgement of which on the one hand and final redemption from which on the other, through the compassionate mercy of God (see for example, Romans 1, 7–8). Homoeroticism, precisely as an expression of human behaviour, therefore, within *this* specific scheme of discourse, is a 'practice' 'of the flesh' (Gal 5, Rom 8). It is immensely significant that the two New Testament texts that explicitly mention such 'practices', Rom 1 and 1 Cor 6, are found in settings dealing with that core Jewish values' debate, idolatry versus the worship of the One true God (with 1 Cor 6 using a Decalogue-type scheme, what's more) and the consequences for 'righteousness'/'justice' and its opposite.[30] That should be enough for New Covenant types! Not least, in view of Romans 12:1–2:

> In view of the mercies of God, I appeal to you therefore, brothers and sisters, to present your bodies as a living sacrifice, holy and acceptable to God, which is your spiritual worship. Do not be conformed to this world/age,[31] but be transformed by the renewing of your minds, so that you may discern what is the will of God— what is good and acceptable and perfect.

Conclusion

The history of the natural sciences gives us a methodology for appraising differing world-views or perspectives upon reality. On the one hand, when the Ptolemaic universe gave way to the Copernican, it was the case that either the

---

30. See also Mark Smith, 'Ancient Bisexuality and the Interpretation of Rom 1:26–7', *Journal of the American Academy of Religion*, 64 (1996): 223–56, where he concludes that Paul clearly condemns sufficiently equivalent ancient homosexual behaviour to that of today. But what is also clear is that Paul universalises the human condition, even as he specifies expressions of this fallenness (1:24f, 26f and 28ff, 2:1).

31. Any society's 'cultural pond', in which people 'naturally swim', is always a crucial manifestation of the aeon of this world, especially on account of its ambivalence given the Christian theology of Creation which views all reality as simultaneously essentially good and yet fundamentally flawed. Just so, the church is exhorted 'to take every design/thought captive to obey Christ' (2 Cor 10:5). This paper is a meagre attempt at just this calling to baptismal 'transformation'.

one or the other was 'correct'. Since the two were mutually exclusive, the one having no room for the other when it came to 'interpreting' phenomena, there is simply no room for both simultaneously. Comparing the Newtonian universe with the Einsteinian however is very different. In this case, we have to conclude that the Newtonian is a subset of the Einsteinian. It is not the case that the Newtonian is exactly 'false'; Newton's laws still prevail. Rather, in cases of the very small or the very large or the very fast, the Newtonian has simply proved 'inadequate'. Additional laws, derived from the likes of Einstein, are seen to have more explanatory power than merely the Newtonian in crucial cases.

In the ecclesiastical world today we are faced with an analogous situation. When the world-wide Anglican Communion seeks consensus over the issue of Bishop Gene Robinson's consecration, which process might prevail? Is it a case of the African and the rest of the Third World Church being the equivalent of the Ptolemaic in their appraisal of this event, this phenomenon? And is the liberal Western paradigm of 'tolerance and pluralism' the equivalent of the Copernican, in the face of 'traditional' values espoused by 'old-fashioned' societies? Or, can we legitimately view the current 'dilemmas' as being akin to Newton versus Einstein? May those views which have arisen in western liberal societies and which most of their population merely take to be 'obvious and natural' today, be reconciled with the more 'traditional' approaches to certain values? Are the two merely differing perspectives upon the whole, which permits complementary versions that are not exactly mutually exclusive and which might co-exist, with now the one being applicable and then now the other, depending upon the precise circumstances of any given case?[32]

This paper has argued for a specific option on this entire phenomenon. It is that a renewed Christian theology of creation, sorely needed in our time in the face of both contemporary science and our contemporary cultures (just as the early church had itself two major cosmological views which it had to deny, the dualism of Gnosticism and Manichaeism as well as forms of pantheism), sets up the view from which the world view of the liberal West and its ensuing discourse and praxis is indeed mutually exclusive. That latter ethos and world

---

32. An example of such ecclesiastical ethics *in via*, of complementary morals for the pilgrim church, might be monogamy in the West and polygamy in missionary settings for, say, two/three further generations after the arrival of the Gospel. Another 'version' altogether is ECUSA's present proposals re the 'local option'.

view, which has historically arisen from the seventeenth century onwards in European societies and those derived from Europe, indeed clashes with a genuine Christian theology of creation and the implications of such for any human cultural mandate, which the Gospel specifically embarks us upon via its unique 'social project'—notably, in the area of human sexuality's expression and fulfilment, our chosen example or 'test case'.[33] The situation is akin to Copernicus versus the Ptolemaic; or Irenaeus versus the Gnostics; or Augustine versus the Manichees. These two are properly separate from each other, and may not co-exist. While both discourses seek to address the same or similar phenomena, in point of fact a more profound appraisal of each will lead to the conclusion that, while apparently similar, in the end there is an essential parting of the ways: such are their respective 'bases and outcomes'. That at least is the claim herein: we must needs 'choose this day whom— which 'gods'—we shall indeed serve' (with deliberate echoes of Deuteronomic theology and praxis, to say nothing of Karl Barth's Barmen Declaration, 1934). Either the triune God of Creation, who is Incarnate in the One Jesus of Nazareth, the Christ of God, whose redemption promises the transformation of our fallen and 'distorted' (Romans) created humanity in the Community of the Church, whose Lord this Jesus is. Or those cultural 'gods' and their 'elemental powers' which have arisen (from the most laudable of intentions, according to many a reading of Western history) and hold sway across certain 'cultural spaces' these days.

The situation is of course a delicate one. To some there is a plausible conviviality between a theology of creation and Western views, while to others the twain cannot meet. The conviviality question is made more acute by certain key traits of liberal Western pluralism having their origins in the Christian faith, being direct fruit of the Gospel's interaction with European culture over many centuries. Yet one needs to ask, what happens when such fruit becomes cut off from the roots over time? And to push the metaphor: is there an increased tendency for the fruit to become sour—or even to drop off altogether, to become another 'expression' of a different culture? One last (metaphorical) observation heightens the stakes yet more. When attempting to

---

33. This conclusion, re the discipline of theology itself, is reached by another route, with important parallels in Reinhard Hütter's *Suffering Divine Things: Theology as Church Practice* (Grand Rapids: Eerdmans, 2000). The significance of this for how the *church* deals with our present 'dilemmas' cannot be overestimated: will its thinking be captured by its cultural, worldly ethos, *or* will it be true to its authentic inheritance?

counterfeit any currency, there is little point in printing a note of any denomination that does not exist in reality. An $80 note simply is pointless! Trying to print a $100 note however has some merit in some people's eyes! Just so, trying to assess the significance of this world's plurality, in nature and our cultural schemas and codes of life, not only has merit but is demanded of us. Like previous cosmological disputes (remember Galileo), it is also a matter of life and death (for some, for many) that we come as close as we may to the truth of our human enterprise and condition—of the divine accommodation and grace among us, should that possibility also be entertained! The promise of pluralism's 'tolerant' 'doctrine of diversity' (almost a studied indifference, to some) claims much indeed: genuine conviviality for a multicultural world laced with differences across many spectra. Globalisation also requires nothing less. But is this truly achievable, given the argument here? Granted, the very emergence of pluralism's social thesis was due, to a large degree, to the failure of the church's 'social project', of one holy catholic and apostolic community, to the lack of ecclesial love to embody its own grace and truth in the face of alternative sovereignties.[34] Yet the counter thesis offered here seeks to warn that, rather than delivering on its promise of a fulfilling life for all, the eventual outcome of secular Western liberalism may very well be *a* counterfeit life that will issue in nothing less than a death, a parody of creation's dazzling variety of forms of life—not least on account of a sterility which has already begun to manifest itself in patterns of sexual homogenisation, incapable of reflecting authentically the fruitful divine image among the human (Gen 1:26–31).

---

34. See also, again, Ephraim Radner's thesis. But will there arise sufficient 'penitence' and/or sacrifice on the part of this divided Western church? While sensing not, Radner leaves us in the Holy Spirit's gracious charge, for there is simply no other Christian 'space'.

11

Sexuality and the Virtues or 'Whose Marriage, which Sexuality?'

Denise Cooper-Clarke

Much has been written about the way biblical rules and principles provide guidance concerning the morality of homosexual practice and the legitimacy of church blessings for homosexual unions. Virtue ethics, with its emphasis on the character of moral agents, and in particular the notion of moral practices, provides an alternative to this focus on rules and principles. This chapter will use a virtue ethics approach to examine sexuality and the practice of marriage within the biblical tradition. According to MacIntyre, a living tradition is not set in stone, but is 'an historically extended, socially embodied argument'.[1] This raises the important question, 'Which features of marriage and sexual morality are inherent in a biblical worldview, and how much is open to reinterpretation?'

1. Let's talk about sex

'Sex' may refer to the act of sexual intercourse. Or it may refer to the quality of being male or female, and by extension, 'the whole domain connected with this distinction'.[2] I will adopt the definition of sexuality as 'that complexity of thoughts, feelings, bodily changes and behaviours that surround the human capacity for one flesh union and which is grounded in human biology'.[3] Sexuality irreducibly connotes both differentiation (Latin *sexus* is akin to *secus*, from *secare*, to cut or divide) and complementarity since it is based on 'reproductive capacities of members of a species that reproduce sexually

---

1. Alasdair MacIntyre, *After Virtue* (2nd edition, Notre Dame: University of Notre Dame Press, 1984), 222.
2. *Chambers Twentieth Century Dictionary* (Edinburgh: W and R Chambers, 1978), 1241.
3. Graham Cole, 'Sexuality and Its Expression: With Special Reference to Homosexuality', *Luke's Journal,* 5/3 (2000): 4–8.

rather than asexually'.[4] Hence the term is out of favour with some writers: 'Sex is a term which erases lesbian desire, sensuality and orgasm'.[5] Indeed, homosexual erotic activity is strictly speaking not sexual activity at all, since it does not express male/female differentiation and complementarity.

Christian sexual ethics were remarkably stable until the second half of the twentieth century. There was general consensus that sexual activity should only take place within marriage, defined as a permanent monogamous union between a man and a woman, and that procreation was a normal purpose of marriage. The only source of dispute was whether celibacy or marriage was morally preferable. During the Middle Ages the Roman Catholic Church regarded celibacy as a higher state of Christian living. But there was no such hierarchy in the Orthodox tradition, which regarded marriage as the norm, at times even describing it as 'a more difficult and courageous decision than celibacy'.[6] The Reformers also rejected the elevation of celibacy and reaffirmed marriage as God's design for humanity.[7]

Today all elements of this consensus are being challenged, or even revolted against, with pressure for the church to revise its position more or less radically. Karen Lebacqz claims that 'a new ethic for single sexuality is needed, for the tradition that requires celibacy in singleness is not adequate'.[8] 'Today's sexual ethic,' writes Beverley Harrison, 'must come to terms with a world where persons come to puberty earlier and earlier but to adulthood later and later . . . Condemnation of sex outside marriage increases pressures for early and premature marriage'.[9] In addition, she claims that the fact that 'people have double the life expectancy and nearly double the years of

---

4. Claudia Card 'The Symbolic Significance of Sex and the Institution of Sexuality', cited by Sarah Hoagland, 'Lesbian Ethics' in *Sexuality: A Reader*, edited by Karen Lebacqz with David Sinacore-Guinn (Cleveland: The Pilgrim Press, 1999), 453–77.

5. Card 'The Symbolic Significance of Sex', 471.

6. Vigen Guroian, 'An Ethic of Marriage and Family', in *From Christ to the World,* edited by Wayne Boulton, Thomas Kennedy and Allen Verhey (Grand Rapids: Eerdmans, 1994), 322–30.

7. Stanley Grenz, *Sexual Ethics: an Evangelical Perspective* (2nd edition Westminster: John Knox Press, 1997), xvi.

8. Karen Lebacqz, 'Appropriate Vulnerability: A Sexual Ethic for Singles' in *Sexuality: A Reader*, edited by Lebacqz, 129–35.

9. Beverley Harrison, 'Misogyny and Homophobia: The Unexplored Connections', in *From Christ to the World*, edited by Boulton, 331–41.

reproductive fertility as they had only a few centuries ago', completely changes the meaning of life-long monogamous sexual relations.[10]

Elizabeth Stuart is even more revisionist:

> It is the attempt to confine sexuality and its expression to marriage that has caused the marginalisation of lesbians and gay men and an emotional overload in marriage which many marriages cannot bear . . . The recognition of the part played by monogamy in the oppression of women has led some Christian lesbian feminists to reject it as an essential ingredient in lesbian and gay relationships.[11]

David McCarthy Matzko does not reject the practice of marriage itself, but assumes that there is no single practice of marriage in the Christian tradition, and that 'certain same sex unions already are functioning within their communities as marriages'.[12]

2. Let's talk about virtue

Ever since the so-called Enlightenment, ethics has been dominated by two competing theories, deontological and utilitarian. The premise of deontological theory may be simply stated as:

> An action is right iff (sic)[13] it is in accordance with a moral rule or principle.

In Christian formulations, a moral rule is one that is either laid on us by God in the Scriptures—Divine Command—or required by natural law, which also reflects the character of God.

The premise of utilitarianism, by contrast, may be stated as:

> An action is right iff it promotes the 'best consequences', where the 'best consequences'are those in which happiness is maximised.[14]

10. Harrison, 'Misogyny and Homophobia', 339.
11. Elizabeth Stuart, 'Lesbian and Gay Relationships: A Lesbian Feminist Perspective', in *Christian Perspectives on Sexuality and Gender*, edited by Adrian Thatcher and Elizabeth Stuart (Grand Rapids: Eerdmans, 1996), 301–17.
12. David McCarthy Matzko, 'Homosexuality and the Practices of Marriage', *Modern Theology*, 13/3 (1987): 371–97.
13. 'Iff' means 'if and only if'.

However, since the early 1980s, we have seen the revival of a third ethical theory, which has as its first premise:

> An action is right iff it is what an agent with a virtuous character would do in the circumstances.[15]

An agent with a virtuous character is 'one who has and exercises the virtues', where 'a virtue is a character trait a human being needs to flourish or live well'.[16] In virtue theory, the primary focus moves from actions to character, from doing to being, from decisions to dispositions, and from discrete moments to a whole life.

It was Alasdair MacIntyre who revived virtue theory, through his savage critique of post-Enlightenment ethics and reworking of the Aristotelian /Thomistic moral tradition. But his voice resonated with others which drew attention to the fact that contemporary ethics is 'the product of a long process of "stripping down"'.[17] In the quest for objective and universal moral principles based solely on reason, ethics lost its anthropological aspect, becoming abstracted from concrete human living. Because reason was also divorced from faith, ethics simultaneously lost its theological character. During the Reformation, Protestant ethics lost its communal aspect, placing moral responsibility on the lone individual making decisions, and at the same time discarding the natural law and virtue stream associated with Aquinas, to focus exclusively on divine command ethics.[18]

The voice of Carol Gilligan urges us to attend to the anthropological aspect of ethics by reminding us that different people see morality differently. Her research on men's and women's moral reasoning convinced her that women have their own distinctive moral development.[19] Gilligan drew

---

14. Rosalind Hursthouse, 'Virtue Theory and Abortion', *Philosophy and Public Affairs*, 20/3 (1991): 224–5.

15. Justin Oakley, 'Varieties of Virtue Ethics', *Ratio*, 9/2 (1996): 2.

16. Hursthouse, 'Virtue Theory and Abortion', 225–6.

17. Brad Kallenberg, 'Positioning MacIntyre within Christian Ethics', in *Virtues and Practices in the Christian Tradition*, edited by Nancey Murphy, Brad Kallenberg and Mark Thiessen Nation (Harrisburg, Pennsylvania: Trinity Press International, 1997), 45–81.

18. Kallenberg, 'Positioning MacIntyre within Christian Ethics', 48.

19. Carol Gilligan, *In a Different Voice* (Cambridge: Harvard University Press, 1982). Some feminists have questioned the validity of Gilligan's findings and deny the 'strong claim' that gender alone results in unique processes of moral decision

attention to moral agents as well as moral acts, and to alternative approaches to rules and principles in moral reasoning.

Alongside the revival of interest in virtue in philosophical ethics, there has been 'a sea change in Christian ethics', led by Stanley Hauerwas.[20] Hauerwas draws on the Aristotelian virtue tradition, but his work is concerned with distinctively Christian character, as nurtured within the Christian community. Character, rather than rational deliberation or obedience to moral norms is the centre of the moral life.[21] Similarly, his emphasis is on stories or narratives rather than doctrinal formulations. It is the narratives of God, as told by the community of Israel and then by the church, which shape Christian character.[22]

Virtue theory in general and the work of Stanley Hauerwas in particular are not without their critics among Christian ethicists. But even the sternest critic will acknowledge that an emphasis on moral excellence and character pervades the Scriptures, although the word *arete* (virtue) itself occurs infrequently in the New Testament.[23] *Arete* (translated as excellence or goodness) is primarily attributed to God, and by derivation to humans as they are conformed to the divine image. This process of conformity, or moral growth, is the work of God, and yet allows human cooperation, even effort.[24]

---

making, while allowing the 'weak claim' that women's different life experiences will colour their moral reflection (see Sidney Callahan, 'Does Gender Make a Difference in Moral Decision Making?', *Second Opinion*, October (1991): 67.) Others are uneasy with a dichotomy between a 'male' ethic of justice (principle based) and a 'female' ethic of care (relationship based) since it tends to reinforce feminine nurturing and mothering stereotypes (Hilde Nelson, 'Against Caring', *The Journal of Clinical Ethics*, Spring (1992): 8.)

20. Nancey Murphy, 'Introduction' in *Virtues and Practices in the Christian Tradition*, *op cit*, 1.

21. James Tubbs, *Christian Theology and Medical Ethics: Four Contemporary Approaches* (Dordrecht: Kluwer Academic, 1996), 96.

22. Stephen Lammers, 'On Stanley Hauerwas: Theology, Medical Ethics and the Church', in *Theological Voices in Medical Ethics* edited by Allen Verhey and Stephen Lammers (Grand Rapids: Eerdmans, 1993), 57–77.

23. Philippians 4:8 (excellence); 1 Peter 2:9; 2 Peter 1:3, 5 (goodness). Paul associates it with what is true, good, just, pure, pleasing, commendable and worthy of praise. Peter speaks of the wonderful deeds (*aretas*) of God, and of supporting our faith with *arete*, our *arete* with knowledge, knowledge with self control, self control with endurance, endurance with godliness, godliness with mutual affection, and mutual affection with love.

24. So Paul designates a list of character traits or virtues as the fruit of the Spirit (Galatians 5:22-23). Believers are instructed to 'be transformed by the renewing of

Much of Jesus' moral teaching focuses on the inner life. The Sermon on the Mount begins with a series of blessings on those who exhibit certain virtues (Matthew 5:1–12). It is not only actions or external behaviour which are morally significant, but attitudes of the heart: anger, lust, thirst for retaliation, and hatred of enemies (Matthew 5:21–8). Words and actions reflect what is in the heart, whether good or evil (Matthew 12:33–5). Those who are clean on the outside, but not inside, are told to clean the inside first (Matthew 23:25–6). Even Oliver O'Donovan, a critic of virtue theory, concedes, 'Jesus took issue with the casuistry of his own day precisely over its fussy concentration on the circumstances of acts and its failure to think seriously about what he called "the heart"'.[25]

3. Virtuous sex redefined?

Virtue theory provides a powerful critique of the principles/rules based approach (including (rule-) utilitarianism, which uses the single principle of maximising good consequences), that has dominated Western ethics since the Enlightenment. Those who would challenge the dominant culture of patriarchy and heterosexism associated by them with this ethical approach thus find in virtue theory a congenial alternative framework.

Central to most contemporary argument for the acceptance of long term committed homosexual unions is a de-emphasis on the importance of specific prohibitions and the morality of particular acts, with a corresponding emphasis on the quality of relationships and the virtues of love, honesty and mutuality. James Nelson argues that 'It has been commonplace in Christian understanding to think of sexual sin in terms of certain acts: sexual acts done with the wrong person, against divine or natural law, or harmful to others and the self'.[26] Instead, he says, we should 'take motives and dispositions as seriously as the physical acts themselves',[27] and argues that ethics must 'find

---

your mind' (Romans 12:2), to 'be renewed in the spirit of your minds, and to clothe yourself with the new self, created according to the righteousness of God' (Ephesians 4:23–4). The passive voice in these texts emphasises that it is God who does the work of renewal, but the exhortations speak of the believer's role in desiring, allowing and cooperating in the ongoing process.

25. Oliver O'Donovan, *Resurrection and Moral Order* (2nd edition Grand Rapids and Leicester: Eerdmans and Apollo, 1994), 205.

26. James Nelson, 'The Liberal Approach to Sexual Ethics' in *From Christ to the World, op cit*, 354–8.

27. Nelson, 'The Liberal Approach to Sexual Ethics', 357.

its centre and direction in love rather than in a series of specific, absolute injunctions'.[28] Such love is honest, faithful, life-serving and joyous, and 'presses us toward a single and not a double standard for sexual morality. The same considerations apply equally to male and female, aged and young, able bodied and disabled, homosexual and heterosexual.'[29]

Similarly, Luke Johnson asks:

> What is the essence of sexual immorality? Is the moral quality of sexual behaviour defined biologically, in terms of certain body parts, or is it defined in terms of personal commitment and attitudes? Is not *porneia* essentially sexual activity that ruptures covenant, just as *castitas* is sexual virtue within or outside marriage because it is sexuality in service to covenant. If sexual virtue and vice are defined covenantally rather than biologically, then it is possible to place homosexual and heterosexual activity in the same context.[30]

And Daniel Helminiak compares the life of the Trinity with the 'ideal of relationships developing within the gay community', arguing that the 'equality among people open to one another in honest and loving relationship', which parallels the equality in God, is more readily fostered by gays, as they are able to transcend 'the limits determined by social sex-role stereotyping'.[31]

Lesbian ethicist Sarah Hoagland draws on virtue theory when she points out that rules and principles cannot guarantee good behaviour: 'they are of no use if individuals are not already acting with integrity'. Similarly, the rules themselves do not tell us how to apply them, or which rules or principles apply in a given situation. To apply principles we must have the 'ability to make judgments' (which virtue theory calls *phronesis*, practical wisdom or prudence).[32] Yet, 'much of what passes for ethics in our culture involves, not the integrity and moral capability of an individual, but rather the extent to which she participates in the structural hierarchy of an organisation by

---

28. Nelson, 'The Liberal Approach to Sexual Ethics', 357.
29. Nelson, 'The Liberal Approach to Sexual Ethics', 358.
30. Luke Johnson, 'Debate and Discernment, Scripture and the Spirit' in *Virtues and Practices in the Christian Tradition, op cit*, 215–20.
31. Daniel Helminiak, 'The Trinitarian Vocation of the Gay Community', in *Christian Perspectives on Sexuality and Gender, op cit*, 318–27.
32. Hoagland, 'Lesbian Ethics', 453–4.

adhering to its rules'.[33] She claims that traditional ethics involves rules of obligation to those higher in the hierarchy, and rules of responsibility to those lower in the hierarchy. Hence, Hoagland rejects traditional virtues: 'The ethical virtues as we know them are master/slave virtues'.[34] But her focus on moral agency, and her emphasis on 'our ability to perceive and judge' and on the 'transformations we undergo as a result of our choices—how we grow and change',[35] locate her thinking within a virtue framework.

4. Does virtue theory demand a new Christian sexual ethic?

We are now in a position to ask: Does the adoption of virtue theory demand a major revision of Christian sexual ethics, such that certain sexual relationships outside of marriage, including gay and lesbian relationships, must be accepted as morally appropriate? Do virtues such as fidelity, love, friendship, honesty, integrity and authenticity justify certain actions which have previously been regarded as wrong because they breach certain moral principles?

4.1 Naked virtue?

The first thing to be clear about is that there is no such thing as naked virtue— all virtues take their shape and content from their context. For example, the virtue of courage takes a different form in different contexts. For Aristotle it was exemplified by willingness to die in battle, but for Aquinas, it was exemplified in martyrdom. For Hauerwas, a pacifist, Aristotle's account of courage cannot be normative, and 'in fact, from a Christian point of view may not be courage at all but rather can only be a semblance of courage or even may be demonic'.[36] Similarly the meaning of virtues like honesty or fidelity is not self-evident. There is no such thing as generic integrity or generic love. Indeed, there is no such thing as a generic virtue theory any more than there is a generic deontological theory. The theory gives us a method of analysis, but its content must be specified. Just as a deontologist uses principles derived from either the Scriptures or from Kant, or some other source of authority, so application of virtue theory similarly requires an independent authority to give content in the form of an account of the good life.

---

33. Hoagland, 'Lesbian Ethics', 455.
34. Hoagland, 'Lesbian Ethics', 455.
35. Hoagland, 'Lesbian Ethics', 456.
36. Stanley Hauerwas, 'The Difference of Virtue and the Difference it Makes: Courage Exemplified', *Modern Theology*, 9 (July 1993): 249–64.

Virtue ethics claims that 'goodness is prior to rightness'. This is in contrast to the view that goodness is derived from notions of rightness, themselves derived from moral principles or rules. But where does our notion of goodness come from? It must be grounded in an independent account of human flourishing (a vision of the ideal life for human beings and communities).[37] Of course, there are any number of competing accounts of human flourishing in our world. Both what counts as a virtue, and the shape that virtue takes, will be very different depending on which account one adopts. So, as Hauerwas says, 'all virtue theories are not created equal'. How the virtues are specified differs from one tradition to another.[38]

4.2 Liberal virtues?

The Christian tradition asserts that the only true account of human flourishing on which to ground our concept of goodness is indeed independent of humans, being revealed by God and reflecting God's own character. But the dominant ideology in Western society—liberal individualism—rejects the promotion of any commonly held concept of the good life or any shared vision of human flourishing.[39] This means that liberalism should be unable to sustain any virtues. However, there is a deep and largely unresolved ambiguity within liberalism in that, paradoxically, the rejection of a common conception of goodness elevates the values of choice and independence of mind[40] and necessitates the strong promotion of individual autonomy (self-rule) as a central moral and political ideal. Hence individual autonomy, together with sincerity and authenticity, may be said to constitute the cardinal virtues of liberalism.[41]

Libertarianism seems to be unavoidable in liberal societies, as obedience to any external rules of morality is regarded as infantile,[42] with the exception of the principle of respect for the autonomy of others. And within the liberal tradition the common criticism of virtue theory, that it can give no guidance in moral decision-making, may well be justified. Moral deliberation without an

---

37. Oakley, 'Varieties of Virtue Ethics', 11.
38. Hauerwas, 'Courage Exemplified', 260.
39. Stephen Macedo, *Liberal Virtues* (Oxford: Clarendon Press, 1990), 253.
40. Stanley Hauerwas and Charles Pinches, *Christians among the Virtues: Theological Conversations with Ancient and Modern Ethics* (Notre Dame: University of Notre Dame Press, 1997), 130.
41. Gilbert Meilaender, *The Theory and Practice of Virtue* (Notre Dame: University of Notre Dame Press, 1984)
42. Patrick Nowell-Smith, cited in Hauerwas and Pinches *Christians among the Virtues*, 130.

independent account of human flourishing becomes a kind of self-interpretation[43]—what is true to my character? An example of this is Nelson's claim that 'more basic than any particular acts, sexual sin is alienation from our divinely intended sexuality . . . alienation within and from the sexual self'[44], and that love 'expresses one's own authentic self-affirmation'.[45] The virtue of integrity offered by liberalism is reducible to personal autonomy and authenticity, and comes close to subjectivism—that what makes an action right or wrong is that someone believes it is right or wrong for her, because it is in accord with her character. Thus lesbian ethicist Sarah Hoagland seems to mean by 'integrity' simply 'the ability to make choices and act'.[46] Such a virtue may not be naked but it is very thinly clothed.

Liberal individualism is not confined to secular ethicists. Theological liberalism shares with political liberalism the Enlightenment attitudes of open mindedness, tolerance, respect for the individual, optimism about human nature, and freedom from tradition.[47] In particular, it involves a privileging of the authority of reason and experience (often invoking modern science) over the moral authority of Scripture and church teaching. Such liberalism has infiltrated much of Protestant, and some Roman Catholic sexual ethics. Sometimes this is explicit, as in the work of James Nelson, who distinguishes between 'a theology of (or about) sexuality', and sexual theology. The former, he claims, has 'assumed essentially a one-way question: what does Christian theology (or the Bible, or the church's tradition) say about human sexuality?' The latter approach, which he endorses, and which comes from liberation theologies, including feminist, gay and lesbian writers, asks as well, ' What does our experience as sexual human beings say about the ways in which we experience God, interpret our religious tradition, and attempt to live the life of faith?'[48]

Nelson claims that in his method 'the concern becomes two directional, dialogical and not monological'. However in practice, those who adopt a sexual theology approach often privilege experience over the Scriptures. As

---

43. O'Donovan, *Resurrection and Moral Order*, 215.
44. Nelson, 'The Liberal Approach to Sexual Ethics', 355.
45. Nelson, 'The Liberal Approach to Sexual Ethics', 358.
46. Hoagland, 'Lesbian Ethics', 455.
47. Michael Alsford and Sally Alsford, 'Liberalism, Theological' in *New Dictionary of Christian Ethics and Pastoral Theology*, edited by David Atkinson and David Field (Downer's Grove, Illinois: Inter Varsity Press, 1995), 552.
48. Nelson, 'The Liberal Approach to Sexual Ethics', 354.

such, sexual theology belongs to the family of praxis theology, which reads
the Scriptures through the situation in the world. So, Elizabeth Stuart writes
that:

> Christian lesbian feminists have no hesitation or
> embarrassment in simply rejecting the biblical and
> traditional prescriptions on homosexuality as wrong and
> non-authoritative, because in the experience of lesbian
> women these precepts, if taken seriously, create brokenness
> rather than wholeness, inequality rather than mutuality,
> injustice rather than justice.[49]

Christians who are committed to standing under the authority of Scripture,
while recognising that all reading of the text takes place within a concrete
historical and cultural situation, regard as problematic the imposition of any
ideological framework on the text, or the use of hermeneutical principles
derived from such a framework to critique the text. Rather, it is the text which
should critique our situation and any ideological framework.

4.3 MacIntyre and moral practices

The whole concept of virtue is problematic within liberalism because the
development of virtue takes place within a community of moral friends, those
who share a thick (that is, contentful) concept of the good. Indeed, the thesis
of MacIntyre's *After Virtue* is that post-Enlightenment moral argument is
incoherent and unsustainable. The only way forward is a return to Aristotelian
virtue ethics. MacIntyre's own version is constructed around four central
concepts: **virtue**, **practice**, **narrative** and **tradition**. MacIntyre does not relate
virtues to life in general, but to specific moral practices. A moral practice is
defined as:

> any coherent and complex form of socially established
> cooperative human activity through which goods internal to
> that form of activity are realised in the course of trying to
> achieve those standards of excellence which are appropriate
> to, and partially definitive of, that form of activity.[50]

---

49. Stuart, 'Lesbian and Gay relationships', 302.
50. MacIntyre, *After Virtue*, 187.

'Internal' goods means goods which cannot be achieved in any other way than by engaging in the practice, and which 'can only be identified and recognised by the experience of participating in the practice in question'.[51]

MacIntyre then defines a virtue in relation to a practice and its internal goods:

> A virtue is an acquired human quality the possession and exercise of which tends to enable us to achieve those goods which are internal to practices and the lack of which effectively prevents us from achieving any such goods.[52]

But virtues and practices themselves can only be understood within a wider context. Neither what qualifies as a practice, nor the virtues of a particular practice can be specified without reference to the narrative which make sense of actions within the unity of each human life. So Aquinas held that charity (love of or friendship for God) is the form of all the virtues, and without it any other virtue is only a false likeness to a genuine virtue.[53] Neither can virtues be specified without reference to a broader tradition of moral enquiry. The narrative of an individual's life is embedded in the narratives of the communities from which she derives her identity.[54] It is the narratives of a community which shape a tradition; MacIntyre defines a tradition as 'an historically extended, socially embodied argument, and an argument precisely in part about the goods which constitute the tradition'.[55] Traditions are not abstract, but embodied in communities of moral friends with shared narratives. They are not static, but develop over time through the reflection and argument of these moral friends. Only people with a shared narrative, who have a common conception of the good, can argue coherently. Hence liberalism while it may be called a tradition in a social and cultural sense is not a tradition of moral enquiry since it lacks the conceptual resources to generate a coherent moral system.[56]

---

51. MacIntyre, *After Virtue*, 189.
52. MacIntyre, *After Virtue*, 191.
53. Hauerwas, 'Courage Exemplified', 256.
54. MacIntyre, *After Virtue*, 221.
55. MacIntyre, *After Virtue*, 222.
56. Alasdair MacIntyre, 'A Partial Response to my Critics', in *After MacIntyre: Critical Perspectives on the Work of Alasdair MacIntyre,* edited by John Horton and Susan Mendus (Cambridge: Polity Press, 1994), 283–304.

4.4 Whose marriage, which sexuality?

This paraphrase of *Whose Justice? Which Rationality?*[57] (MacIntyre's sequel to *After Virtue*) reminds us that an understanding of both the practice of marriage and the meaning of sexuality depends on one's location within a particular tradition, and which narrative shapes that tradition. The narrative which pre-eminently shapes Christian virtues and practices is the story of God's dealings with his people in the Scriptures. Indeed, the Christian tradition claims that narrative is not only the story of a particular community, the church, but a story about humankind and its relationship to ultimate reality[58]—a meta narrative which claims to be true for all people, for all communities. We are now in a position to ask, which practices in relation to human sexuality are shaped by and coherent within this narrative, and which corresponding virtues do they require? This is a very different project from that of identifying certain virtues (naked or thinly clothed) such as honesty, fidelity or love, and claiming that the presence of these virtues is sufficient justification for certain practices. The moral practices in relation to sexuality which are shaped by liberalism are different to those shaped by the Christian tradition, and their correlative virtues are specified very differently.

5. Sexual practices within the Christian tradition

5.1 Marriage

The foundation for a Christian understanding of sexuality and marriage comes from the creation and fall narrative in Genesis 1–3. Sexuality, the differentiation of male and female, is fundamental to being human, reflects our creation in the image of God, and is good (Genesis 1:27). But this does not mean that all varieties of sexual expression are good. The sexual practice which is ordained by God is marriage, a one flesh union between a man and a woman (Genesis 2:24). In his radical interpretation of this passage, Jesus affirmed that marriage is to be life-long and monogamous: 'So they are no longer two, but one flesh. Therefore what God has joined together, let no one separate' (Matthew 19:6).

The image of God is not reflected in either male or female alone but in male and female together (Genesis 1:27). This complementarity is also expressed in the statement that it is not good for the man to be alone, and that

---

57. Alasdair MacIntyre, *Whose Justice? Which Rationality?* (Notre Dame: University of Notre Dame Press, 1988)

58. Richard Mouw, *The God Who Commands* (Notre Dame: University of Notre Dame Press, 1990), 122.

the woman is an appropriate, complementary partner for him (Genesis 2:18-23). Although Matzko claims that the notion of male/female complementarity is a theological innovation, a '"stopgap measure" against homosexuality'[59], it is clear from the biblical text that it is a constitutive element of marriage. After the woman has been created and recognised as the same ('bone of my bones') yet different, the text continues 'therefore a man leaves his father and his mother and clings to his wife, and they become one flesh', thus inextricably linking the practice of marriage to male/female complementarity. A man marries a woman *because* he and she are complementary. That theologians have been slow to understand this is hardly surprising given the misogyny of the Christian tradition up until the second half of the twentieth century. As the texts dealing with the equality of women have been re-examined and in some cases 'rediscovered', so the biblical notion of marriage as partnership between two different but equal people, a 'unity in diversity', has emerged, in addition to an understanding of the truly complementary roles of women and men in church leadership.

Robert Williams, one writer who urges that the church should recognise homosexual as well as heterosexual marriages without distinction, is honest enough to admit that it would need to be grounded in a quite different narrative, an alternative to the 'Genesis creation myth'. Plato's *Symposium* contains the story of human beings who were created as doubles, with four arms, four legs and two heads. Some of these original double human beings were male/male, some female/female and some male/female. They were split in half by the gods because of their arrogance, leaving 'each half with a desperate longing for the other'. Williams claims that this story is 'in many ways, more accurate and certainly more humane than most Christian theologies'.[60] He recognises that the biblical narrative simply cannot support the concept of homosexual 'marriage'.

Another attempt to justify different sexual practices does use the biblical narrative. From the description of man and woman in Eden as 'naked and not ashamed' (Genesis 2:25), Karen Lebacqz argues that as well as procreation and one flesh union (the proper context for which is marriage), sexuality has a third 'redemptive purpose'—appropriate vulnerability. This 'basic intention for human life, which may be experienced in part through the gift of sexuality . . . is the precondition for both procreation and one flesh union', but may be

59. Matzko, 'Homosexuality and the Practices of Marriage', 383.

60. Robert Williams, 'Toward a Theology for Lesbian and Gay Marriage', in *Christian Perspectives on Sexuality and Gender, op cit*, 79–300.

separated from them. This means that sexual intercourse may be appropriate in some relationships between single people, homosexual or heterosexual.[61] But it is artificial to abstract this one aspect (vulnerability) from the other features of the relationship of the man and woman. Further, the statement that the man and woman were 'naked and not ashamed' does not refer only or primarily to sexuality but to the intimacy and unbroken fellowship of the first couple with each other and with God. It serves as a prologue to the events about to unfold in chapter 3 when this fellowship was shattered. Then they knew they were naked and were ashamed (they hid from God) and afraid.

There are many goods associated with the practice of marriage which vary from one historical and cultural context to another. These include social stability, sexual pleasure, romance, companionship, and economic security. But according to the biblical narrative, there are only three internal goods, goods intrinsic to the practice of marriage, and these are complementarity (Genesis 2:18), procreation (Genesis 1:28)[62] and one flesh union (Genesis 2:24) where sexual intercourse symbolises the relational bond of those who are no longer two but one. Similarly there are many virtues required for a good marriage, but two are essential: chastity and fidelity. Chastity has often been understood in a narrow and restrictive way, as abstinence from forbidden sexual acts. But it refers more broadly to the morally responsible exercise of human sexuality.[63] One aspect of the virtue of chastity in marriage is openness to procreation.[64] 'Because this is a virtue, it is a disposition which relates to married life viewed in its totality rather than as series of unrelated sexual acts each and every one of which must be open to procreation.'[65]

Fidelity in a minimalist or proscriptive sense, is sexual exclusivity.[66] But this is to treat fidelity as simply the expression of a rule, 'Do not commit adultery'. Fidelity is much more than this, although it would be a mistake to suppose that there is no place in virtue ethics for rules at all. In MacIntyre's

---

61. Lebacqz, ' Appropriate Vulnerability', 131–3.
62. I distinguish here between procreation and reproduction, which may occur in the context of other sexual relationships, or apart from them (as in artificial reproductive technologies) or even asexually, through reproductive cloning (currently only possible in certain animals but theoretically possible in the future for humans).
63. JH Olthuis, 'Chastity' in *New Dictionary of Christian Ethics and Pastoral Theology*, 223.
64. O'Donovan, *Resurrection and Moral Order*, 210.
65. O'Donovan, *Resurrection and Moral Order*, 210.
66. Catherine Wallace, *For Fidelity: How Intimacy and Commitment Enrich our Lives*, (New York: Alfred A. Knopf Inc., 1998), 13.

scheme, some rules are necessary for practices to be possible at all.[67] For example, the practice of playing chess is constituted by certain rules, but playing well requires certain skills or virtues. 'No adultery' is a rule which constitutes the practice of marriage in general, but Christian marriage may be distinguished from marriage in general, and requires the virtue of fidelity.[68] According to Lewis Smedes, 'The Christian concept of fidelity is based on the model offered to us by the marriage between God and his people . . . a picture of someone who makes a solemn vow to enduring partnership and whose fidelity is measured in terms of his creative love for his partner'.[69] Within marriage two people care for each other's total welfare. 'Each is dedicated to the growth, healing, pleasure and freedom of the other'.[70]

The narrative of the fall tells us that sexual relationships now are warped by sin. Instead of equality, there is domination of the woman by the man, and procreation becomes subject to pain and difficulties (Genesis 3:16). The Apostle Paul sees homosexual behaviour as one consequences of God giving up rebellious creatures to their own futile thinking and desires: it is one of the symptoms of the underlying sickness of turning away from God (Romans 1:18–32). Homosexual behaviour is *para physin* (contrary to nature) not in the sense of an individual acting contrary to his or her 'natural' sexual orientation, (which would be anachronistic since Paul knew nothing of sexual orientation and only ever speaks of homosexual acts), but in the sense that it is a distortion of the created order, where male and female are differentiated and complementary.[71]

5.2 Celibacy

Marriage is the only moral practice constituted by the Old Testament in relation to sexuality. 'It is not good that the man should be alone' (Genesis 2:18) so woman is created. But in the New Testament we find Paul saying to the unmarried and the widows, 'it is well for them to remain unmarried as I am' (1 Corinthians 7:8). Paul personally prefers celibacy, but affirms that both

---

67. Nancey Murphy, 'Using MacIntyre's Method in Christian Ethics', in *Virtues and Practices in the Christian Tradition, op cit*, 39.

68. Murphy, 'Using MacIntyre's Method in Christian Ethics', 39.

69. Lewis Smedes, *Sex for Christians* (Grand Rapids: Eerdmans, 1976), 169.

70. Lewis Smedes, 'Respect for Covenant' in *From Christ to the World, op cit*, 347–53.

71. Richard Hays, 'Awaiting the Redemption of Our Bodies' in *Virtues and Practices in the Christian Tradition, op cit*, 210.

celibacy and marriage have a legitimate place in the present age,[72] since 'each has a particular gift from God' (1 Cor 7:7). One internal good of celibacy is single minded service to God, being free from the anxieties and limitations associated with a spouse and family (1 Cor 7:32–4). John Stott reflected on his ministry: 'I began to believe that God meant me to remain single . . . Looking back, with the benefit of hindsight, I think I know why. I could never have travelled or written as extensively as I have done if I had had the responsibilities of a wife and family'.[73]

To be celibate requires the virtue of self-control, but it does not require the denial of one's sexuality. Sexuality is the desire for intimacy and community, one expression of which is sexual intercourse. To be celibate does not mean to be asexual, or to be alone. Friendship is a good for all people, but particularly important in the celibate life. [74] Single people can and should develop a wide range of intimate (non erotic) friendships with men and women.[75] Celibacy, like marriage, is a 'sub-practice within the broader constitutive Christian practice of witness'.[76] Just as fidelity in marriage witnesses to the faithfulness of God, celibacy witnesses to the eschatological hope of belonging to a community in which the fidelity and love of the marriage relationship will be extended to all believers. Marriage witnesses to the goodness of the created order, celibacy its future fulfilment. They are alternative vocations, which together comprise the whole Christian witness to the quality of loving community.[77] Celibacy, says Hauerwas, is that practice, which reminds us as the church that we live by hope, not biology. 'We believe that every Christian in one generation could be called to singleness, yet God will create the church anew'.[78]

5.3 Sexual practices within liberalism

Contentful reflection about sexual practices cannot be sustained by the moral vacuum at the heart of liberalism and so it tends to draw on alternative narratives and to borrow from the practices of law and economics. The myth

---

72. GJ Laughery, 'Paul: Anti-marriage? Anti-sex? Ascetic? A Dialogue with 1 Corinthians 7:1–40', *The Evangelical Quarterly*, 69/2 (1997): 109–28.

73. In Albert Hsu, *The Single Issue* (IVP: Leicester, 1997), 200–1.

74. Hauerwas and Pinches, *Christians among the Virtues*, 31.

75. Robin Payne, *Embracing the Single Life* (Melbourne: Acorn Press, 1994), 112–13.

76. Murphy, 'Using Macintyre's Method in Christian Ethics', 39. The other two practices of the church are worship and works of mercy.

77. O'Donovan, *Resurrection and Moral Order*, 70.

78. Stanley Hauerwas, *After Christendom?* (Nashville: Abingdon Press, 1991), 128.

of romantic love has been described as 'one of the master stories . . . of liberal, advanced, capitalistic society'.[79] This myth arose in the Middle Ages and is exemplified in the story of Tristan and Isolde, and its core elements are that true love falls on people like a spell, but it is essentially tragic in that it can only ever be realised fleetingly, clandestinely and in opposition to society. 'Quintessential love is understood as unsatisfied yearning, as desire exquisitely deprived. It cannot end in consummation or steady, unfolding fulfilment but only in death.'[80] This myth is so potent that we may be unable to shake it off, but once we recognise that it is no part of the Christian tradition, we can begin to challenge it.

In the Christian tradition, sexual relations cannot be separated from marriage but romantic love is not an essential element. In liberal sexual ethics by contrast, romantic love and sexual expression must not be separated, but marriage is not essential.[81] Marriage is, in fact, antithetical to romantic love, which requires a series of sexual relationships in the never-ending quest for fulfilment. In the sexual practices sustained by this myth, the quintessential virtue is 'commitment'. Turner calls this 'a virtue for the tentative' and a 'modern substitute for chastity', which is basically a sincere dedication to testing the quality of a relationship.[82] Since relationships tested this way will almost always be found wanting, they are of limited duration. The resulting limited trust in liberal sexual practices necessitates recourse to legal patterns of relationship—a contract may be required for even casual sexual encounters. Such practices may also be specified in the language of economics: 'It is worth noting how well the narrative of romantic love supports the ethos of advanced capitalism, which demands that the ideal consumer be perpetually frustrated and never really contented'.[83]

6. Conclusion

The adoption of a virtue theory framework does not necessitate a revision of Christian sexual ethics, so long as we are clear which tradition, which narrative, which practices and which virtues we are talking about. Liberalism

---

79. Rodney Clapp, 'From Family Values to Family Virtues', in *Virtues and Practices in the Christian Tradition*, 185–201.

80. Clapp, 'From Family Values to Family Virtues', 196–7.

81. Philip Turner, 'Excerpts from *Limited Engagements*', in *From Christ to the World, op cit*, 359.

82. Turner, 'Excerpts from *Limited Engagements*', 360.

83. Clapp, 'From Family Values to Family Virtues', 198.

sustains a number of sexual practices and speaks of a number of virtues, some of which have apparent similarities to Christian virtues. But in the Christian tradition the virtues relating to sexuality can only be specified within the practices of marriage and celibacy, which are in turn sub-practices of the church's practice of witness.

12

(Homo)Sex and the City of God

Gordon R Preece

Introduction

This concluding chapter firstly examines the homosexuality issue in the context of the disillusioned 'morning after' modernity feeling of the influential US TV show *Sex and the City*'s portrayal of postmodern sex etiquette or bed manners. It will secondly contrast this with the Augustinian City of God motif, presenting a narrative theology of homosexuality in a creation, fall and redemption framework that illuminates the mystery of sexuality. We will look at our created 'sexual ecology', our fallen condition of sexual idolatry and ideology and the redemptive possibilities of sexual therapy set within a Christian form of social construction aimed at the City of God.

Sex and the City is set in that most postmodern, exciting, and mobile city, New York. Yet New York symbolises the almost infinite consumerised desire and sexual decadence doing so much damage to so many. It also aroused the wrath of extremist Islam on 9/11. I offer an alternative, but not that of fundamentalist Islamic or some Christian fundamentalist family values moralists like Jerry Falwell who blamed New York and the US's denial of such values for 9/11. Instead, while contrasting the city of God and bride of Christ with the city or whore of Babylon, I will stress that misguided sexuality is cause not for condemnation, but compassion. Jesus memorably showed this to the woman caught in adultery—yet a compassion guided by his moral compass—'go and sin no more' (Jn 8:8). The biblical narrative of creation, fall and redemption both affirms and critiques our sexuality and points us to true north in the City of God.

1. Sex and the City

Sex and the City is based on a book by columnist Candace Bushnell. It follows Carrie, a sex columnist or sexual anthropologist and her observations of New York's sexual mores. It is based on her own, and her successful, smart, thirty-something friends', largely fruitless search for meaningful sexual relationships. Each is sadly unsuccessful, each fills the empty hole in their heart in their own way. 'Sexy Samantha, who is in PR, sleeps with pretty much anyone [and does just about anything]; Miranda the lawyer dallies with a man with whom the sex is great but whom she will definitely not marry; Charlotte, the art gallery buyer, is Ivy League, somewhat preppie and, relatively speaking, inhibited'.[1]

Carrie's provocative prone advertising pose bears the caption: 'Carrie Bradshaw knows good sex'—without a hint there might be a theological or ethical, not merely aesthetic or technical, sense of 'good sex'. Carrie's friends' conversation rarely rises above the navel, but masks a poignancy and longing for love in the midst of a succession of one or several night stands. It represents the nihilistic nadir of the modern romantic myth as shown in the following excerpt from the programmatic first episode.

An attractive young Englishwoman of Carrie's acquaintance arrives in New York and is wooed off her feet into a whirlwind romance with a Manhattan male. They have candlelight dinners, make love, even look at houses together before Carrie's all-knowing voice-over says:

> Then I realized, no-one had told her about the end of love in Manhattan. Welcome to the end of innocence. No-one has breakfast at Tiffany's and affairs we like to remember. Instead, we have breakfast at 7 am and affairs we try to forget as quickly as possible. Self-protection and closing the deal are paramount. Cupid has flown the coop. How the hell did we get into this mess? There are thousands and thousands of women like this in the city. They spend $400 on a pair of strappy sandals, and they're alone.[2]

A sad comment in *Sex and the City* was 'how can you believe in love at first sight in a city where a guy jerks off next to you on the subway'. Such is the postmodern, post-AIDs, post-most-divorced-generation-in-history's sense of betrayal by the modern master narrative of romantic love. Yet they keep coming back for more. All the cynicism barely covers great wistfulness.

Two themes often arise in contemporary disillusioned media romances. Firstly, many movies—such as *Four Weddings and a Funeral, My Best Friend's Wedding, American Beauty*—shift the traditional romantic tragic plot

---

1.   Mark Greene, *Of Love, Life and Cafe Latte* (London: Azure, 2000), 9.
2.   See 'Sexual Heeling: Everything you wanted to know about *Sex and the City* but were afraid to ask', *Who,* 10 February 2003, 38–42.

of star-crossed heterosexual lovers to portray women who find the best guys and relationships are gay. As Carrie's gay friend Stanford Jones says: 'You know I'm beginning to think that the only place where you can still find love and romance in New York is the gay community. Straight love has become closeted'. TV shows like *Ellen*, *Six Feet Under*, *Queer Eye for the Straight Guy* and *Queer as Folk* display fascination with, and partial idealisation of, gay relationships and stereotypically dysfunctional heterosexual marriages and families.

Secondly, in *Sex and the City* postmodern *mobility* of bourgeois bohemians, or 'bobos',[3] has been mistakenly translated into a consumerist and relativistic *morality*. This is a category mistake. Nonetheless it shows why the bedroom must not be divorced from the boardroom because the global cosmopolitan urban economy generates hyper-capitalist development of narrower market niches with attached life, spirituality and sexual styles. Think of the powerful pink dollar and the new class of sexually expressive individualism that dominates much media, arts and parts of the city and church. RR Reno, before turning Catholic, captured well the class captivity of the American Episcopalian push to marry and ordain practicing homosexuals:

> The gay lobby, while unappealing in some of its excesses, is fundamentally congenial to the sensibilities of Bourgeois Bohemians. The typical Episcopalian is not very likely to be committed to the homosexual agenda in any focused sense . . . The general relaxation of traditional sexual morality is the decisive element. The experience of many upper-class Americans [and Australians] is that it is OK to sleep around a bit—it did not destroy their lives . . . 'Hey', says the Bourgeois Bohemian, 'if we can neglect the Scriptures on matters of fornication, adultery, and divorce, then why not on homosexuality?' This helps to explain why homosexuality is so important in the Episcopal Church. It symbolizes the Bourgeois Bohemian confidence that liberated sexual practices can be prudently and wisely absorbed into a socially respectable way of life . . . Homosexuality is also important *because it* reassures . . . If homosexuality is OK, then our transgressions are OK . . .

---

3.   David Brooks, *Bobos in Paradise: The New Upper-Class and How They Got There* (New York: Simon and Schuster, 2000).

> otherwise we would have to confront the uglier sides of the
> sexual revolution and would begin to feel the necessity of
> judgments and condemnations that might threaten our happy
> marriage of sexual freedom and upper-class respectability.[4]

Contrast the largely old middle class Christian and other family-values advocates of the suburbs or 'burbos'. The split between them and sexually expressive 'bobos' is sociologically where many of our contemporary social, ethical and church conflicts brew. The elitism that despises the suburbs is rampant in our inner-cities, media circles and church social justice bureaucracies. And its hostility is returned in kind in an unedifying spectacle. As Christians our identity does not consist in our gender or social location. Neither heterosexual family values nor homosexual sexual expressivism, neither suburbs nor inner-city is to be idolatrously identified with the city of God, our ultimate end and destination. Such utopias inevitably end as dystopias, denying others entrance through the gates of the New Jerusalem.

Christian convictions about permanent commitment in sexual and family relationships are often conveniently co-opted by politicians in the UK, US and Australia, stronger on family values rhetoric than pro-family employment, tax and welfare policies. Both right-wing economic individualism's short-term contractualism and leftist sexual libertarianism undermine stable relationships and the family. Casualisation of work and sex go together. This galloping consumerist individualism is mimicked by *Sex- and- the- City*-style women from men, especially Samantha who has 'sex like a man' and leaves them floundering the next morning. Such individualism is a fair-weather philosophy only for those (temporarily) on top.

Nicholas Boyle helpfully sets postmodernity's celebration of homo-sexuality in the context of this disembodied, non-reproductive logic of global consumerism and individualism:

> Sexual preference, once detached from the process of bodily
> reproduction loses touch with the necessities and enters the
> realm of play—it becomes part of the entertainment
> industry, a choice to be catered for, but not a constraint on
> producers. Indeed, worldwide consumerism makes use of
> homosexuality as a means of eliminating the political
> constraints which regulate our role as producers: if marriage

---

4. RR Reno, *In the Ruins of the Church* (Grand Rapids: Brazos Press, 2002), 116–18 using Brooks.

is redefined as a long-term affective partnership, so that it may be either homosexual or heterosexual, the essentially reproductive nature of male and female bodies is no longer given institutional (and therefore political) expression. Bodies are seen as the locus only of consumption, not of production . . . [5]

Compare D Stephen Long, who relativises Victor Paul Furnish's representative relativising of all scriptural standards as time and culture bound.

His apologia for gay unions is easily construed as reflecting the dominance of exchange values in late capitalist culture, where what a thing is (male or female body) has no bearing on its 'values', but how it is exchanged through what the will wants (orientation or preference) gives it its value.[6]

Sociologist Richard Sennett further shows how the inroads of individualism and the cracking of capitalism's moral and spiritual base are exacerbated in our increasingly placeless and virtual global economy. The rapid turnover of jobs and consequent mobility causes what he calls *The Corrosion of Character*[7]—an erosion of vocational, locational and familial loyalty, even for the previously stable middle class. 'The global economy does not "grow" personal skills, durable purposes, social trust, loyalty, or commitment' in his view.[8] This is true whether we inhabit the world of *Sex and the City* or the suburbs.

Sennett recognises that neither private family values, nor the sexual liberation that his gay friend Michel Foucault sought, are enough to snatch back sexual relationships from the grasp of public economic individualism

---

5. Nicholas Boyle, *Who Are We Now? Christian Humanism and the Global Market from Hegel to Heaney* (Notre Dame: University of Notre Dame Press, 1998), 59.

6. D Stephen Long *The Goodness of God: Theology, the Church, and Social Order* (Grand Rapids: Brazos, 2001), 207, see also 202–18.

7. Richard Sennett *The Corrosion of Character: The Personal Consequences of Work in the New Capitalism* (New York: WW Norton, 1998).

8. Richard Sennett, 'The New Political Economy', *Echoes*, 1/3 (Winter 1997): 15. See also Max L Stackhouse, 'General Introduction' to his and Peter J Paris, editors, *Religion and the Powers of the Common Life*, volume 1, *Of God and Globalization* (Harrisburg, Pennsylvania: Trinity Press International, 2000).

and mobility. As he says, 'If liberating the body from Victorian sexual constraints was a great event in modern culture, this liberation also entailed the narrowing of physical sensibility to sexual desire'. The physical sensuality of the city is increasingly reduced to the sexual as compensation for urban ugliness. Sennett's book *Flesh and Stone* shows how bodies are not merely natural, but are also microcosms of the macrocosm of the city and the socio-political visions it embodies, whether in Greco-Roman, Enlightenment, postmodern or Christian form. The 'Heavenly City' of the Enlightenment sought absolute bodily autonomy, freedom from suffering and freedom for economic goods to pass unimpeded through empty space. In contrast a Christian view of the body's goodness, but insufficiency, its pain and exile, in need of God and others, can nurture an alternative vision of sexual relationships and the city as a public place in pilgrimage to the City of God.[9] That vision—joining the personal and political, the body physical and body politic—is provided by the biblical and Augustinian narrative of the City of God, to which we now turn.

2. The City of God: the true story of our sexuality

Augustine's *City of God* was written in the early fifth century AD at a time of barbarism within and without Rome. It was written to a Roman imperial age, not dissimilar to our own American imperial age, of sexual decadence and frenetic restlessness symptomatic of the decay of Western civilization.[10] *Sex and the City* is truest when Carrie confesses herself 'restless'. Compare EL Doctorow's recent New York novel about a spiritually and sexually restless Episcopalian priest, entitled *City of God*.[11] Both are reminders of Augustine's sexually and spiritually restless pre-Christian state described famously in his

---

9. R Sennett, *Flesh and Stone: the Body and the City in Western Civilization* (New York: WW Norton, 1994), 370–6 on 'Civic Bodies' and chapter 5 and especially 26–7. See also Peter Brown, *The Body and Society: Men, Women, and Sexual Renunciation in Early Christianity* (New York: Columbia University Press, 1988), chapter 1 on 'Body and City' and chapters 15, 19 and Epilogue. Compare also Pierre Manet, *The City of Man*, translated by Marc A Le Pain (Princeton University Press, 1998) and Carl E Braaten and Robert W Jenson, editors, *The Two Cities of God: The Church's Responsibility for the Earthly City* (Grand Rapids: Eerdmans, 1997) and Carl L Becker, *The Heavenly City of the Eighteenth-Century Philosophers* (1932).

10. See Patrick Riley, *Civilising Sex: On Chastity and the Common Good* (Edinburgh: T and T Clark, 2000), chapter 4 and Eva Cantarella, *Bisexuality in the Ancient World* (New Haven: Yale University Press, 1992) chapter 8.

11. EL Doctorow, *The City of God* (London: Little Brown and Co, 2000).

Confessions as 'lord make me chaste, but not yet' and 'Lord we are restless until we find our rest in Thee'. Augustine restlessly tried and discarded many ancient philosophies and lifestyles.

Augustine's Christian legacy is partly ambiguous. Witness his pessimism, his occasional confusion of sin (concupiscence, or disordered desire) and sex, his over-valuation of virginity and of procreation compared with companionship in marriage. Yet he has been scapegoated for all the ills of the Western theological tradition. None of the above denies his profound understanding of sexuality in its created, fallen and redeemed reality.[12] Augustine's attempt at discerning the goodness of the created order, the body and its gendered destiny in resurrection in *The City of God*,[13] shows how far he has put his neo-Platonic and Manichean dualism behind him with its devilish denial of the goodness of the body, sex and marriage for the grandeur of being 'created to embrace the material world'.[14]

Despite some of the Augustinian tradition's ambiguities on sexuality, today's 'naked public square'[15] needs re-clothing, not in the romantic myths of modernity, discredited by *Sex and the City*, but in the biblical and Augustinian narrative of the City of God. This story, with its realistic and prophetic vision of the future city or polity of God,[16] out-narrates all other stories of utopian cities and sexual freedom without consequence. The story of the City of God can transform the earthly city as it did when it inspired Christendom (but minus its coercive and repressive features), the best of early liberal modernity,[17] and some of the world's most urbane cities or public places.[18]

---

12. Michael Banner, *Christian Ethics and Contemporary Moral Problems* (Cambridge University Press, 1999), 25–6. See also 297–307.

13. Augustine, *City of God*, translated by H Bettenson (London: Pelican Books,1972) especially xiv; see also: xxii, 17.

14. Brown, *The Body and Society*, 425.

15. Richard John Neuhaus, *The Naked Public Square: Religion and Democracy in America* (Grand Rapids: Eerdmans, 1984).

16. Robert Jenson, 'Toward a Christian Theory of the Public,' in *Essays in Theology of Culture* (Grand Rapids: Eerdmans, 1995), 142 notes that 'a polity is, indeed, the institutionalization of an eschatology'.

17. See Oliver O'Donovan's seminal *The Desire of the Nations: Rediscovering the Roots of Political Theology* (Cambridge: Cambridge University Press, 1996), 275–6 and see also 226–30.

18. See Ian Barns, 'Another City: Theology and the Ecology of Urban Life', *St Mark's Review*, 181 (Autumn 2000): 3–10, and William T Cavanagh, 'The City: Beyond

2.1 Created order: sexual ecology

The created order, provides, in postmodern-speak, the pattern of our sexual *ecology*. We are gradually rediscovering our natural ecology, that everything is connected and has ecological consequences, from the butterfly flapping its wings in Cairns to the hurricane in Florida. It is ironic, then, that even the most left and green assume that somehow our humanity and sexuality stands outside this natural order in a subjective, consumerist erogenous zone of pure choice.

By sexual ecology, I mean that creation is in *kinds* or species (Gen 1) not just in our *minds*. This contrasts strongly with the tragic recent Australian case of 'Kevin', a female to male transsexual, lacking male genitalia, whose marriage to 'Jennifer' has been recognised by the Family Court because 'Kevin' has been living as a male for several years and *perceives* himself and *is perceived by society* as male.[19] This ruling capitulates to a Gnostic and Alice-in-Wonderland-like social constructionist view of sexuality. A word like 'man' in the marriage act can now mean 'just what I choose it to mean,' according to Humpty Dumpty. Thus our own personally or socially produced biography trumps biology. As masters of the universe, we make up our own personal master-narratives. Oliver O'Donovan supports an English judge's verdict against the validity of an alleged marriage in a similar case, saying this leaves our gender floating above our biological sex like oil on water.[20] The Australian Government contested (but lost) the case on the grounds that 'marriage' in the Marriage Act means people of the opposite biological sex (including, normally, reproductive potential), not just social gender. The ruling opened the way for homosexual marriage. The government promptly closed the loophole, with agreement of the Labor Opposition, by making the implicit and assumed opposite sex nature of 'marriage' in the Marriage Act explicit.

Gordon Watson rightly takes the Australian Uniting Church Assembly's Sexuality Task Group to task for making the same subjective, solipsistic, and social constructionist mistake. They urge 'that we must understand relationships in the Christian *koinonia* in terms of each individual's self-

---

Secular Parodies,' chapter 9 in *Radical Orthodoxy*, edited by J Milbank, C Pickstock and G Ward (London: Routledge, 1999) which compare favourably with Graham Ward's sexual constructionism. See Graham Ward *Cities of God* (London: Routledge, 2000), 177–200.

19. Shown on ABC TV's *Australian* Story, 31 March 2003 as background to their transsexual lawyer's story.

20. Oliver O'Donovan *Transsexualism* (Bramcote: Grove, 1982), 6. Judge Ormrod presided in *Corbett v Corbett,* 1970.

understanding', that is, 'perceived sexual orientation'. The church is to adopt the homosexual person's sexual self-understanding as an expression of compassion or unconditional acceptance. But this is compassion without a moral compass. 'God's "compassion", at great cost, recreates the creature as a creature'. Based on Gen 1:26–8's depiction of the image of God reflected or represented in our biological male and femaleness, Watson states that the argument 'for legitimating homosexuality as a complementary Christian lifestyle or sexual orientation in fact breaks the co-humanity of the human species as male and female and creates another species called homosexual'.[21]

This created order or 'structured being (ordered ontology)'[22] includes the basic *difference* or *otherness* (also postmodern terms), or more conventionally, *complementarity* of male and female. This is designed so we image or represent God, to each other relationally and sexually, and to creation through responsible rule (Gen 1:26–8) and care (Gen 2). Homosexual practice is therefore wrong because it is a sexist (yet another postmodernism) rejection of that basic difference, and an overturning of the created order, exchanging natural relations for unnatural ones (Rom 1:26–7ff.).

Some argue against this that God's image refers to our intellectual, moral and spiritual similarity to God expressed in undifferentiated loving relationships. Therefore if homosexual relationships are loving (and monogomous) they are to be approved and recognised by marriage. However Ray Anderson, building on Karl Barth, critiques Emil Brunner's advocacy of this more vague view of God's image as expressed in I-thou relationships. Anderson and Barth show that God's image is spelt out specifically in terms of male and female biological and sexual differentiation. Diagram 2 below reflects Brunner's now common contemporary view of the moral and spiritual image not overlapping with biological sexual difference. Contrast Barth's view of this overlap in Diagram 1 which also better reflects the diversity of the

---

21. Gordon Watson, 'The "Compassion" of God as a Basis for Christian Ethical Claims', in Murray A Rae and Graham Redding, editors, *More than a Single Issue* (Hindmarsh: Australian Theological Forum, 2000), 245–6, 250. Watson adds: 'The homosexual relationship cannot in principle be an image of such a compassionate relationship as is established by God in Christ's relationship with the Church [compared to marriage, for instance (Gen 2, Eph 5:21ff)], since it presupposes a relationship of *like to like* (that is, *homo*). The relationship of Christ to the church, however, is not one of *like to like* (250–1)'.

22. Ray S Anderson, 'Homosexuality and the Ministry of the Church: Theological and Pastoral Considerations', *More than a Single Issue*, edited by Rae and Redding, 61.

three persons within the unity of the Trinity. Eve's creation was more than a cloning of Adam for Genesis. As Anderson summarises Barth, 'the solitariness of Adam would not have been overcome by another male for such a one could not confront him as 'another' but he would only recognise himself in it . . .' Consequently, Barth condemned homosexual practice as 'humanity without the fellow man'.[23]

Diagram 1: Brunner's Dualistic Biological versus Personal View

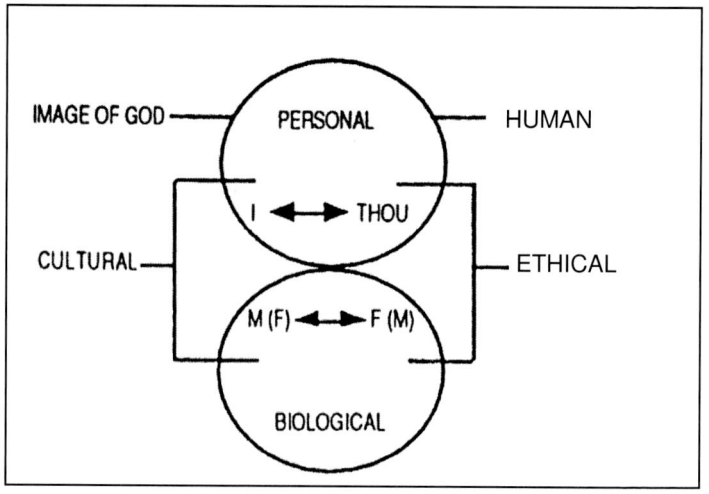

---

23. Anderson, 'Homosexuality', 58–62 citing Karl Barth, *Church Dogmatics* III/4 (Edinburgh: T and T Clark, 1961), 166.

Diagram 2: Barth's Integrated Biological–Personal View

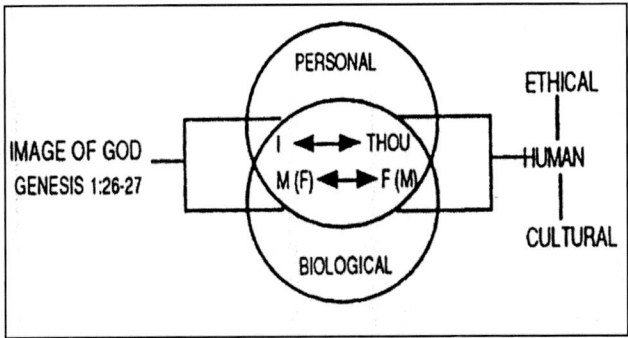

Further, creation comes not only in differentiated kinds in a static or non-evolving way but also with God-given *ends* or purposes built in.[24] These include particular purposes. So, for example, a knife is made to cut; humans are made to be kind; sexuality is for companionship, sexual satisfaction and procreation and as preparation for the loving, universal relationships of the City of God.

A secondary reason for rejecting homosexual practice (not persons) is that it is fruitless or non-procreational, frustrating part of the natural purpose of our bodily sexuality as Greco-Roman natural law recognises. But Genesis 2:23 does not mention procreation as primary. Adam cries with joy: 'This at last is bone of my bones and flesh of my flesh; she shall be called Woman, for from man she was taken'. Adam doesn't say; 'This at last is big hips for child-bearing and big breasts for child-feeding!' Nor does Paul mention procreation as his main reason for rejection of homosexual practice in Romans 1:24–7, even though it was an urgent imperative in ancient society and soon will be in many Western societies with less than replacement population rates.

This basic idea of sexual ecology (though not the rejection of homosexual practice) was supported recently by gay health activist Gabriell Rotello's book entitled *Sexual Ecology*. He bravely challenges various gay myths which are killing gays especially: 'the pervasive myth that humans have somehow transcended the limits of the biological world'. Rotello argues that:

---

24. Following Oliver O'Donovan 'The Natural Ethic,' in *Essays in Evangelical Social Ethics*, edited by DF Wright (Exeter: Paternoster Press, 1979), 19–25.

the highly selective spread of HIV around the world shows
that AIDS is . . . an ecological epidemic that exploits certain
behaviors, chief among them the practice of having large
numbers of partners, straight or gay [and] the single riskiest
sexual practice of all: anal sex.[25]

While recognising some usefulness of safe sex campaigns and condoms,
Rotello rightly challenges sole reliance on 'the condom code' as 'anti-
ecological', a classic 'technological fix'. The church and wider community
have relied on consequences alone for too long.[26] Rotello's argument is
'rooted not in traditional morality, but implacable biology'. But unless the
moral and biological are arbitrarily separated, the logic of his argument leads
towards a moral version of sexual ecology or 'moral ecology'.[27] In this way,
Rotello's logic supports my argument that biology and ecology back up the
Bible. God's two books, Scripture and nature, in that order, agree.

2.1.1. Knowing creation/nature

Well before postmodernity, Emil Brunner recognised this created ecology:
'the world is not a shapeless mass of matter, it is not a chaos which we have to
reduce to form and order. It was formed long ago . . . in a rich variety of form
. . . In its form the will of God is stamped upon that which exists'.[28] The
world is a God-shaped cosmos, for Brunner, not a chaos awaiting us to redraw
the sexual wheel.

Yet how do we discern what is divine order and what is human disorder?
Michel Foucault claims that notions of natural and unnatural are historically,
socio-culturally and politically constructed and that almost any cultural and
institutional configuration of pleasure can be constructed and depicted as
natural.[29] Theological 'postmodernists', like Stanley Hauerwas, rightly note

---

25. Gabriell Rotello, *Sexual Ecology: Aids and the Destiny of Gay Men* (London:
    Plume, 1998), 188.
26. Rotello, *Sexual Ecology*, 8–10, 187. Though consequences do have a rightful place
    in Patrick Dixon, *The Rising Price of Love: The True Cost of the Sexual
    Revolution* (London: Hodder and Stoughton, 1995).
27. See Michael Novak, 'Awakening from Nihilism,' *First Things* (August/September
    1994): 18–22 and *The Catholic Ethic and the Spirit of Capitalism* (New York: Free
    Press, 1993), 215–37. See also, John Paul II, *Centesimus Annus*, number 50.
28. Emil Brunner, *The Divine Imperative* (London: Lutterworth Press, 1937), 124–5.
29. Michel Foucault, *History of Sexuality*, volume 1, Introduction (New York: Vintage
    Books, 1980), 105. See also JJ Winkler, *The Constraints of Desire* (London:
    Routledge, 1990), 17.

that 'appeals to creation too often amount to legitimating strategies for the principalities and powers that determine our lives', leading us to project our present 'twilight of good and evil' onto the canvas/screen of creation.[30] They cite the misuse of the doctrine of the orders of creation to justify Nazi racism and by some contemporary Christians to justify sexism or homophobia.

This misuse of arguments from nature has led to the near rejection of creation as part of the Christian master-narrative or the idea of a master narrative at all, as justifying the mastery of some over others.[31] Yet James Gustafson correctly sees Hauerwas abandoning the distinction between right use and abuse of nature. Thus: 'Nature is . . . of no ethical significance as a source of direction in Hauerwas's ethics. Hauerwas becomes a twentieth-century version of Marcion'.[32] Similarly, much postmodern theology is now 'an Omega that has no Alpha', an end without a beginning.[33] The contemporary social location of such views can be found among the sexually expressive urban elites or cosmopolitan new middle class who can choose who, when, and where to relate to, and how. Sociologist David Reisman anticipated their looking down on 'the provinciality of being born to a particular family in a particular place [and looking forward to the desired time] when ties based on *conscious relatedness* would replace those of blood and soil'.[34]

Yesterday's sociology, often justifying a particular academic and social location, regularly becomes today's theology. Liberal Catholic theologian JJ

---

30. Stanley Hauerwas, *Dispatches from the Front: Theological Engagements with the Secular* (Durham, North Carolina: Duke University Press, 1994), 111. Despite Hauerwas' disavowal of the label 'postmodernist', he is so here.

31. See Pim Pronk, *Against Nature: Types of Moral Argumentation* (Grand Rapids: Eerdmans, 1993).

32. J Gustafson, 'A Response to Critics,' *Journal of Religious Ethics,* 13 (1985): 191 cited in Banner, *Christian Ethics*, 20 who notes Gustafson should speak more theologically of 'creation' not 'nature'. Despite Hauerwas' *With the Grain of the Universe: The Church's Witness and Natural Theology* (London: SCM, 2002) he still, like Barth, confuses our subjective epistemological difficulty of accessing the created order and its objective ontology. Thus Hauerwas is ambivalent about homosexual practice in 'Capitalism' and 'Why Gays (as a group) are Morally Superior to Christians (as a group)', in Hauerwas, *Dispatches*, chapter 6.

33. As Hans Urs von Balthasar said, cited by Banner, *Christian Ethics, 19.*

34. David Reisman with Nathan Glazer and Reuel Denney, *The Lonely Crowd* (Hartford: Yale University Press, 1950), xlvii.

McNeill is typical in going to the social constructionist extreme. He argues that:

> the call of the Gospel to man is not one of conforming passively to biological givens; rather that call is to transform and humanize the natural order through the power of love . . . what it means to be a man or woman in any given society is a free human cultural creation.[35]

This is a Gnostic rejection of creation or biology altogether. Likewise, former Uniting Church minister and continuing lesbian Dorothy McRae-McMahon, who resigned soon after 'coming out', said, like many, 'this is the way God created me'. But this is an individualistic and subjective distortion of Luther's existential emphasis on 'God created *me*' in his *Shorter Catechism*. For theologians like the above (not Luther), creation 'lacks any inherent good apart from this grasping and humanising',[36] something any ecologist should recognise as very anthropocentric and arbitrary.

How do we tell if we have grasped this order well or badly without an ontological reference point? It is like trying to grasp a jellyfish, there's no backbone structure or form to hold onto. We are left with vague values of 'justice and love',[37] which are loosely used to justify sex outside heterosexual marriage in many mainline liberal church sexuality reports.

Yet, without some 'authoritative nature' it is difficult to deny the wrongness of pedophilia, bestiality or incest if such relationships are loving, non-painful, or possibly consensual.[38] These practices are likely to be the next battlegrounds as some in the American Psychiatric Association want them recognised as harmless and delisted as disorders.

Postmodern social constructionism is fallacious like the projection theory of religious needs; just because we are hungry does not mean that food doesn't really exist. Further, just because people ideologically abuse the notion of the natural for their own power doesn't deny the existence of the natural. Abuse

---

35. JJ McNeill, *The Church and the Homosexual* (London: 1977, 102–4).
36. Banner, *Christian Ethics,* 279.
37. McNeill, *Church,* 148.
38. Banner, *Christian Ethics,* 272, footnote 5. A new Dutch single-issue political group seeks to legalise pedophilia. Recently Australian philosopher Peter Singer supported (non-painful) bestiality. See Gordon Preece, *Rethinking Peter Singer* (Downers Grove: IVP, 2002), 23–6. Former Australian Governor General, Bishop Peter Hollingworth notoriously suggested on ABC TV's *Australian Story* (2002) that the case of a 14-year-old's sexual relationship with a priest, later bishop, was justified as consensual.

of the notion of creation order does not deny its use, it just disciplines our critical discernment of it, or we would do away with sex too, the most abused of all precious human goods.

We can reject reading natural laws from analogies to animals (for example, monogamy from the documentary *The March of the Penguins*—pity it's only temporary) or from genitals being seen as only or primarily for procreation (pity about the clitoris) as unbiblical, un-holistic and impersonal. And we can reject wrong notions of the natural or biologism (biological determinism) without rejecting all notions of the natural or biological. This misuse of nature cuts both ways, however. Outspoken bisexual Camille Paglia speaks disparagingly of how gay activist:

> fibs and fabrications continue, now about the still-fragmentary evidence for a genetic link to homosexuality and for homosexual behavior among animals. The incidence of the latter is enormously exaggerated, in proportion to conventional procreative pairings throughout nature, and acknowledgment is rarely made of the exceptional conditions of environmental stress or population pressure under which it occurs. I am also unpersuaded, thus far, by multigenerational and twin studies that claim to have found evidence for a genetic basis for homosexuality . . . [39]

What we need is not to throw the baby of nature out with the bathwater of ideological constructions or deconstructions of it. Instead we need 'a corrected account of creation; that is, one which does not crassly identify what is the case with God's will for the world?'[40] A corrected account begins by seeing the three theological tenses of any narrative of nature as:

1.   Past: Edenic natural laws/ideals of marriage, including comple-mentarity and procreation, which should no more be ignored than we should write a sex manual ignoring the laws of gravity;
2.   Present: fallen nature (Gen 3) subject to idolatry and vanity (Eccles, Rom 1:20 ff; 8:18 ff) but partially restored in Christ now;

---

39. Camille Paglia, *Vamps and Tramps* (London: Viking, 1995), 74.
40. Banner, *Christian Ethics,* 17. See also Robert Scharleman, *Happiness and Benevolence* (Edinburgh: T and T Clark, 2000) from a more Catholic, philosophical perspective affirming the teleology or goal of nature.

3.   Future: nature redeemed to reach its goal, for which it, our bodies and
     the Spirit groan with the pangs of the new creation like a mother in
     childbirth (Rom 8:18ff).

In Matthew's Gospel Jesus Christ enables us to see all three aspects of
sexuality in response to the Pharisees' and Sadducees' questions regarding
divorce and marriage in heaven respectively:

1.   God's original, created purpose: one man, one wife for life (19:3–6)
2.   God's permissions, like divorce, for hardness of heart (19:7–9)
3.   Celibacy or 'eunuchs for the sake of the kingdom' (19:12). 'For in
     the resurrection they neither marry nor are given in marriage, but are
     like angels in heaven' (22:30).

Because of the Fall's disruption to the natural order and our ability to know it
(Rom 1:18–32), the Bible and Augustine leave sexuality not 'merely to the
endless rhythms of nature' but incorporate it in the Christian narrative or
redemptive rhythm of creation, fall and redemption. John Calvin and Karl
Barth follow Augustine here. For Barth, the ethical question regarding sex is
'essentially a question of things that are natural and right', but not 'securely
naturally know'.[41] Our access to the natural is revelational. Calvin describes
how Christ, the true natural human or Last Adam, puts the Spirit's spectacles
on us to see creation clearly.

    It is biblical revelation of our being made in God's image that enables us
to see sexuality's personal and relational aspects. This can be seen against the
background of a perverted form of naturalism which absolutises nature as it is
now, fallen nature—not natural law, but natural flaw.[42] An example is the
aptly named The Bloodhounds song line: 'you and me baby ain't nothing but
mammals, let's do it like they do on the Discovery channel'. Another example
is that infamous collector of wasps and deviant sexual behaviors from
unrepresentative prison and university student populations, Alfred Kinsey.[43]

---

41. Barth, *Church Dogmatics*, III/4, 120.
42. See Bruce S Thornton, *Eros: The Myth of Greek Sexuality* (Boulder: Westview
     Press, 1997), 7 on Greek ambivalence or negativity about nature as something to be
     controlled, if possible, by culture.
43. See *Kinsey, Sex and Fraud: The Indoctrination of a People*, edited by Judith A
     Reisman, Edward Eichel, W J Gordon Muir and John H Court (Lafayette,
     Louisiana: Huntington House, 1990) and James H Jones, *Alfred C Kinsey* (New
     York: WW Norton, 1998) which show that Kinsey was bisexual, a voyeur, an
     exhibitionist, and masochist.

His fraudulent report set the agenda for the sexual revolution, and especially the homosexual revolution, with its inflated and oft-cited figure of ten per cent of the population being homosexual.[44]

Instead of being a form of sexual solitaire and animalistic stimulation, sex is an expression of our personal, relational nature as men and women made in God's relational, trinitarian image. This God is the ground and goal of our identity, whether we are married or single.[45] When the two become one there is a mysterious image of that trinitarian oneness in difference, where there is a basic complementarity and completeness, unity and non-competitive equality (Gen 2:24, Mt 19:5, Eph 5: 28–33).

2.2 Sexual idolatry and ideology: the Fall

In Romans 1:24ff Paul depicts homosexual practice as a symptom of Gentile idolatry and God's giving them up to disordered and unnatural desires. In Romans 7:13–25 Paul graphically describes the Adamic self (still existing within the Christian) divided by all-demanding desire, including sexual desire. Following Paul, Augustine partially deconstructed the Greeks' Olympian harmonious soul-body dualism. Autobiographically in his *Confessions*, he explored humanity's broken sexuality in a much more fundamental way than any postmodern de-centering or fragmentation of the self. Augustine found its source in the Pauline 'dissociation of body, reason and will'.[46] This leads to a disordering of our now competing loves and desires. Desires become

---

44. Paglia, *Vamps and Tramps*, 74, says 'As a teacher of twenty-three years, most . . . in art schools, I have been struck by the rarity, not the frequency, of homosexuality. From the start of my media career, I attacked the much-touted activist claim that 10 per cent of the population is gay—which was always a distortion of Kinsey's finding that 10 per cent had some homosexual experience over their lifetime. Tracking my students, acquaintances, and the world in general, I guessed the number hovered at 3 per cent, and recent surveys [ranging from 1 or 2 to 4 per cent, including *The Australian Study of Health and Relationships*] have borne this out. The 10 per cent figure, servilely repeated by the media, was pure propaganda, and it made me, as a scholar, despise gay activists for their unscrupulous disregard for the truth'.

45. Barth, *Church Dogmatics*, III/2.

46. Banner, *Christian Ethics*, 298 citing Augustine, *Confessions*, Book viii, 10, 22.

demands, captive to the law of sin competing with the mind/conscience's recognition of the goodness of God's law.[47]

According to Romans 1:20ff, anarchic or disordered, anonymous or depersonalised desire flows from idolatry. Idolatry means worshipping the creature, including sex, not the Creator. It makes good things into gods. As Augustine notes, the basic problem of the earthly city is that it does not do justice to God's worth, by refusing to worship him, and by sacrificing to other gods. One of the most powerful of these gods in Augustine's and our age, is clearly Eros, the god of sex.

Idolatry infects the whole person, mind and body. It means not thinking thankfully with our minds (1:21), not worshipping, honoring God with our bodies. Contrast Rom 12:1–2 where we are called to present our bodies as 'living sacrifices' and 'be transformed by the renewing of our minds'.

One of the insights of postmodernity is that our thinking is never neutral or universal, it is always determined by a particular vantage point. The Bible takes this insight deeper; post-Fall, we are not so much rational creatures as rationalising creatures, trying to justify ourselves and our idolatry (Rom 1:20ff). Augustine saw the way the will drags our reason behind it more profoundly than any postmodern questioning of modern rationality.

Wilful idolatry or divinised desire therefore leads to ideology, rationalising or justifying our wrong worship and lust, our objectifying exercise of power against God and others. E Michael Jones' deconstructive and idolatry detection skills uncover many examples of such modern sexual rationalisation. Prominent sexual theorists, such as Jung, project their own parochial Western, class-based mores onto a universal canvas to justify their own practices, because 'everybody's doing it'. For instance, Jones cites anthropologist Derek Freeman's demolition job on Margaret Mead's trend-setting sexual anthropology. Her *Coming of Age in Samoa* justified the swinging sixties, as well as her own lesbianism and adultery, by claiming that Samoan adolescents were engaged in a wholesale process of sexual experimentation and free love. They were just pulling her leg.[48]

---

47. Francis Watson, *Agape and Eros: Pauline Sexual Ethics* (Cambridge: Cambridge University Press), 2000. See also Paul Ramsey, 'Human Sexuality in the History of Redemption,' *Journal of Religious Ethics*, 16, (1988): 56.

48. See E Michael Jones, *Degenerate Moderns: Modernity as Rationalized Sexual Misconduct* (San Francisco: Ignatius Press, 1993), chapter 1, 'Samoa Lost: Margaret Mead, Cultural Relativism, and the Guilty Imagination', drawing on Derek Freeman, *Margaret Mead and Samoa: The Making and Unmaking of an Anthropological Myth* (Cambridge, Massachusetts: Harvard University Press, 1983). David Williamson's play *Heretic* is based on Freeman's exposure of Mead.

Further prominent examples of ideologically induced mistakes of methodology and misuse of data regarding sexuality and psychology are described in a range of recent studies. The Kinsey Report demonstrated more about its author's own kinkiness than normal sexual practices. His research into child orgasm was probably based on experimental sexual abuse of children.[49] Further, the American Psychiatric Association's (APA) de-classification of homosexuality as a disorder came about under strong political pressure from the gay lobby, not due to any scientific advances, as Jeffrey Satinover shows in *The Politics of Truth*.[50] Finally, censorship is common for both Christian and other counsellors/psychiatrists engaged in corrective therapy for homosexuals and of television advertisements by 'Exodus' in US regarding the possibility of change.

The danger of ideological misreading of sexual history is shown by Bruce Thornton's *Eros: The Myth of Greek Sexuality*. This myth or ideology had its modern social location in mid-nineteenth-century English single-sex boarding schools and Oxford University around the time of Oscar Wilde.[51] It projected its own view of homosexuality's higher love onto the ancient Greek city to provide a classical precedent for its own urbane view of homosexuality. Similarly, Foucault's claim that the Greeks were bisexuals, indiscriminately appreciating beauty wherever it may be found, is a myth.[52]

---

49. See also: Jones, *Degenerate Moderns*, chapter 5.

50. Jeffrey Satinover, *Homosexuality and the Politics of Truth* (Grand Rapids: Baker, 1996), chapter 1.

51. Charles Seltman, *Women in Antiquity* (London and New York: 1956), 137 says: 'The all-male life of the 19th-century public school and college inclined too many scholars to retrospective wishful thinking. In their day-dreams they wanted to think of their beloved Athenians as people unencumbered like themselves, by femininity'. Oscar Wilde, interestingly, made a death-bed repentance and returned to the Catholic Church as did many of his fellow decadents. See Joseph Pearce, *The Unmasking of Oscar Wilde* (London: HarperCollins, 2000), chapters 26 and 27.

52. Thornton, *Eros*, 256–7, notes that 'recent writing on homosexuality in ancient Greece is overwhelmingly influenced by KJ Dover's *Greek Homosexuality* [New York: Vintage Books, 1978] . . . Dover excited the advocacy scholars with his thesis that the Greeks were indifferent to same-sex relations considering them "perfectly normal" if they reflected the political dominance of the older male over the teenage boy expressed in pederastic penetration of the boy's thighs. David Cohen, in *Law, Sexuality, and Society,* 171–202, demonstrates the oversimplicity of the Dover model as elaborated by Foucault, the way it glosses over the ambivalence and anxiety surrounding same-sex relations in ancient Greece, as well

Thornton shows that the Greeks see Eros is one of the anthropomorphic gods at creation, foundational to the cosmos and an 'inhuman force of sexual attraction'. 'Eros needs to be tamed so his potentially destructive powers, which will always exist, can be redirected to human purposes. This was accomplished in the institution of marriage and by the sexual fidelity of husband and wife' and children.[53]

2.3 Creation healed: therapy and community

The biblical story of the Kingdom of God is the source of complete sexual liberation and wholeness —'creation healed' as Hans Kung calls it. Its healing powers radiate out from the city of God which has within it the tree of life 'for the healing of the nations' (Rev 22:2). Redemptive ethics or therapy buys back creation by re-channeling our sexuality within creaturely limits. This demythologises the modern sexual liberationist and consumerist myth that allows uncontrolled, covetous desire to flood every part of life. In this redemptive way eros, or desire, is healed and made part of the whole of Christ's sacrificial love or agape.[54] Only the love of the crucified and resurrected Christ can liberate us from this body of deathly, disordered desire because it is stronger than death.

Though intimately related to identity, sexuality (whether hetero-, homo-, or bi-) is not to be idolatrously equated with our identity, as Richard Hays' late gay friend discovered from much hard experience in the homosexual community.[55] Sexuality is not the soul or the whole of the person, though it has taken over its role in modernity, as Foucault notes.

If our sexuality is not the basis of our identity, then sex will not save, or bring wholeness. National Gay and Lesbian Task Force (NGLTF) executive director, Torie Osborne, summed up the more sober post-AIDS view of some:

> The radicals won the 'sex wars', but we lost the truly radical
> vision of full human liberation in the process. The idea of
> sex as salvation and as self, which dominates gay male—and
> now young lesbian—culture [and many straights], holds no

---

as passing over or rationalising away the very real evidence of disgust toward the passive homosexual irrespective of the presumed pederastic protocols'.

53. Thornton, *Eros*, chapter 1.

54. So eros is not eternally opposed to agape as is Augustine's tendency and Anders Nygren's in *Agape and Eros* (London: SPCK, 1954) especially section I.2, 'Two Opposed Fundamental Motifs' and II.3, III and IV.

55. Richard Hays, *The Moral Vision of the New Testament* (San Francisco: Harper, 1998), 379.

promise for real change; it is consumeristic and ultimately hollow.[56]

Sexuality is not the transcendent liberation many seek. People mistake the sign for the reality it signifies or points to. Instead, sexuality is a sign or sacrament of relationship with a trinitarian relational God. Sexuality and its stabilisation in marriage is a sign or metaphor of God's propositioning us, God's marrying his people, in an exclusive, intimate, purifying relationship (Hosea, Eph 5:21ff, Rev 21:1, 2). Unlike modern romantic myths, this is a realistic and robust divine romance that can re-enchant cynical postmodern sexuality.[57]

2.3.1 Sexual bodies and the body of Christ

It is vital not only that romance and love be re-framed or re-stor(i)ed[58] but that our bodily sexuality be re-narrated. We live in a society that promotes bodily hatred of in order to sell products to perfect 'bad' bodies. We need to hear the New Testament story of the body, condensed in 1 Corinthians 6 and connected with the corporate story of the body of Christ.

To set the scene: Corinth was an infamous sea-port where sailors found a good time. In fact, just as the Red Hot Chile Peppers can sing of 'Californication', so 'Corinthifornication' was a byword of the ancient world. The individualistic and over-spiritual Corinthians (some of whom had 'spiritual' marriages (1 Cor 7:1–7) thought that whatever they did with their bodily appetites is irrelevant to their soul, and so they visited prostitutes.[59]

---

56. In her *Advocate* column in late 1994 cited in Rotello, *Sexual Ecology,* 288.

57. See also Charles Williams, *An Outline of Romantic Theology: Religion and Love in Dante*, edited by Alice Mary Hadfield (Grand Rapids: Eerdmans, 1990), and James Wm McClendon Jr, *Ethics: Systematic Theology*, volume I (Nashville: Abingdon), 1986, chapter 5, 'The Romance of Orthodoxy'.

58. Audrey N Grant's 'Towards Restor(y)ing a Vision for Education for the Third Millenium', *Ridley College Centre of Applied Christian Ethics Newsletter*, III/1 (April 1998): 3–6 (www.ridley.unimelb.edu.au/cace). Ian Barns advocates doctrinal 'reframing' of the 'fiduciary framework' of modern secular existence. See 'Going Public: Reflections on *Zadok*'s Role in Australian Society,' *Zadok Paper*, S86, (Autumn 1997): 8–11.

59. See Gordon D Fee, *The First Epistle to the Corinthians*, NICNT (Grand Rapids: Eerdmans, 1987) on this passage. Compare the Corinthians to James Nelson's influential but dualistic *Embodiment: An Approach to Sexuality and Christian*

But Paul has an earthier view of our bodily sexuality. He describes the body holistically, not as something irrelevant to the soul or self.[60] Paul locates the body within the story of salvation and sanctification: through Jesus' death on the cross on Good Friday 'you were bought with a price' (verse 19); through the resurrection of Jesus' body on Easter Sunday our bodies are bound to Christ's in the body of the church (verses 14–17). Through the Spirit of Pentecost 'your body is a temple of the Holy Spirit'. 'You are not your own . . . So glorify God in your body' (verse 19).

There are many sexually soiled and damaged people in our society and church. In this context Paul first has bad news: 'Neither the immoral, nor idolaters, nor adulterers, nor sexual perverts . . . will inherit the kingdom of God'. But he then boldly proclaims the good news of redemption: 'And such were some of you. But you were washed, you were sanctified, you were justified in the name of the Lord Jesus Christ and in the Spirit of our God' (verses 9–11). So many of us have been stained or polluted sexually, that we need to recapture the old biblical language of cleansing to be restored.

We also need to recapture Paul's corporate view of the Christian's body as primarily a member of the body of Christ. Social anthropologists note the way the physical body is perceived through the social body, in a never-ending exchange of meanings and bodily experiences. The corporeal body is part of the corporate body of Christ, the church, which functions as a body politic. There is no such thing as sex being a purely private thing. The personal is political. When we bed people we are representatives of the body of Christ (see 1 Cor chapters 6, 10, 11, 12).

This corporate view of the body and of bodily church discipline on sexual issues appears harsh to individualistic modern Christians. But the early church had no concrete signs such as the sabbath, circumcision or food laws to maintain its distinctiveness like its Jewish parent/brother. One of its primary

---

Theology (London: SPCK,1979) where 'moral agents float above their bodies' (Banner, *Christian Ethics,* 280).

60. Augustine says that just as dead bodies and even their clothes are honoured, how much more should we honour our actual bodies 'since we wear them in a much closer and more intimate way than any clothing. A man's body is no mere adornment, or external convenience; it belongs to his very nature as a man' (*City of God,* i, 13). Although Augustine and many early Christians had problems with the body, it was problematic primarily because it was to be 'loved and cherished' (Brown, *Body and Society,* 425).

signs or practices was its bodily discipline or heightened sexual ethic, which set it apart as a holy people, a third race:[61]

> Modern Christians who feel that traditional Christianity attached undue importance to sexual morality and made it too restrictive need to be aware that their own lack of sympathy with the traditional discipline arises not only from sexual liberation but also from a different ecclesiology, from a lowering of boundaries between the Church and the world. The broad questions of the . . . precise sense in which the Christian should be in the world but not of it, need to be . . . resolved before the sexual ethic of traditional Christianity can be rightly understood and fairly judged.[62]

Paul and the early church engaged in a form of Christian social and political construction, which we need to recapture our integrity and distinctiveness as the body of Christ. When Christian bodies engage sexually with other bodies they do so first and foremost as members of the body of Christ.[63] In a world of *The Clash of Civilizations* and *Global Sex*[64] we need to think how the body of Christ can regain a notion of discipleship of and discipline over the bodies of Christians.

The real contest today is between Third World Christianity and Islam. Western Christianity is too flabby and weak to be in the contest. It is no accident that the growing churches were those leading the way for sexual purity at the Lambeth Anglican Bishops Congress in 1998. The African bishops were not only biblical, but preventatively pastoral with an eye on their massive AIDS crisis, and missiological concerning Muslims who see

---

61. Richard M Price, 'The Distinctiveness of Early Christian Sexual Ethics,' in *Christian Perspectives on Sexuality and Gender*, edited by A Thatcher and E Stuart (Herefordshire/Grand Rapids: Gracewing/Eerdmans, 1996), 29. See also Peter Brown, *Body and Society,* chapter 1 and Epilogue, especially 428.

62. Price, 'The Distinctiveness of Early Christian Sexual Ethics', 29.

63. See Dale Martin, *The Corinthian Body* (New Haven: Yale University Press, 1995) for background on Paul's semi-medical view of sexual pollution, although he fails to read Paul sympathetically.

64. Samuel Huntington, *The Clash of Civilizations and the Remaking of World Order* (New York: Simon and Schuster, 1997); Denis Altman, *Global Sex* (St Leonards: Allen and Unwin, 2001).

Christianity as accommodated to a sexually decadent West. We should share their concern, and not parochially sell out our sexual ethics to inner-city Westerners, while still being hospitable to them.

The really difficult issue though, is how to recapture a thick or strong enough community or church life to model committed Christ-like relationships for younger people under much pressure to conform sexually. Like the ancient Greeks we need to mentor and apprentice young people, not just boys, into mature, sexual adulthood and citizenship of the city or polis, not in pederastic, homosexual style, as some wrongly claim they advocated,[65] but into citizenship of the city of God, an even higher good than the created good of sexuality.

The eroticisation of everyday life has caused the sad decline of non-sexual opposite-sex friendship and cast suspicion on same-sex friendships. We need to recover a range of committed, even covenantal relationships: marriage and parenthood; same-sex non-sexual friendships like Jonathon and David, Ruth and Naomi; same and mixed sex communities and flatmates. These could help meet the need for intimacy, even touch ('greet one another with a holy kiss' 1 Cor 16:20), but not genital intimacy (unless heterosexually married).[66]

2.3.2 Heavenly sex

Lesbian theologian Elizabeth Stuart only slightly exaggerates that 'No one has yet attempted to do sexual theology from an eschatological perspective'. We

---

65. See Cantarella, *Bisexuality in the Ancient World* and contrast Thornton, *Eros*, 256–7.

66. On same-sex friendship see Michael Vasey, *Strangers and Friends: A New Exploration of Homosexuality* (London: Hodder and Stoughton, 1995); Stanley Hauerwas, 'Gay Friendship: A Thought Experiment in Catholic Moral Theology,' in his *Sanctify Them in the Truth: Holiness Exemplified* (Edinburgh: T and T Clark, 1998), chapter 6 and Peter Carnley's chapter in The Doctrine Panel of General Synod, *Faithfulness in Fellowship: Reflections on Homosexuality and the Church* (Melbourne: John Garret, 2001). However, Carnley smuggles the meaning of marriage into gay friendships to avoid confrontation over gay marriages and because of the association of marriage with procreation. However, theologically the primary problem is lack of sexual difference/complementarity and for many gays the basic problem is monogamy. Carnley favours church-blessed covenants for same-sex friendships modelled on David and Jonathon (1 Sam 20:42). But there was no church blessing attached to this informal covenant. John Dunnill in the same volume notes that David and Jonathon's same-sex friendship was probably non-erotic. Biblical and traditional covenants reinforce creation norms, that is, heterosexual marriage or chaste same-sex friendships as in monasticism.

have responded to her challenge in locating sex in relation to the eschatological city of God. For Stuart we have become like Sadducees, who did not believe in the resurrection. Fundamentalist family values advocates often collapse heaven 'into the eternal nuclear family' even 'while the nuclear family itself is breaking up'.[67]

By contrast the nineteenth-century novelist Charles Kingsley 'thought heaven would be one perpetual copulation in a literal, physical sense, with his wife, Fanny, and illustrated his belief'.[68] He believed that Jesus only ruled out getting married in heaven, while earthly marriage continued. But Jesus said there would be no marriage in heaven, not just marriage ceremonies (Mk 12:18–27).

Gay theologians like Stuart see this as part of Jesus' common questioning of the patriarchal, heterosexual family. Similarly, Michael Vasey says that modern evangelical Christianity is unaware that: 'Its recurring anxiety over "family issues" is a measure of how deeply it has sold its soul to the destructive idols of Western culture'—heterosexism and commodities not communities. Evangelical hostility to gays is less due to its biblical loyalty than to its idolatry.[69] For Hauerwas also, family values is 'how Americans talk about "blood and soil"'.[70] In fact, for many, the heterosexual family is heaven.

It is important to hear this challenge without hearing it uncritically. We do make good things like family and heterosexuality into gods, but contrary to gay theologians, that doesn't mean that they are not good, just not God. Sadly, Stuart perversely pretends that the anonymous, no-name sex of many singles and gay bars and bathhouses is an anticipation of our universal, unmarried relations in the city of God, rather than an expression of the anonymity of the city of Babel leading to our remaining strangers to one another even in the most intimate of acts.[71]

---

67. Elizabeth Stuart, 'Sex in Heaven: The Queering of Theological Discourse on Sexuality', in Davies and Loughlin, *Sex These Days,* 193–204, here: 196–201.

68. Stuart, 'Sex in Heaven', 200 citing Susan Chity, *The Beast and the Monk: the Life of Charles Kingsley* (London: Hodder and Stoughton, 1975), 17.

69. Vasey, *Strangers and Friends*, 248–9.

70. Hauerwas, *Dispatches from the Front*, 158.

71. Contrast Rotello's *Sexual Ecology* and Michael Arditti's *Easter* (London: Arcadia, 2000), 201ff more realistic depictions of anonymous gay sex with Stuart's ('Sex in Heaven', 193–204) and Kathy Rudy's (*Sex and the Church: Gender, Homosexuality and Christian Ethics* [Boston: Beacon, 1997], 75–7, 128) bizarre

A reminder for the church of the priority of God and the city of God over sex and family is the place of celibacy. Martin Luther rightly rejected a corrupted Gnostic and medieval Catholic form of celibacy as a salvific work. He reaffirmed the created goodness of marriage and family, but did not affirm celibacy as a sign, for some, of the kingdom's priority, even above family. Although celibacy has been scapegoated for the Catholic sexual abuse scandal, and it should be non-compulsory, its important role as an anticipation of God's kingdom should not be lost.

The truth between the two extremes, or heresies, of Sadduceeism and Gnosticism is found in 1 Cor 7:25–40. There Paul encourages singular devotion to God, with a preference for singleness, but liberty to marry for those so gifted, lest they be distracted by their sexual needs. Nonetheless, 'the appointed time has grown very short; from now on those who have wives should live as though they had none . . . for the form of this world is passing away' (verses 29–31). Paul may be accommodating himself to the Corinthian ascetics. He may have in mind a particular crisis or a famine. Or, as I believe, he may be highlighting the perpetual state that we are in short of the second coming. Marriage is good, but not God; it is not the meaning of life, only a sign of it, like celibacy. A reaffirmation of voluntary celibacy, and celibate communities, may be a way to pastorally support the homosexually inclined, and counter the eroticisation of same-sex relations and the sexual fetishisation of friendship.

2.3.3 Sexual liberation: back to the garden or on to God's city?

Paul's realistic narrative and eschatological theology is foreign to many contemporary family values advocates' quest for heaven in family and also to many sexual liberals quest for an Eden of free sexual expression. The Woodstock generation sang their anthem along with Joni Mitchell and Crosby, Stills, Nash and Young: 'we are stardust, we are billion year old carbon, and we've got to get ourselves back to the garden' as they romped and played naked in rain and mud, like Israel before the Golden Calf (1 Cor 10:6–8). Sex was salvation, paradise, the Garden of Eden.

---

advocacy of the promiscuous yet faithful (!) brotherhood and sisterhood of gay anonymous, heavenly sex. Biblically, sexual relationships are kingdom apprenticeships, but as they re-create truly personal, embodied, gendered, not anonymous, disembodied, de-gendered relationships. They move from the personal to the universal, when there will be no marriage feast in heaven, only that reuniting the heavenly City of God to the new earth, beautifully bedecked as the Bride of Christ (Rev 21:2). But the sexually immoral, with other sinners, find no place in that city (Rev 22:15).

Rotello adopts a more realistic ecological and cultural perspective. He says: 'Deep ecology recognizes that our thoughts, beliefs, and social systems are as much a part of nature's web as any other factor in ecology' and 'require fundamental changes in human organization and philosophy' if we want 'sustainable solutions'.[72] Contrary to the notion of gay sex as historically unchangeable, the relatively recent gay gym culture with its incredible discipline over the body shows how cultural discipline can bring change.[73] Rotello wants to restore the more Greek-type of spiritualised, self-controlled sex[74] through social incentives encouraging universally recognised monogamy. However, Rotello has no moral motivation to back up his purely naturalistic approach: 'I have no moral or ideological argument with promiscuity whatsoever when it doesn't kill people'. 'One can be a promiscuous saint, I believe, or a monogamous creep'.[75] For all his positive health proposals for gays context, Rotello is a moral relativist. He also fails to reckon with Thornton's demonstration that the Greek form of therapy for erratic eros was *heterosexual* marriage.

Theologians too can mimic a seventies romanticism about sexual liberation. James Nelson, whose books were eagerly cited by many mainline liberal sexual reports in the nineties, wrote a book entitled *Between Two Gardens*. But Nelson is utterly utopian in thinking that sex now is unambiguously good, with no flaming sword blocking our way back to the garden of pure sexual delight. He highlights the idyllic romanticism of the garden in Song of Songs over the fallen garden of Eden with its tension between the innocence and ambiguity of sex. Nelson has no sense of the eschatological end of sex, no sense of the garden's goal within the city of God, and therefore no reason for sexual restraint.[76]

So much of the liberal utopian sexual agenda sees our sexuality as our property, merely limited by the rights of others, rather than part of our person. It shows a Pelagian naivety about human nature and unfettered, neutral freedom, limitless liberty, as if each sinful act is atomistic with no long chain of after-effects. It assumes that a utopian view of the sexual body—as ongoing

---

72. Rotello, *Sexual Ecology*, 187–8.

73. Rotello, *Sexual Ecology*, 254, 299–300.

74. Rotello, *Sexual Ecology*, 225–7.

75. Rotello, *Sexual Ecology*, 250–1.

76. See James Nelson, *Between Two Gardens* (New York: Pilgrim, 1983), 7–9.

incarnational sexual revelation,[77] divorced from the finality of Christ's Incarnation, Cross and resurrection, plus a bit of sexual therapy and technique —will solve all our sexual problems.

Sadly, we have replaced the biblical and Augustinian city of God with the modern Enlightenment quest for the Heavenly City on earth, originally through reason, increasingly through sexual passion. As Foucault says:

> A great sexual sermon—which has had its subtle theologians and its popular voices—has swept through our societies over the last decades; it has chastised the old order [of Christian and Victorian repression], denounced hypocrisy [which is the only thing that stands between us and shameless, cynical decadence, the compliment we pay to having some standards] and praised the rights of the immediate and real; it has made people dream of a New City.[78]

People seeking this New City foolishly think of it as a god-like *creatio ex nihilo,* out of nothing, as if God did not create in the first place. Like an erratic jazz musician, they seek to culturally and sexually improvise without any created rhythm to improvise upon.[79] Yet 'the word "culture" comes originally from agriculture [see Gen 2:15]; culture is nature humanised, not abrogated'.[80] Oliver O'Donovan captures this fine biblical balance between nature and culture (social construction) in the city of God:

> It is the last word of the Gospel as it is of the New Testament. Itself a natural environment rather than possessing a natural environment; a city that has overcome the antinomies of nature and culture, worship and politics

---

77. James Nelson, *Body Theology* (Louisville: WJKP, 1992), 9. Contrast Woodhead, 'Sex in a Wider Context', 102–3.

78. Michel Foucault, *The History of Sexuality*, volume 1, translated by Robert Hurley (New York: Vintage Books, 1980), 7–8.

79. Bonhoeffer calls this a *'cantus firmus'* or 'ground bass' in God's love holding all our polyphonous human loves together. *Letters and Papers from Prison* (London: SCM, 1953), 99–100. Contrast this with Richard Holloway's use of jazz as a model for moral improvisation in his *Godless Morality* (Edinburgh: Canongate Books, 2000).

80. Spaemann, *Happiness and Benevolence*, 167. See also C Westermann, *Creation* (London: SPCK, 1971).

> . . . a city with a Valley of Hinnom, which does not
> therefore have to carry within the cheapness and
> tawdriness that have made all other cities mean.[81]

All impurity or lack of created wholeness will be cast out of the city of God. Allow me to use an imperfect analogy to illustrate.[82] The first time I went to Times Square New York with my wife in the early 1980s, it was known aptly as Hell's Bedroom. It was full of prostitutes and intimidating pimps. We were scared and got out of there as soon as possible, not even going to Broadway. The second time we went, with teenage kids, was 1997. The transformation was astonishing. The city centre had been cleaned-up and we felt safe walking the streets at night with the children and had a wonderful time. This is a vision of what could happen if we sought seriously to transform our cities into analogues of the city of God. But to do so Christians will need to challenge the public boardrooms as well as the private bedrooms of our culture, the whole commodification of sex and persons in the light of a comprehensive vision of the city of God.

Conclusion

I conclude and summarise with a final image of how the Bible and Augustine reframe our sexual story. Rembrandt's painting 'Bathsheeba' uses a similar framework of creation-fall-redemption, characteristic of Rembrandt, over against the classical legacy of the city of Rome.[83] The beautiful, naked Bathsheba reflects the created glory of the human body bathed in golden light. But she wears the melancholy look of the Fall and shame at her nakedness before the distant gaze of the adulterous King David high on the hill. Also unnoticed by her, perhaps, is 'a figure who attends her as she bathes, washing her feet, one who will later be borne of her genealogy' (Mt 1: 6–7), one who came to serve (Lk 22:27) and clean our feet (often a coy euphemism for

---

81. O'Donovan, *Desire of the Nations*, 285.
82. The analogy is imperfect as the prostitutes and homeless were forced out through zero tolerance policing. And the city of God will have a place for the homeless and former prostitutes. Nonetheless, the comparison concerning cleaning up is apt. For a similar but different use of New York as a sign of the city of God see Peter Berger, 'New York City 1976—A signal of transcendence', chapter 18, of his *Facing up to Modernity: Excursions in Society, Politics, and Religion* (New York: Basic Books, 1977.
83. Kenneth Clark, *Introduction to Rembrandt* (London: HarperCollins 1978), 115.

genitals in Scripture), indeed our whole selves, with the complete cleansing of the Cross (Jn 13). 'Thus the light that falls on Bathsheba is not only the light of Eden, but the light of the 'holy city' the new Jerusalem'.[84] It is this light, this cleansing, that we need for the New York of *Sex and the City*, the archetypal postmodern city, and for our morose postmodern sexual mores.

Rembrandt's 'Bathsheeba'.

---

84. Banner, *Christian Ethics,* 308–9 who pointed me to Clark and Rembrandt's 'Bathsheeba'.